Aspects of the Grammar and Lexica of Artificial Languages

Alan Reed Libert / Christo Moskovsky

Aspects of the Grammar and Lexica of Artificial Languages

PETER LANG

Frankfurt am Main · Berlin · Bern · Bruxelles · New York · Oxford · Wien

Bibliographic Information published by the Deutsche Nationalbibliothek
The Deutsche Nationalbibliothek lists this publication in the Deutsche Nationalbibliografie; detailed bibliographic data is available in the internet at http://dnb.d-nb.de.

Cover Design:
Olaf Gloeckler, Atelier Platen, Friedberg

Printed with the financial support
of the University of Newcastle

ISBN 978-3-631-59678-4
© Peter Lang GmbH
Internationaler Verlag der Wissenschaften
Frankfurt am Main 2011
All rights reserved.

All parts of this publication are protected by copyright. Any utilisation outside the strict limits of the copyright law, without the permission of the publisher, is forbidden and liable to prosecution. This applies in particular to reproductions, translations, microfilming, and storage and processing in electronic retrieval systems.

www.peterlang.de

Table of Contents

Preface ... vii

List of Abbreviations ... ix

Part I: Phonetics, Phonology, and Orthography ... 1

Chapter 1: Nasals in Artificial Languages ... 1

Chapter 2: Affricates in Artificial Languages ... 7

Chapter 3: Consonantal Digraphs of Artificial Languages ... 15

Chapter 4: Stress Systems of Artificial Languages ... 21

Part II: Morphology and Syntax ... 35

Chapter 5: Nominal Plural Formation in Artificial Languages ... 35

Chapter 6: The Forms and Uses of Demonstratives in Artificial Languages ... 47

Chapter 7: On Case Assignment by Prepositions in Artificial Languages ... 55

Chapter 8: Indirect Objects in Artificial Languages ... 59

Chapter 9: Comitative and Instrumental Marking in Artificial Languages ... 75

Part III: Lexicon ... 85

Chapter 10: Color Terminology of Artificial Languages ... 86

Chapter 11: Terms for Metals in Artificial Languages ... 105

Chapter 12: Terms for Beverages in Artificial Languages ... 123

Chapter 13: Describing the Weather in Artificial Languages ... 137

Chapter 14: Terms for Time Periods in Artificial Languages ... 157

References ... 171

Preface

As in our previous work, in general we restrict ourselves to ALs which seem to be reasonably serious in purpose, and hence do not treat fictional languages, "art languages", or personal languages.[1] Even with this narrowing of our field of inquiry, the number of ALs is so large that we cannot hope to discuss more than a fraction of them, but we trust that the following chapters will give some idea of tendencies in ALs.

Several artificial languages that we treat here have their own alphabet or writing system, but one may also use the Roman alphabet to write them, or at least the designer often or usually uses the Roman alphabet when presenting his language. For example, Algilez has an "optional" (Giles 2010a: 1) alphabet. We use the Roman alphabet for these languages (as it is used by the designers for their languages), which also include aUI, Esata, NOXILO, and Ygyde. Chabé Abane also has its own alphabet, but our source for this language, C&L (1903), uses the Roman alphabet to represent it (as perhaps its designer sometimes did; we do not have access to his book presenting it), and we shall do the same.

In the chapters on the lexicon usually Esata roots are shown, rather than entire words. This is because generally only roots are given in the "Basic Esata to English Vocabulary" and "Basic English to Esata Vocabulary" parts of Bothi (2006), Appendix B and Appendix C respectively.[2] An example of an entire word occurring in (one or both of) these appendixes is *riyo* 'river'. In the case of words consisting of only two segments, the entire word consists of the root (or less than the whole root, v. later in this paragraph), as these words have no word class suffixes; only one such word/root will come up in Part III of the present book, *ka* 'car'. These items (in their one-syllable form; v. infra) do not appear in Appendixes B or C of Bothi (2006), but are listed in Section 4, "One-Syllable Words: the Primary List". (However, Bothi (ibid.) says, "One-syllable words are abbreviations of 2 syllable words ending in **he**". This means, for example, that the full form of the word for 'car' would be **kahe*, and the form *kah-* does appear in Appendix B of Bothi (ibid.). Should one therefore conclude that the root of this word should be seen as *kah-*, and not *ka-*? Further, since (as we shall see in the next paragraph) "an unvoiced vowel *e* ... may be dropped in the written form, to reduce character count" (ibid.),[3] the form *kah* can occur, and is found once in Bothi (2006).)

---

[1] The designer of the Scientific Dial System, Andrew Hallner, apparently viewed his creation not as an international auxiliary language, but as "A Substitute for Universal Language" (Hallner 1912: 16). It at least resembles an artificial language designed for a serious purpose, and we discuss it in this book.

[2] We only present items with three or more segments given in these parts, not those appearing only in Appendix D, "English to Esata Transcription", of Bothi (2006).

[3] Bothi does not explain what is meant by "an unvoiced vowel *e*".

vii

Note also the following remark (ibid.) about the omission of <e> (which occurs in some words given in Appendix C): "The format of Esata words is ... consonant followed by vowel until the end of the word. An exception is made in the case of an unvoiced vowel *e* which may be dropped in the written form, to reduce character count. An *e* is generally assumed to be present when two consonants are written together, or a word ends in a consonant. In these cases the vowel *e* it is pronounced as though present." Since *-e* is the word class ending for nouns (although we do not know when it would be "unvoiced"), it potentially occurs every often and (if "unvoiced") could be omitted very often. Thus for example, one of the roots meaning 'day' is *dey-*, so the full nominal form of the word should be *deye, but in fact this form never occurs in Bothi (2006), while the form *dey* occurs three times in texts there.

We have hyphens in the compounds of Idiom Neutral, since that is how they appear in our main source for this language, Holmes (1903). However, Holmes (ibid.: 27) states that "Compound words ... may be formed ... by simple juxtaposition, with a hyphen or (usually) without it". He later (p. 31) says of compounds, "the hyphen need not be employed in the actual use of the language".

As one might expect, glosses, definitions, and meanings of words generally come from our sources and are not original with us (but are sometimes modified and/or translated by us), although we often do not note this. We do not always give a full morphological breakdown of words in the examples, if it is not relevant to the point being discussed. Translations of passages originally in languages other than English were made by one of us.

We have sometimes, but not always, changed punctuation in glosses from our sources: one or more sources may always put semi-colons between words in glosses, even when they are closely related in meaning, and where, one might think, there should be commas between them if one is using commas between closely related meanings and semi-colons between meanings that are not closely related. There is also the sometimes difficult decision to make about how close meanings have to be for them to be separated by commas (rather than by semi-colons), and different people might make different decisions on this. Therefore, not too much should be read into the occurrence of commas or semi-colons in glosses.

The Interlibrary Services of the library of the University of Newcastle has been of considerable assistance in obtaining sources for the writing of this book. We thank Hongge Libert for her help in preparing the manuscript. Of course we alone are responsible for all errors and flaws. One of us (Libert) was provided with funding for teaching relief during part of the writing of this book by the Endangered Languages Documentation, Theory, and Application Program of the Humanities Research Institute of the University of Newcastle, for which we are most grateful. We also acknowdge the financial support that was provided by the School of Humanities and Social Science towards the publication of this book.

List of Abbreviations

ACC	–	accusative
adj(s).	–	adjective(s) (or adjectival roots with reference to American)
AG	–	agent
Art.	–	"artificial" root in Ruggles' Universal Language[4]
ATT	–	marker of attributive (as opposed to predicative) adjectives
BL	–	the Blue Language (Bolak)
C&L	–	Couturat and Leau
CN	–	common gender (apparently including neuter)
DAT	–	dative
Eng.	–	English
EXCL	–	exclusive
F	–	feminine
FUT	–	future
GEN	–	genitive
Ger.	–	German
Gk.	–	Greek
Gmc.	–	Germanic
Hom-id.	–	Hom-idyomo
Id. Neut.	–	Idiom Neutral
Indon.	–	Indonesian
Int. IALA	–	Interlingua (IALA)[5]
It.	–	Italian
Lat.	–	Latin
LdP	–	Lingwa de Planeta
LFN	–	Lingua Franca Nova
Ling. Int.	–	Lingua Internacional (by Adam Zakrzewski)
LOC	–	locative
M	–	masculine
MIE	–	Modern IndoEuropean
NN	–	word class marker for nouns
NOM	–	nominative
OT	–	our translation (as opposed to one made by a source)
PASS	–	passive
PAT	–	patient
pl., PL	–	plural
POSS	–	possessive
PRES	–	present

---

4   "Artificial radices are those which are not derived directly from the Latin, but [are] analogously constituted." (Ruggles 1829: 82)
5   IALA = International Auxiliary Language Association

PST	–	past
PTCP	–	participle
REFL	–	reflexive pronoun
Rom.	–	Romance
Rug.	–	James Ruggles' Universal Language
Sci. Dial	–	the Scientific Dial System
sec.	–	section
SG	–	singular
Sot.	–	Lengua Universal (by Bonifacio Sotos Ochando)[6]
Sp.	–	Spanish
SY	–	Short Ygyde[7]
tr.	–	translation
TRA	–	transitive suffix
Univ.Spr.	–	UniversalSprache (by Pirro)
vb.	–	verb
Welt. V+F)	–	Weltsprache (by Volk and Fuchs)

---

6   We shall refer to this as "Sotos Ochando's language".
7   The *Ygyde Language Introduction* (anon. 2010a) states:
    There are three versions of Ygyde: Short, Standard, and Long. Standard Ygyde has short, two letter syllables described above. Some 6 and 7 letters long words of the Standard Ygyde sound like a staccato. Short Ygyde makes them sound better by removing either [the] second identical vowel or [the] second identical consonant. The removed letter cannot be the last letter of the word. The letter can be removed only if letters adjacent to the removed letter are different and the shorter word is easy to pronounce. For example, osotate == osotae and apupipe == apuipe == apupie are correct, but okekebo == okekbo is too difficult to pronounce.

Part I: Phonetics, Phonology, and Orthography

Chapter 1: Nasals in Artificial Languages

There are many varieties of nasals in natural languages: they have places of articulation from bilabial to uvular, and they can be voiced or voiceless. Nasals usually occur in the onsets or codas of syllables (i.e. as non-syllabic sounds) but they can also occur in syllable nuclei (i.e. as syllabic sounds). In this chapter we shall examine what different types of nasals are found in artificial languages (henceforth ALs). We can start by saying that to our knowledge no AL designer has said anything about the occurrence of voiceless nasals, either phonemically or allophonically, in his language.

Allophones and Assimilation

In natural languages, there are often two or more allophones of nasal phonemes, e.g. English has the labiodental nasal [ɱ] as an allophone of /m/. However, designers of ALs do not often talk about allophones. We suspect that in practice (if an AL were ever spoken), assimilatory processes would cause e.g. labiodental and velar nasals to occur allophonically, even if their designers did not explicitly allow them.

An example of a work presenting an AL which brings up allophonic variation of a nasal is Gode and Blair (1951: 4) about Interlingua (IALA). They say, "The sounds of **g** and **k** assimilate a preceding **n** as in English".

Voksigid has phonemic bilabial and alveolar nasals, represented by <m> and <n> respectively. The latter is realized as a velar nasal when preceding a velar stop, and is still represented by <n>: Gilson's (2009a) description of the pronunciation of <n> is: "Eng. sun; before **k** or **g**, as in Eng. sung".

Quiles (2009: 119) says with respect to MIE, "**b, d, h, l, m, n**, are pronounced as in English. **n** might also be pronounced as guttural [ŋ] when it is followed by another guttural, as in Eng. *sing* or *bank*". Kisa (2009) says about the letter <n> in Toki Pona (which has phonemic bilabial and alveolar nasals), "When **n** appears at the end of a syllable, it represents any nasal consonant. It usually matches the sound that comes after it. For example, **nanpa** ['number'] and **unpa** ['to have sex with; sex; sexual'] sound like **nampa** and **umpa**, and the **n** in **ma Sonko** ['China'] sounds like the English *ng* in *ding dong*".

Wennergren (2005: 25), a detailed grammar of Esperanto, discusses allophones of nasals:

> N estas denta naza konsonanto. Ĝi kontrastas al la alia naza konsonanto M, kiu estas lipa. Kiam N staras antaŭ gingiva aŭ vela sono, oni emas ŝanĝi N en gingivan sonon (malgranda diferenco), aŭ velan sonon (granda diferenco),

por faciligi la elparolon: *tranĉi, mangi, longa, banko* k.a. Tio estas senprobleme, ĉar ne ekzistas gingiva aŭ vela nazaj sonoj, kun kiuj N povus konfuziĝi. Simile oni emas elparoli M lipdente antaŭ alia lipdenta sono: *amforo, ŝaŭmvino* k.a. Ankaŭ tio estas senprobleme. Sed oni atentu, ke oni ne elparolu N lipdente: *infero, enveni* k.a., ĉar tiam oni konfuzus N kaj M, kio ne estas akceptebla. Kompreneble oni povas ĉiam uzi la bazan elparolon de N kaj M. (p. 25)

('N is a dental nasal consonant. It contrasts with the other nasal consonant M, which is labial. When N is before and alveolar or velar sound, one tends to change N into an alveolar sound (a small difference), or a velar sound (a big difference), in order to facilitate the pronunciation: ... This is not problematic, because there do not exist alveolar or velar nasal sounds with which N could be confused. Similarly one tends to pronounce M labiodentally before another labiodental sound: ... This also is not problematic. But one should pay attention that one not pronounce N labiodentally: ..., because then one would confuse N and M, which is not acceptable. Of course one can always use the basic pronunciation of N and M.')

Syllabic Nasals

Many natural languages (e.g. English, Swahili) have allophonic syllabic nasals, but these are rarely discussed in works on ALs. An exception is Quiles (2009: 120), who says about Modern Indo-European:

Indo-European has also consonant-only syllables. It is possible to hear similar sound sequences in English *cattle* or *bottom*, in German *Haben*, in Czech *hlt*, Serbian *srpski*, etc. In this kind of syllables [sic], it is the vocalic sonant [r], [l], [m], or [n] – constrained allophones of [r], [l], [m], [n] –, the one which functions as syllabic centre, instead of a vowel proper: **kr̥-di**, *heart*, **wl̥-qos**, *wolf*, **de-km̥**, *ten*, **nō-mn̥**, *name*.[8]

Quiles (ibid.: 127) makes the following remark on the representation of syllabic consonants: "The vocallic [sic] allophones [r], [l], [m], [n] may be written, as in Latin transliterations of Sanskrit texts, as r̥, l̥, m̥, and n̥, to help the reader clearly identify the sonants; therefore, alternative writings **n̥mr̥tós**, *inmortal*, **km̥tóm**, *hundred*, **wodr̥**, *water*, etc. are also possible."

Loglan also has syllabic nasals, and as in Modern Indo-European one can optionally indicate their syllabicity: <mm> and <nn> stand for the syllabic bilabial and alveolar nasals respectively. (In addition /n/ has a velar allophone.)

Amerikan seems to have at least one syllabic nasal, given the existence of words such as *wesn* 'essence, affair, concern' and *gesivn* 'civilized'. Tutonish,

---

8   One will notice that Quiles uses the under-ring, which is the IPA symbol for voicelessness, in his phonetic symbols for syllabic consonants.

created by the same designer (Elias Molee), also apparently has at least one syllabic nasal, as in e.g. *havn* 'haven, port'.

Places of Articulation

We shall now give examples of different sets of (presumably) phonemic nasals in ALs.[9]

Languages with One Nasal

Fitusa, which has seven consonantal phonemes, has only a bilabial nasal.

Languages with Bilabial and Dental or Alveolar Nasals

The following ALs have bilabial and dental or alveolar nasals: Algilez, aUI, Babm, Chabé Abane, Desa *Chat*, Euransi, Europal, Fremdu, Idiom Neutral, Letellier's Langue Universelle, Lingua, Myrana, Neo, Neo Patwa, Olingo,[10] Omnial, Orba, Panamerikan, Pasifika, Romanova, the Scientific Dial System, SPL, Spokil,[11] Temenia,[12] UNI, Universal-Sprache, Uropa, Vela, Veltparl, Volapük, Voldu, Weltsprache (Eichhorn), Weltsprache (Volk and Fuchs), and Ygyde.

---

9 If a sound is represented by its own letter (or digraph), it is generally a safe assumption that it is phonemic, and we have followed this assumption, though one cannot be certain about this when dealing with ALs. We have sometimes given examples of words in which nasal sounds under discussion occur, and in which their appearance is not due to assimilation, in order to show that they are phonemic.
  Of course we cannot take into account nasal phonemes that our (primary or secondary) sources do not mention. To take a hypothetical example, a simplified version of English may have the velar nasal as a separate phoneme (perhaps spelled <ng>), but the designer of the language may not explicitly state that it exists in his language, perhaps because he is unaware that it exists in English.
10 One might think that at least allophonically Olingo has a velar nasal, as in the name of the language itself, but Jaque (1944: 33) states that "the consonants [are pronounced] as in English, save that each letter has only one sound". This may not rule out the possibility of allophones, depending on what he means by "only one sound". Descriptions of various other ALs may also say something about <n> (and other sounds) being pronounced "as in English", e.g. Elhassi (2008) states that in Ardano the prounciation of <n> is "like English n". Does this mean that <n> is always pronounced as an alveolar, the default prounciation of English <n>, or that it is pronounced as a velar when preceding a velar, as happens in English?
11 Conceivably there could be nasals in other places of articulation in borrowed words.
12 In Temenia, which uses the Greek alphabet, the dental/alveolar nasal is represented not by <ν>, as in Greek, but by <η>. (We use the cover term "dental/alveolar nasal" when it is not clear to us whether an AL has a dental or an alveolar nasal.)

The Langue Fédérale has bilabial and dental/alveolar nasals; Barral (n.d.: 27) seems to rather emphatically indicate that the language does not have palatal or velar nasals, saying, "**gn** = g + n; **ng** = n + g [pronuncendi separat!]".

Languages with Bilabial, Dental or Alveolar, and Velar Nasals

Eurasto, which is based on English, has bilabial, alveolar, and velar nasals; the printed letter for the last of these is <n′>, as in *livo′n′* 'a lover'. American, which has the same three nasals, has a very similar letter for its velar nasal, <ń>, as in *máń* 'among'.

The Pandunia letter for its velar nasal is the same as the IPA symbol for that sound, <ŋ>, but Kupsala (n.d. a) says, "In case the proper symbols are not available for typing, <ŋ> can be replaced with <q>". Pandunia also has bilabial and alveolar nasals. In Amerikan as well <ŋ> stands for a velar nasal and there are also bilabial and alveolar nasals.

In Ro (1913) and Ro (1921) there are bilabial, alveolar, and velar nasals, with <q> standing for the last of these, as in the word *aq*, which is glossed 'same, même, derselbe' in Foster (1913: 16) and 'self' in Foster (1921: 5). Ro (1931) also has this set of nasals, stood for by the same letters, and we would guess that this is true of Ro (1919), since it has the letters <m>, <n>, and <q>, but Foster (1919) does not explicitly say so.

Konya has bilabial and alveolar nasals; in addition, the letter <q> in its alphabet stands for a velar nasal, but this is one of the "[f]oreign letters" (Sulky 2005a) which are "[o]nly used in foreign (non-Konya) words and names" (ibid.). The letter <q> seems to be a relatively popular one for representing the velar nasal, since it has this phonetic value as well in Minyeva (e.g. in *fluqo* 'an onion') and Sasxsek (e.g. in *iaq* 'a sheep'), both of which also have bilabial and alevolar nasals (or perhaps a dental nasal in the case of Sasxsek).[13] Ceqli is another language with bilabial, alveolar, and velar nasals with <q> standing for the last of these; May (2007) explains this as follows: "Q was chosen to represent the consonant in siNG because it had no other obvious use, and because the NG sound rarely has a symbol in any language."

In Eurolang there are biblabial, alveolar, and velar nasals, the last one represented by the digraph <ng>. In Lingone <ngh> stands for the velar nasal, as in *longhe* 'long'; Bollen (n.d. a) says, "The hard 'g' is dropped [when this sequence of letters is pronounced], as opposed to –ng w[h]ere the hard 'g' is audible". Lingone also has bilabial and dental/alveolar nasals, spelled by <m> and <n> respectively.

---

13 Nutter (n.d. a: 6) gives the IPA symbol [n] to represent the pronunciation of <n> in Sasxsek and indicates that it is to be pronounced "[l]ike **n** in ni**n**e", but calls it a "[d]ental nasal". He has the same sort of inconsistency (ibid.: 6-7) with respect to <d> and <t> (but not with respect to <s> and <z>).

Ande has bilabial, alveolar, and velar nasals. Anderson (n.d.: 20) gives <n'> as the letter for the last of these, but in actual use it may never show up as such; Anderson (ibid.: 21) states:

> Where "n' " occurs in compounds with "k", or "g", the apostrophe is omitted thus "nk", "ng"; the "n" is here pronounced as "n' ". Where "n' " occurs as the final letter of a word, only the apostrophe is written thus "Sa' ", i.e., "San' ". Such words as "Angi' " or "Bankio' " exemplify both the above provisions concerning "n' "; in all other associations the apostrophe is used alone.

This might mean that the velar nasal is represented in a different manner when it appears as an allophone of the dental/alveolar nasal phoneme than when it is the realization of a separate velar phoneme, with both the dental/alveolar and the velar allophones of /n/ being represented by <n>.

In LdP the digraph <ng> can sometimes, but not always, represent [ŋ], and indeed one is not ever required to use a velar nasal in this language: the *Lingwa de Planeta Grammar* (anon. n.d. a: 2) states, "The combination «ng» at the end of a word is pronounced as one sound: [ŋ] (like in «doing») is preferred, but [n] is also possible. In the middle of a word this combination is read exactly as [a] combination of «n» plus «g»".

Languages with Palatal Nasals

There are bilabial, dental/alveolar, and palatal nasals in Tal, the last of which is spelled as <x>. Perio apparently also has (something like) a palatal nasal (as well as bilabial and dental/alveolar nasals); C&L (1907/1979: 4) state that the letter <q> is "prononcé à peu près *gn*" ('pronounced approximately *gn*'). There are bilabial, dental/alveolar, and palatal nasals in Panamane; the sequence <jn> stands for the palatal nasal, e.g. in *gajner* 'to win'. Dilpok and Pantos-Dimou-Glossa have the same set of nasals, with the palatal nasal being represented by <ñ> in both languages. Auxil has bilabial, dental/alveolar, and palatal nasals: according to Rodríguez Hernández (2002: 16) <gn> "= /nj hispana ñ/" ('= /nj Spanish ñ/').

Conclusion

We have found limited variation in the inventories of nasals in ALs. We know of no AL that lacks nasals (and of only one that has a single nasal), and of no AL that clearly has more than 3 phonemic nasals. Allophones of nasals (including syllabic nasals) are occasionally discussed by AL designers or presenters.

Chapter 2: Affricates in Artificial Languages

Affricates occur in many, but not all natural languages, and they also occur in many ALs. In this paper, after a few words on affricates in natural languages, we shall look at their occurrence in ALs.

Natural Languages

Affricates involve a range of places of articulation in natural languages. For example, German has the "labiodental" affricate [pf], Sherpa has the alveolar affricate [ts], English has the palato-alveolar affricate [tʃ], and Nez Perce has the uvular affricate [qχ]. Some languages have aspirated affricates as separate phonemes from their unaspirated counterparts. Various more exotic affricate types also occur, including lateral affricates (e.g. the [tɬ] of Classical Nahuatl) and ejective affricates (e.g the [ts'] of Tigre).

Artificial Languages

We now look at affricates in ALs. As with natural languages, it may be sometimes difficult to determine whether an AL has a (phonemic) affricate or simply a sequence of a stop followed by a fricative, and with most ALs we are not able to use instrumental means to resolve this question, given the lack of speakers. We assume that if a sequence stop – (close to) homorganic fricative is signified by one letter, it is an affricate. Below is a list of presumably phonemic affricates of some ALs.[14][15]

	dental/alveolar	palato-alveolar	
Algilez		[tʃ] <c>	[dʒ] <j>
American		[tʃ] <ć>	[dʒ] <ģ>
Amerikan	[ts] <z>	[tʃ] <ɉ>[16]	[dʒ] <j>
Ardano			[dʒ] <j>

---

14 Although we are dealing with "presumably phonemic affricates", we use square brackets rather than slashes. One issue that we are concerned with is how a particular letter in a language is to be pronounced, and pronunciation is a phonetic issue. The square brackets here can be interpreted to indicate the most general (or only) allophone of a phoneme, e.g. "[ts] <c>" means that a language has the phoneme /ts/, which is generally or always realized as [ts], and which is represented by the letter <c>.

15 In the case of Algilez and NOXILO, which have non-Roman alphabets, we give the letters from the Roman alphabet which are used to represent the affricates present in the language (rather than giving the symbols from their alphabets), which is reasonable, considering that the non-Roman alphabet is optional and/or is used less than the Roman alphabet in the presentation of the language.

16 Molee (1888: 220) says that this letter "is *t* and *j* combined".

Arulo	[ts] <c>		[tʃ] <ch>	
Auxil	[ts] <c>[17]		[tʃ] <ch>	[dʒ] <j>, <g>[18]
Blue Language			[tʃ] <ɥ>[19]	
Ceqli			[tʃ] <c>	[dʒ] <j>
Desa *Chat*	[ts] <c>[20]		[tʃ] <q>	[dʒ] <j>[21]
Ekselsioro			[tʃ] <c>	
Esata			[tʃ] <c>	[dʒ] <j>
Esperadunye			[tʃ] <c>	[dʒ] <q>
Esperanto	[ts] <c>		[tʃ] <ĉ>	[dʒ] <ĝ>
Esperingle			[tʃ] <c>	[dʒ] <j>
Euransi			[tʃ] <c>	[dʒ] <j>
Europal	[ts] <z>[22]			
Eurasto			[tʃ] <c>	[dʒ] <j>[23]
Eurolang			[tʃ] <ch>	
Eurolengo			[tʃ] <ch>	[dʒ] <j>
Fremdu	[ts] <c>			
Hom-idyomo			[tʃ] <c̃>	[24]
Idiom Neutral			[tʃ] <c>[25]	

---

17 Rodríguez Hernández (2002: 16) states, "C = /k/ antaŭ a, o, u   C = /s/ aŭ /ts/ antaŭ e, i" ('C = /k/ before a, o, u   C = /s/ or /ts/ before e, i').

18 Rodríguez Hernández (2002: 16) says, "G = [Esperanto] /ĝ/ antaŭ e kaj i   J = /ĝ/" ('G = /ĝ/ before e and i ...'). (In other environments <g> has the phonetic value [g].)

19 One apparently is permitted to pronounce <ɥ> as [ʃ]: while Bollack (1900: 2) states that <ɥ> "corresponds to the English *compound sound* TCH or CH", Bollack (1904: 4) says that it is "prononcé DCHE (ou, si l'on veut, CHE)" ('pronounced DCHE (or, if one wants, CHE)'). Perhaps the difference between the two sources is due to the intended audience for each, i.e. anglophones and francophones.

20 We assume that Desa *Chat*'s <c> stands for (something like) [ts]; the instructions on its pronunciation in Davis (1999/2000) are not entirely clear. He first says that <c> "has the sound of the ts in hats, not the c in cat or cent" and shortly thereafter states, "Note that c is NOT the sound of t followed by s. It is the sound of a short s made with the tongue initially pressed hard against the top of the mouth".

21 We assume that in Desa *Chat* <j> is pronounced [dʒ], since Davis (1999/2000) says, "Pronunciation of the consonants is similar to that of UK English, with some important exceptions", and <j> is not one of the exceptions given.

22 Weisbart (n.d.: 6) gives the pronunciation of <z> as "ts or ds".

23 We assume that <j> stand for [dʒ], although it is not explicitly stated in Tacchi (n.d.), since this letter is used for the first sound in the names 'James' and 'John', which are written /jEmz/ and /john/ in Eurasto orthography (the slash indicating capital letters).

24 It seems likely that [dʒ] exists in Hom-idyomo and that <j> stands for it, but Cárdenas' (1923: 2) description of the pronunciation of <j> is not clear; he states that it is "pronounced as in English and a little less strongly than in French. This sound is similar to that of Spanish *y* in *yegua*, assuming that here *y* has a consonant sound different from that of *i*. In French and Italian, *g* followed by *e* or *i* has very nearly the correct sound of *j* here described".

Ido	[ts] <c>	[tʃ] <ch>	[26]
Ingli		[tʃ] <c>	[dʒ] <j>
Lingone	[ts] <c>	[tʃ] <ch>	[dʒ] <j>
Lingua	[dz] <z>	[tʃ] <c'>[27]	[dʒ] <j>[28]
Ling. Int.	[ts] <c>	[tʃ] <q>[29]	
LdP	[dz] <z>	[tʃ] <ch>	[dʒ] <j>
Meso		[tʃ] <c>	
Mondlingvo	[ts] <z>	[tʃ] <ĉ>	[dʒ] <ĝ>
Myrana		[tʃ] <c>	
Neo		[tʃ] <c>	[dʒ] <j>
Neo Patwa		[tʃ] <c>[30]	([dʒ] <j>)[31]
NOXILO	[ts] <C>	[tʃ] <Q>	[dʒ] <J>
Olingo		[tʃ] <ch>	[dʒ] <j>
Orba		[tʃ] <h>	
Panamerikan		[tʃ] <c>	[dʒ] <q>
Parla	[ts] <c>		
Pasifika		[tʃ] <c>	[dʒ] <j>
Perio		[tʃ] <ch>	[dʒ] zs>/<sz>[32]
Ro (1931)			[dʒ] <j>[33]

---

25 The use of <c> to represent [tʃ] was not approved of by C&L (1903/1979: 498): "par une curieuse inconséquence, l'*Idiom neutral* donne à **c** le son complex *tch*, et représente au contraire le son simple *ch* par deux lettres: **sh**" ('by a curious inconsistency [or 'thoughtlessness'], Idiom Neutral gives to [the letter] **c** the complex sound *tch*, and represents on the other hand the simple sound *ch* with two letters: **sh**').

26 The letter <j> has the the phonetic value [ʒ], but one is permitted to realize it as [dʒ], "se on ne povas pronuncar ol tale" ('if one cannot pronounce it in such a way', De Beaufront (1925/2005: 8)).

27 The letter <c> (i.e. with no apostrophe) stands for [k]; <ch> stands for [kʰ].

28 The letter <j'> (i.e. <j> with an apostrophe) stands for [ʒ].

29 According to C&L (1907/1979: 81), "Si l'on répugnait trop à donner à **q** le son *tch*, l'auteur propose de donner ce son à **c**, et de remplacer la lettre **c** par la lettre **s**" ('If one is too reluctant to give the sound *tch* to **q**, the author proposes to give this sound to **c**, and to replace the letter **c** with the letter **s**').

30 Wilkinson and Wilkinson (2010) state, "C is pronounced either as English 'ch' or 'sh'".

31 [dʒ] is not listed among the consonants of Neo Patwa. Wilkinson and Wilkinson (2010) say of it, and of [v] and [z], "there are consonants that can be used in Neo Patwa, but are not used in the core vocabulary except for some exceptional cases. These sounds are used in specific cultural terms and in proper nouns, for example".

32 C&L (1907/1979: 4) say that "**zs ou sz**" ('**zs** or **sz**') stands for [dʒ]; we do not know what determines the choice between them, or whether one can use either of them freely.

33 One has a choice of phonetic values for <j> in this version of Ro; Foster (1931: 1) says, "Roleb J uz Francais J in Jour, ur English G in Edge" (which we believe means something like 'Pronounce J like French J in Jour, or English G in Edge'). In Ro (1913) <j> apparently could not be pronounced as an affricate, as Foster (1913: 15) says, "**J** is like *zh* or French *j*"; the same is true of Ro (1921).

Romániço	[ts] <ç>/<cz>, <c>[34]		[tʃ] <çh>	
Sasxsek			[tʃ] <c>	[dʒ] <j>
Sci. Dial			[tʃ] <x>	[dʒ] <j>[35]
Sintezo	[ts] <c>		[tʃ] <ch>	[dʒ] <j>[36]
Sona	([ts] <z>)	([dz] <z>)[37]	[tʃ] <c>	[dʒ] <j>[38]
Tutonish	[ts] <z>[39]		[tʃ] <ch>	
Veltparl	[ts] <z>		[tʃ] <c>	[dʒ] <h>
Virgoranto	[ts] <c>			
Voksigid			[tʃ] <c>[40]	[dʒ] <j>[41]
Volapük	[ts] <z>			[dʒ] <c>
Voldu			[tʃ] <c>	

Afrihili has the affricate [tʃ], spelled by <ch>, and apparently also [ts], since there is the sequence <ts>, which is pronounced "as in tsetsefly" (Attobrah 1973). It is likely that it also has the affricate [dʒ], represented by <j>; this letter of Afrihili presumably does not have the phonetic value [j], since there is a letter <y> in Afrihili (which probably does not stand for [y]).

SPL has the affricate [ts], as the letter <c> has this phonetic value "before E, I, AE, OE, Y" (Dominicus 1982: 4) (otherwise it has the phonetic value [k]). The letter <č>, which stands for [tʃ], is one of the two "Symbols Used in Geographic Names" (ibid.:5), as in *Čilia* 'Chile'; no other letter has this phonetic value and thus [tʃ] is probably not to be regarded as one of the native sounds of SPL.[42]

According to Kupsala (n.d. a) the "[p]honetic range" of the Pandunia letter <ȷ>[43] is "[ʒ] [z̞] [dʒ]"; we do not know whether this means that one has a choice

---

34 One uses <ç> or <cz> to represent [ts] in any other context than preceding <e> or <i>, where one uses <c>.
35 One might think that the Scientific Dial Ssystem also has an alveolar affricate, since according to Hallner (1912: 19) the pronunciation of <z> is "as 'dsee' in zebra, hazel, zone", but we would guess that <z> simply stands for a voiced alveolar fricative.
36 There are two permitted phonetic values of <j>, [ʒ] and [dʒ]; we would guess that a speaker has a free choice between them.
37 Searight (1935: 30) says that in Sona <z> "is sounded as in E[nglish] 'zeal', but may have the Italian variation of dz, or the German ts".
38 Again there are two permitted phonetic values of <j>; Searight (1935: 29) says, "*j* may be sounded as in E[nglish] dʒ or F[rench] ʒ = zh".
39 Molee (1902: 109) says, "'z' b [= is] hard as in german n [= and] italian; as zero (tsero), e [= the] more good t [= to] distinguish it from 's'. we need some hard sounds for variety".
40 One has a choice of pronouncing <c> as [tʃ] or as [ʃ].
41 One has a choice of pronouncing <j> as [dʒ] or as [ʒ].
42 SPL has the digraph <ch>, but it has the phonetic value [k].
43 This letter is apparently meant to be an undotted <j>. Kupsala (n.d. a) allows for the use of a lowered capital letter <J> instead of it (which we have not lowered for technical reasons), "[i]n case the proper symbols are not available for typing" (other than in this situation there are no capital letters in Pandunia), and says, "In practice the dotless j symbol (J) is almost always unavailable on computers because it doesn't belong to the Unicode standard yet".

of pronunciations or that <J> represents different sounds in different environments, though we suspect that the former may be the case.[44] However, Kupsala (n.d. b) gives only one possibility for this letter, stating that "**J** is pronounced as Z in 'azure'".

Spokil has no affricates but Nicolas (1904: 3) more or less allows <j> to be pronounced as a voiced palato-alveolar affricate rather than as a fricative, stating, "**J** a le son français: *jour*; mais il n'aucun inconvénient à le pronouncer *dj*" ('J has the French sound: *jour*; but there is no drawback in pronouncing it *dj*').

ALs (apparently) without affricates include aUI, Babm, Fitusa (which has seven consonantal phonemes), Kotava, the Master Language, pan-kel (as described in Wald 1909) (with 14 consonantal phonemes), Tal, Temenia, Toki Pona (which has nine consonantal phonemes), UNI (which has 15 consonantal phonemes), Uropa, Uropi, and Weltsprache (Volk and Fuchs).

In Konya the letter <c> stands for [tʃ], but it is a "[f]oreign letter" (Sulky 2005a) and "[o]nly used in foreign (non-Konya) words and names" (ibid.). Otherwise the language has no affricates.

To our knowledge no AL (designed for serious purposes) has an affricate which is not dental/alveolar or palato-alveolar, although many ALs have bilabial and velar stops. Likewise we know of no AL which has phonemic aspirated affricates, or ejective or lateral affricates. Some of these facts are not surprising, since ejective and lateral affricates are relatively rare among natural languages, but the absence of [pf] may be unexpected, given that some ALs have borrowed a considerable amount of material from German.

The table below summarizes the different ways in which affricates are represented in the orthography of ALs:

[ts]	<c> (e.g. Lingone) <c>, <ç>/<cz> (Romániço) <z> (e.g. Veltparl)
[dz]	<z> (e.g. LdP)
[tʃ]	<c> (e.g. Veltparl) <ć> (American) <ĉ> (e.g. Esperanto) <č> (Hom-idyomo) <c'> (Lingua) <ch> (e.g. Perio) <çh> (Romániço) <h> (Orba) <q> (e.g. Ling. Int.)

---

44 With respect to the "phonetic range" of some other letters, we believe that the latter type of situation may hold.

11

	<x> (Sci. Dial)
	<ɥ> (Blue Language)
[dʒ]	<c> (Volapük)
	<g>, <j> (Auxil)
	<ġ> (American)
	<ĝ> (e.g. Esperanto)
	<h> (Veltparl)
	<j> (e.g. Sasxsek)
	<q> (e.g. Panamerikan)
	<zs>/<sz> (Perio)

Table 1: *Letters for Affricates in Some ALs*

It can be seen that a wide range of letters has been used to represent the palato-alveolar affricates. Although the voiceless dental/alveolar affricate occurs in a fair number of languages, there is much less variation in its representation. The next table shows letters used to represent affricates (and the different affricates that they have been used to represent):

<c>	[ts] (e.g. Lingone), [tʃ] (e.g. Sasxsek), [dʒ] (Volapük)
<ć>	[tʃ] (American)
<ĉ>	[tʃ] (Esperanto)
<c'>	[tʃ] (Lingua)
<ch>	[tʃ] (e.g. Perio)
<g>	[dʒ] (Auxil in some environments)
<ġ>	[dʒ] (American)
<ĝ>	[dʒ] (Esperanto)
<h>	[tʃ] (Orba)
<j>	[dʒ] (e.g. Sasxsek)
<q>	[tʃ] (e.g. Ling. Int.), [dʒ] (Panamerikan)
<sz>	[dʒ] (Perio)
<x>	[tʃ] (Sci. Dial)
<z>	[ts] (e.g. Veltparl), [dz] (e.g. LdP)
<zs>	[dʒ] (Perio)

Table 2: A *Summary of Which Affricates are Represented by Which Letters in Some ALs*

Let us now look at the combinations of affricates found in ALs:

number of affricates	affricate combination	example languages
1	[ts]	Parla
	[tʃ]	Orba
	[dʒ]	Ardano
2	[ts], [tʃ]	Arulo
	[ts], [dʒ]	Volapük
	[tʃ], [dʒ]	Algilez
3	[ts], [tʃ], [dʒ]	Auxil
	[dz], [tʃ], [dʒ]	LdP

Table 3: *Combinations of Affricates Occurring in ALs*

Some, but not all, of the possible combinations occur, and some that do occur are rarer than others among our sample of ALs. There is no AL with only one affricate whose affricate is [dz] (and [dz] is not found often among ALs generally). The most common affricate among ALs with a single affricate is [tʃ], followed by [ts]; [dʒ] rarely appears as an AL's sole affricate. All combinations of two affricates include at one voiceless affricate, i.e. the combination [dz], [dʒ] is not found (although the combination [ts], [tʃ] is). Such facts are in line with the "avoidance of voiced sibilant affricates" in natural languages discussed by Żygis (2008). All combinations of two affricates include at least one palato-alveolar affricate, i.e. the combination [ts], [dz] never occurs (although [tʃ], [dʒ] does). It thus appears that palato-alveolar affricates are preferred relative to dental/alveolar ones, just as voiceless affricates are preferred relative to voiced ones.

Overall, it appears that ALs are conservative with respect to affricates, only using a few of those that are found in natural languages (which is probably due at least in part to an effort to avoid sounds regarded as difficult for prospective learners), and not using all of the possible combinations of those few affricates.

Chapter 3: Consonantal Digraphs of Artificial Languages

In this chapter we look at digraphs used to represent consonants in ALs, including the range of sounds in languages which are spelled by them and the range of digraphs used to represent some sounds. There is some degree of overlap between this chapter and the previous one, as digraphs, both in natural and artificial languages, often stand for affricates (e.g. English <ch> for [tʃ]), and affricates are often stood for by digraphs. However, there are many cases, in both natural and artificial languages, of digraphs standing for sounds which are not affricates (e.g. English <sh> for [ʃ]), and of affricates which are stood for by single letters. There are ALs with at least one affricate which do not have digraphs (e.g. Orba), while Uropa has one digraph but no affricates. As with other chapters, we only present information about a limited number of ALs, but this information should give some idea of the situation in such languages.

There may be some difficulty in determining what counts as a digraph (just as there may be some question of what counts as an affricate). For example, in English are <mb> as in *lamb* and <ck> as in *back* (standing for [m] and [k] respectively) digraphs? For the purposes of this chapter we use a narrow notion of *digraph*: we do not consider a sequence of letters to be a digraph unless it stands for a sound different from the sound generally represented by either of the single letters in it, i.e. we do not regard as digraphs sequences in which one letter is "silent". Thus we do not treat e.g. <mb> and <ck> in English as digraphs. Consider now the situation when a digraph represents a sound that one of its component letters also frequently represents, but with there being some common contexts in which this letter does not stand for that sound. For example, in Italian the sequence <ch> stands for [k], which <c> by itself also often represents. However, there is a well-defined set of circumstances in which <c> does not represent [k] (but rather [tʃ]). In such cases we do consider the sequence of letters to be a digraph.

Also, for us a digraph must represent a sound (significantly) different from what is represented by its two letters when in the same sequence and not part of a digraph. For example, if <ts> stood for the affricate [ts] in some language we would not consider it a digraph.

We do not deal with sequences such as <qu> or <kv> (at least the latter can be seen as simply representing the sequence of sounds that its component letters stand for when in the same order) or with digraphs for nasal sounds; for the latter v. Chapter 1. We also do not discuss digraphs such as <aw> and <ay> (which are at least partly vocalic), or the sequence <ks>, as it does not stand for a single sound.

In some languages, both natural and artificial, digraphs are part of the alphabet of a language, i.e. are counted as letters, while in some they are not, but we do not take account of this here.

There are many ALs which (as far as we can determine) do not use consonantal digraphs in their spelling system (not counting <qu>, etc.). These include Amerikan, Ardano, Balta, the Blue Language, Ceqli, Desa *Chat*, Dil, Esperanto, Esperingle, Euransi, Fitusa, Fremdu, Hom-idyomo, Ingli, Konya, Letellier's Langue Universelle, Meso, Mondlingvo, Neo Patwa, Omnial, Panamerikan, pan-kel, Pasifika, Sasxsek, the Scientific Dial System, Sona, Spelin, Suma, Tal, Toki Pona, UNI, Uropi, Vela, Volapük, Voksigid, Voldu, Weltsprache (Volk and Fuchs), and Zakrzewski's Lingua Internacional. The presence or absence of consonantal digraphs in a language can, to some degree, be linked to two factors: how many consonantal phonemes there are in a language (as the more phonemes there are, the greater the need there is to go beyond simple letters) and whether and to what extent a language uses diacritical marks, as letters with such marks can be used instead of digraphs (or vice versa). Esperanto uses several letters with circumflexes, and this is a feature of it that has been criticized; in some modified versions of it, e.g. Perilo, digraphs are used to replace them. However, it is possible for an AL to have neither digraphs nor diacritics; Mondlango is an example of such a language.

The table gives lists of digraphs (again leaving aside those that we are not discussing) in some ALs:

Language (no. of digraphs)	Digraphs (and what they stand for)[45]
Anglo-Franca (2)	<ch> ([tʃ]), <çh> ([ʃ])
Arulo (2)	<ch> ([tʃ]), <sh> ([ʃ])
Eurolang (4)	<ch> ([tʃ]), <sh> ([ʃ]), <th> ([θ]),[46] <zh> [ʒ][47]
Europal (1)	<ch> ([ʃ])
Id. Neut (1)	<sh> ([ʃ])[48]
Ido (2)	<ch> ([tʃ]), <sh> ([ʃ])
Lingua (4)	<ch> ([kʰ]), <ph> ([pʰ]), <sh> ([ʃ]), <th> ([tʰ])[49]
LdP (2)	<ch> ([tʃ]),[50] <sh> ([ʃ])

---

[45] As in the previous chapter we use square brackets rather than slashes to represent what letters stand for.

[46] Hunt (1998a) says, "If you have difficulty pronouncing [T] [i.e. [θ]], you can pronounce this phoneme as [t]".

[47] This digraph seems to be rare in Eurolang: there are no words containing it in the *Eurolang to English Dictionary* (Hunt 1998b), or indeed to our knowledge in any of the publicly available materials on Eurolang by Hunt.

[48] The digraphs <gh>, <kh>, and <th> can occur "[i]n the phonetic writing of proper names and foreign words" (Holmes 1903: 2).

[49] According to C&L (1903/1979: 382) <ch>, <ph>, and <th> stand for "*k, p*, et *t* aspirés" ('aspirated *k, p*, and *t*').

[50] In LdP <c> does not occur outside of this digraph, i.e. it does not occur on its own.

Mundolingue (2)	<ch> ([k]),[51] <sh> ([ʃ])
Myrana (2)	<ch> [x], <sh> ([ʃ])
Neo (1)	<sh> ([ʃ])
Nuove-Roman (1)	<ch> ([k])[52]
Olingo (3)	<ch> ([tʃ]),[53] <sh> ([ʃ]), <th>[54]
Perilo (4)	<cx> ([tʃ]), <gx> ([dʒ]), <jx> ([ʒ]), <sx> ([ʃ])
Ro (1913) (3)	<dh> ([ð]), <th> ([θ]), <wh> [ʍ][55]
Romániço (6)	<ch> ([k]),[56] <cz> ([ts]),[57] <çh> ([tʃ]), <kh> ([x]),[58] <sh> ([ʃ]), <th> ([θ])[59]
Sintezo (2)	<ch> ([tʃ]), <sh> ([ʃ])
Slovio (4)	<cx> ([tʃ]), <gx> ([dʒ]), <sx> ([ʃ]), <zx> ([ʒ])
Tutonish (2)	<ch> ([tʃ]), <sh> ([ʃ])
Uropa (1)	<th> ([ð])
Veltparl (1)	<sh> ([ʃ])
Virgoranto (1)	<sh> ([ʃ])

Table 1: *Sets of Digraphs in Some ALs*

[51] In Mundolingue both <ch> and <c> represent [k]; <c> has this phonetic value when it precedes <a>, <o>, or <u> (or a consonant?); when it precedes <e> or <i> it has the value [ts] or [tʃ].

[52] Both <ch> and <q> stand for [k] in Nuove-Roman, which does not have the letter <k>. In addition, <c> has the phonetic value [k] when not preceding <e>, <i>, or <y> (in which contexts it stands for [s]).

[53] The letter <c> is not found outside of this digraph in Olingo.

[54] Jaque (1944: 33) indicates that in Olingo <th> stands for "th", without saying whether it stands for the voiceless slit dental fricative or the voiced dental slit fricative; one might think that it cannot stand for both since "each letter has only one sound" (ibid.).

[55] Foster (1913: 15) indicates that the pronunciation of this digraph is "like *wh* in when"; <hw> can be used to represent the same sound. It is not clear to us what determines the choice between <wh> and <hw>, or whether one may choose freely between them. In fact, these sequences appear to be very rare or non-existent in Ro (1913). For that matter, the digraphs <dh> and <th> seem to be found in very few words in Ro (1913); the same is true of <dh> and <th> in Ro (1921). Ro (1913) also has the sequence <dj>, which is "like English j" (Foster 1913: 15), but we would not label this a digraph, since the sound it represents can be seen as the sum of the sounds represented by its component parts.

[56] Both <ch> and <c> represent [k] in Romániço; <c> has this phonetic value when it is not preceding <e> or <i> (when it has the value [ts]); <ch> can only precede <e> or <i> (at least as a digraph), and when it does, it stands for [k].

[57] One has a choice of using <ç> or <cz> to represent [ts] before letters other than <e> and <i>.

[58] In Romániço the letter <k> does not occur outside of this digraph, which, along with the sound that it represents, is "only used in a few words of non-Latin origin" (Morales n. d. a).

[59] The version of Morales (n.d. a) downloaded on May 21, 2010 does not mention this digraph, but the version viewed on October 31, 2010 does and gives as the "example" of its pronunciation "t̲hank (or t̲ank, whichever's easier)"

17

We would not claim that this is a representative sample of ALs with digraph (in fact it might be difficult to know what counted as a representative sample of ALs) but we can make some observations about it, which might be indicative of some general tendencies. The most frequent digraphs (in terms of number of languages they are found in) are <ch> and <sh>, each occurring in roughly 2/3 of the languages (14 and 15 out of 22 respectively). The next most common digraph, <th> occurs only in half as many languages (seven). Seven of these ALs have only one digraph, and that one is usually <sh> (found in four such ALs, with <ch> found in two and <th> in one). By far the most common sound to be represented by a digraph is [ʃ], this happens in 19 of the languages shown above; [tʃ] is represented by a digraph in 11 of them.

In most ALs with digraphs, the second component of most or all of their digraphs is the same, usually <h>, but <x> in and Perilo and Slovio. The same situation holds in some natural languages as well, e.g. English, in which most digraphs (in our narrow sense) have <h> as their second component. This means that the distinction between digraphs and letters with diacritics is not clear. (Indeed, <x> is used as a replacement for the circumflex when writing Esperanto in situations when one cannot type diacritics.) If we were to restrict our concept of *digraph* so as to eliminate such cases, there would be very few diagraphs in ALs. The status of these "diacritical letters" differs; in some languages it never occurs outside of digraphs, as is the case of <x> in Perilo and <h> in Pantos-Dimou-Glossa (see the next table), and in such languages one could make a stronger case for it being simply a diacritic (as diacritics do not occur without their letters either). However, in other languages these letters can occur on their own, as is the case with the <x> of Slovio. One would think that whatever letter is chosen as a "diacritical letter" is one that is not very common in the language generally, or least is excluded from some contexts, for otherwise there might be confusion between the digraph and a sequence of simple letters.

Note that Slovio's representation of [ʒ] is different from that of Esperanto: in addition to having <x> instead of a circumflex; the letter that is modified is not the same, for Esperanto uses <ĵ> for [ʒ] while Slovio uses <zx>.

The table on the next page shows some digraphs occurring in ALs (including some not brought up in the previous table[60]), and what sounds they stand for.

Although both <ch> and <sh> are found in relatively large numbers of languages, <ch> is used to represent a variety of sounds while <sh> is only used to stand for one sound, [ʃ]; further, <ch> is used to stand for different kinds of sounds, stops, fricatives, and an affricate.

---

60 Table 1 is supposed to give what we believe to be complete sets of digraphs of the languages listed in it (subject to the restrictions and omissions mentioned above); if an AL appears only in Table 2 we may or may not be giving all of its digraphs.

<ch>	[k] Mundolingue, Nuove-Roman, Romániço; [kʰ] Lingua; [ʃ] Adelfeal lingw, Europal; [tʃ] Afrihili, Alteutonik, Anglo-Franca, Arulo, Auxil, Eurolang, Ido, LdP, Olingo, Pantos-Dimou-Glossa,[61] Perio,[62] Sintezo, Tutonish; [x] Myrana
<cs>	[ts] Linguna
<cx>	[tʃ] Perilo, Slovio
<cz>	[ts] Romániço; [tʃ] Linguna
<çh>	[ʃ] Anglo-Franca; [tʃ] Romániço
<dh>	[ð] Ro (1913), Ro (1921); [dʒ] Adelfeal lingw
<dz>	[ð] Linguna
<gx>	[dʒ] Perilo, Slovio
<jx>	[ʒ] Perilo
<kh>	[x] Adelfeal lingw, Romániço
<lh>	stands for "*ll* mouillées" (C&L 1903/1979:247) in Pantos-Dimou-Glossa
<ph>	[pʰ] Lingua; [f] Communia, Int. IALA, SPL[63]
<qh>	[ç] Linguna
<sh>	[ʃ] Afrihili, Alteutonik, Arulo, Auxil, Eurolang, Id. Neut., Ido, Linguna, Lingua, LdP, Mundolingue, Myrana, Neo, Olingo, Pantos-Dimou-Glossa, Romániço, Sintezo, Tutonish, Veltparl, Virgoranto
<ss>	[s] Linguna[64]
<sx>	[ʃ] Perilo, Slovio
<sz>	[s] Linguna;[65] [dʒ] Perio
<th>	[θ] Eurolang, Ro (1913),[66] Romániço; [ð] Afrihili, Uropa
<wh>	[ʍ] Ro (1913)
<zh>	[ʒ] Eurolang; [tʃ] Communia
<zs>	[dʒ] Perio
<zx>	[ʒ] Slovio
<zz>	[ts] Linguna

Table 2: *Some Digraphs of ALs and Sounds Represented by Them*

---

61 The letter <h> does not occur outside of digraphs in Pantos-Dimou-Glossa.
62 Note that Perilo and Perio are different languages.
63 All three of these languages also have the letter <f>.
64 In Linguna <s> stands for [z].
65 Publicly available materials on Linguna, such as Goeres (2004), are not entirely clear on the matter, but <sz> may sometimes stand for [θ], although this sound is usually represented by <z>.
66 One might suspect that Ro (1921) also has this diagraph (and that it stands for [θ]), given the existence of e.g. the word *ith* 'according to', although Foster (1921) does not explicitly say so.

The next table presents some sounds (other than affricates and nasals) which are represented by digraphs in some ALs; the third column shows some monographs which are used to represent the same sound in other (or the same) ALs:

[k]	<ch> e.g. Mundolingue	<c> e.g. Mundolinco, <k> e.g. Esperanto
[f]	<ph> e.g. Int. IALA	<f> e.g. Int. IALA
[θ]	<th> e.g. Ro (1913)	<c> Hom-idyomo, <j> Ande, <z> Linguna
[ð]	<dh> Ro (1913), <dz> Linguna, <th> e.g. Uropa	<q> Ande, <z> Dilpok
[s]	<ss> Linguna, <sz> Linguna	<s> e.g. Esperanto
[ç]	<qh> Linguna	
[ʃ]	<ch> e.g. Europal, <sh> e.g. Olingo, <sx> e.g. Slovio	<c> e.g. Perio, <ç> Dilpok, <h> e.g. Tal, <j> e.g. Dil, <ŝ> Esperanto, <x> e.g. Orba, <y> Ling. Int., <σ> Universal-Sprache
[ʒ]	<jx> Perilo, <zh> Eurolang, <zx> Slovio	<j> e.g. Perio, <ĵ> Esperanto, <j'> Lingua
[x]	<ch> Myrana, <kh> e.g. Romániço	<h> Omo, <ĥ> Esperanto
[ʍ]	<wh> Ro (1913)	

Table 3: *Some Sounds Represented by Digraphs in Artificial Languages*

A range of sounds are represented by digraphs (generally fricatives and affricates), although there are some sounds that we have never seen spelled by a digraph, e.g. [b] and [v] (nor do we recall having seen these sounds represented by digraphs in natural languages). Although [ʒ] is not often represented by digraphs, in the languages that we have examined here three different digraphs have been used to spell it.

Conclusion

Many ALs use digraphs, although usually they do not use a large number of different ones, and many ALs do not have digraphs at all. Digraphs vary widely in how commonly they are found across ALs, with some occurring in many or most ALs that use digraphs, and some occurring in only a small number of ALs.

Chapter 4: Stress Systems of Artificial Languages

Stress can be a difficult feature for second language learners of some natural languages to master. One might therefore be tempted to agree with Monnerot-Dumaine's (1960: 27) remark about stress in ALs, "une L.I. [= langue internationale] doit avoir des règles [for stress] réduites au minimum" ('an international language should have rules reduced to the minimum'). In this chapter we shall see whether AL designers have followed this principle.

Languages with Simple Fixed Stress

We begin with languages in which stress is usually or always on the same syllable of the word.

Languages with Stress on the First Syllable

Toki Pona words receive stress on their initial syllable. The same is true of Ling, Suma, and Virgoranto. Kupsala (n.d. b) states with respect to Pandunia, "First [sic] syllable of every word is stressed. The stressed syllable is *higher and louder* than the rest of the syllables". Prist (1998b: 3) says of Vela, "Where are the stresses, in the old languages? Can anyone remember them all? In Vela, there is a weak stress on the first syllable in every word".

Languages with Stress on the Second Syllable

Attobrah (1973) states that in Afrihili, "The accent ... is usually on the second syllable".

Languages with Stress on the Penultimate Syllable

Languages in which stress is on the penultimate syllable include American,[67] Arlipo,[68] Ayola,[69] Esperanto, Eurolang, Fremdu, Mondlango, Mundolinco, Olingo, pan-kel, Parla, Salveto,[70] Sintezo, and Veltparl.

---

67 O'Connor (1917: 8) does not express this in the most concise way: "Every word of more than two syllables is accented on the syllable next to the last. Words of two syllables are accented on the first syllable."
68 Although Vitek (n.d.) states that the stress is "Omnam sur avanlasta silabo di vorto" ('Always on the penultimate syllable of the word'), he also says (ibid.), "En parolado au poezio esat ellasebla adjektiva au adverba finazho, anstate kvo on skribat apostrofo; akcento daurat sur la sama silabo" ('In speaking or in poetry an adjectival or adverbial ending is elidable, instead of which one writes an apostrophe; the accent remains on the same syllable'). In such cases then the stress would be on the last (actually present) syllable.

Uropa generally, but not always, has penultimate stress; Donisthorpe (1913) states, "the accent is always on the last syllable but one, EXCEPT when that syllable happens to be -yr, -yt, -ym or -ys. The letter 'y' is short. Thus is 'ludera,' a playground, the accent is on the 'er,' ... but in 'dolyre,' to hurt, the accent is on the first syllable". From his example, one would conclude that those words that are not stressed on the penult receive stress on the antepenult.

Concerning Atlango Antonius (2009a) says, "Stress falls most often on the second-last syllable. [...] There are also words with stress on the last syllable, which are ended by -all and even by -arr".

Rodríguez Hernández (2002: 16) states about Auxil, "La akcento ĉiam estas sur la antaŭlastan silabo, kiel in Esperanto. Escepte en la vortoj devenitaj de orient-europaj lingvoj, ĉi-kaze la akcento estas simila al tiu de la originala vorto" ('The stress is always on the penultimate syllable, as in Esperanto, except in words derived from East European languages; in these cases the stress is similar to that of the original word').

In Romániço as well the basic pattern involves penultimate stress, but not all words follow this pattern; Morales (n.d. a) states,

> Generally speaking, words in Romániço are stressed on the next-to-the-last syllable, as in **fortuno** [for-'tu-no] and **mentiono** [men-'tjo-no]. The exceptions to this rule are infinitive verbs, which are stressed on the last syllable (eg., **parler**, "to speak", pronounced [par-'ler]), and words whose stress falls on the third-to-the-last syllable, indicated by an accute accent mark (eg., **ópero, ásino**). These last words go back to being stressed on the penultimate syllable, however, when suffixes that change the stressed vowels' position in the words are added: **herédito** "inheritance", but **hereditanto** [he-re-di-'tan-to] "heir".

---

69 Ayola Research Group (2007: sec. 2.9) says, "Names from other languages can be approximated by the string of Ayola sounds which is closest to the native pronuncation by using the twenty-eight symbols of the Ayola alphabet along with the acute accent (´) indicating irregular stress (stress not on the next-to-the-last syllable) and the grave accent (`) indicating the absence of stress". Further, "There are no native Ayola interjections. All interjections are treated as adopted foreign words, e.g. **waw** (*wow*), **hurá** (*hurrah*), **olé** (*olé*). Because they are foreign words, they may use one of Ayola's two stress accents" (ibid.: sec. 1.3.6).

70 Non-native words and proper nouns can have stress on a different syllable; Lorenz (2010) says,

> An acute accent may be placed over a vowel for proper names and foreign imported words that are spelled phonetically, to indicate stress if Salveto's natural stress would result in a different pronunciation (e.g. América, Nu Mécsico, Wásington, Óregon, Bárbara). This does not change the sound of the vowel, only the stress. In the case of an "i" or "u" followed by a vowel, if either of the vowel pair is accented, the two are pronounced separately, not melded together as they normally would be (e.g. María, Perúa, Dián).
>
> If the word contains an accent or any non-Salveto letters, it must either be capitalized (a name) or italicized (a foreign word).

These accent marks, while useful in print, need not be used in handwriting, and, if so desired, can be ignored altogether. (Words like **spectáculo** are generally more recognizable in speech with the accent mark left in, but the marks are not critical for understanding.)

The same general situation holds of Unitario:

> As a rule of thumb, stress is put on the penultimate syllable. Exceptions are possible and can be indicated by underlining the stressed vowel. The infinitive is stressed on the last syllable. If no consonant follows the stressed vowel (as would be the case in 'rad_i_o'), the stress is moved foreward [sic] by one syllable 'r_a_dio'. The vowel 'i' is not always counted as a syllable for itself and forms sometimes an irregular version of stress. (Pleyer 1990: 104)

In the absence of an accent mark in the written form of a word, Voldu words have penultimate stress. Stadelmann (1945: 3) describes the situations when the accent mark occurs:[71]

> The accent [mark] is employed:
> A) to conserve the stress of any word whenever it would have to contradict the above accentuation rule when taking flexion [sic] endings. For the same reason the accent disappears when it becomes superfluous.
> Ex: Grande ['great, tall, big'], grándere, grándeste.
> Tic ['teach'], ticer ['teacher'], tíceros ['teacher' (GEN)], tícera ['female teacher'].
> Akús ['accuse'], akusen ['accused' [PST PTCP]], akuser ['accuser'], akúseno ['the accused'].
> Frekwént ['frequent(ly), often'], frekwenter ['more frequent(ly), often'].
> B) in proper names.
> Ex: Amérika, Méxiko, Sókrates.

As we see with *akús*, as well as with e.g. *anúns* 'announce' and *advertís* 'advertize', infinitive forms apparently are stressed on their final syllable. Several derivational suffixes bear stress, including *-és* (as in *byulés* 'beauty, from *byul* 'beautiful') and *-íst* '-er, -ist' (as in *sapíst* 'shoemaker, from *sap-* 'shoe').[72] Some underived nouns and adjectives are stressed on the ultima, e.g. *enzín* 'engine' and *egál* 'equal'.[73] Given the following statement (ibid.: 19), it appears that prepositions do not have stress, unless Stadelmann is discussing sentence stress rather than word stress: "Some prepositions (most of space) may take an adverbial

---

71 Stadelmann (1945: 4) says, "The accent [mark] can be abandoned later", which might mean that advanced speakers do not have to use it.

72 Cf. the suffix *-er*, which has a similar or the same meaning, but which does not bear stress, e.g. *beker* 'baker', from *bek* 'bake'. A difference between these suffixes is that *-ist* is attached to nominal stems, while it is verbal stems to which *-er* is usually attached.

73 Voldu would appear to have syllabic consonants, given words such as *probábl* 'probable'. However, to our knowledge Stadelmann (1945) says nothing about them, and the fact that the accent mark is over the <a> in this word indicates that he thinks that the syllable containing it is the ultima and not the penult (since otherwise it would not need the accent mark), i.e. that the lateral is not in the nucleus of a separate syllable.

23

function, when standing alone and stressed. [...] Ex: [...] Tu hav sie hat ná. *To have one's hat on.* [...] Tu stap méztu. *To step between.*"

In Arulo there is penultimate stress in all words except infinitives, in which the ultima receives stress, and except for the following situation: "Simple (non-compound) words in which the **i** or **u** precedes immediately the grammatical ending ... have the accent on the third vowel from the end: ... **perpétua**, perpetual; **asócias**, he associates ... but **omnadía**, daily; **fishglúo**, fishglue" (Talmey 1925: 2).

Languages with Stress on the Final Syllable

The ultima is the stressed syllable of Volapük words, with the exception that hyphenated suffixes, of which there are two (the subjunctive suffix *-la* and the interrogative affix *-li*[74]), do not bear stress; the syllable immediately before them is stressed.[75] Dil (which is a modified version of Volapük) has word-final stress. Wilkinson and Wilkinson (2010) say, "Though stress varies to some extent by speakers, stress in Neo Patwa is basically on the final syllable of the word. For compound words, the stress is usually placed on the last syllable of the compound."

Languages with Stress on the Root

We now look at languages in which a particular syllable of a word is (generally) stressed; however, that syllable is not one defined by its position relative to the beginning or end of the word, but by its occurrence in the root. Concerning stress in Uropi Landais (n.d. a: 3) states:

En général **l'accent tonique** tombe sur la **racine**; ce qui implique que ni les **préfixes**, ni les **suffixes**, ni les **terminaisons** ne sont accentués. [...]
Exceptions: sont accentués sur la **dernière syllabe:**
- Les substantifs **internationaux** terminés par une **voyelle** ex. *taksì* taxi ...
- les verbes au **passé** ex. ex: *i vizì* j'ai vu ...
- Les suffixes **-èl** *(instrument)*, **-ìst** *(spécialiste)* ex: *kotèl* couteau ...

('In general **the tonic accent** falls on the **root**, which means that neither **prefixes** nor [derivational] **suffixes** nor **grammatical endings** are stressed. Exceptions: the following are stressed on the last syllable:
– **International** nouns ending in a **vowel**, e.g. *taksì* 'taxi' ...[76]

---

74 The latter marker can also be a prefix, again hyphenated.
75 However, Schleyer (1887: 3) permits stressing of a syllable other than the ultima in limited circumstances: "In every word the stress, the accent, must be put on the last syllable. (Only in poetry this rule allows some freedom.)".
76 In fact, this is not an exception, since presumably *taksì* is a root. It is an exception to the rule given in Landais (n.d. b: 3) that "l'accent se place ... sur **l'avant-dernière syllabe** ... qui correspond à la racine" ('the stress is placed on the **penultimate syllable** ... which

- Verbs in the **past**, e.g. *i vizì* 'I saw' ...
- The suffixes -**èl** *(instrument)*, -**ìst** *(specialist)*, e.g. *kotèl* 'knife' ...)

With at least some of these "exceptions" it is required to place a grave accent over the vowel of the stressed syllable, as with *vizì*. Further, Landais (n.d. b: 3) says, "Dans les mots de **plus de trois syllabes** (rares), il est préférable d'**indiquer l'accent** tonique à l'aide d'un **accent grave**" ('In words of **more than three syllables** (rare) it is preferable to **indicate the** tonic **accent** with the help of a **grave accent'**). One of his examples is *anincèpli* 'incomprehensible'.

Bond (1926: 1) says of Meso, "**Akcentio;** kadi semper epi silab last de stem. Eks. sáltir, epistóles, kanadál ... plantlogí ... mesó" ('**Stress:** falls always on the last syllable of the stem. E.g. ...'). One might think he means "root" rather than "stem", given the example in his next sentence, "Kwando esti ple ka un sufiks, una akcentio lejer kadi also epi silab last: perféktibilitá" ('When there is more than one suffix, a light stress also falls on the last syllable ...'). Bond is thus one of the few language designers who brings up secondary stress.

According to C&L (1903/1979: 402) in Myrana, "L'accent se place sur la syllabe principale du mot" ('The accent is placed on the principal syllable of the word'). However they do not say how one identifies the "principal syllable"; one might guess that it is the one containing the root, but some roots have more than one syllable.

Languages with Stress Rules Based on Syllable Structure/Contents

Some ALs have slightly more complicated stress rules; stress is not always on the same syllable of words but is placed according to what is contained in syllables. In Lingua Komun, "L'accent porte en général sur la dernière syllabe fermée (par une consonne)" ('The stress rests in general on the last syllable which is closed (by a consonant)') (C&L 1903/1979: 481). Zilengo's stress rule is similar, but not identical; Lins (2001/n.d.) says, "Der Akzent liegt auf dem Vokal vor dem letzten Konsonanten" ('The accent is on the vowel before the last consonant').[77] These rules do not give identical results: in a word which ends V-CV Zilengo would have the stress on the penult, while Lingua Komun would have it on the antepenult or conceivably on an earlier syllable, since the penult is not closed, the

---

corresponds to the root'). The problem here is that not all roots are monosyllabic, as these stress rules seem to presuppose. Although it is not explicitly stated, it seems that in general if a word consists of a root of more than one syllable and no suffix it will be stressed on the penult; if such a word has stress on the ultima, this is marked, and can happen whether the last segment is a vowel or a consonant, e.g. *arànʒ* 'orange'. One might wonder where the stress occurs in the word *tilie* '1000'.

77 We assume that in a word such as *dio* 'day', which has no vowel before the last consonant (which is the only consonant), the first syllable is stressed. This is the case in Idiom Neutral, as we shall see presently.

consonant being part of the ultima (if we assume that by "syllabe fermée (par une consonne)" C&L mean 'closed syllable' in the usual sense (and not 'a syllable whose vowel is followed by a consonant which need not be in the same syllable')).

Idiom Neutral has the same stress rule as Zilengo, with exceptions. Holmes (1903: 2-3) describes it as follows (and brings up the situation mentioned in footnote 77):

> The accent (or stress of voice) is on the vowel that immediately precedes the last consonant, if there be such vowel, e.g. **fortun** (pronounced **fortùn**) fortune, **manu** (pr. **mànu**) hand, **aloe** (pr. **àloe**), **filio** (pr. **filio**) son; otherwise it is on the first vowel, e.g. **mai** (pr. **mài**) May, **Deo** (pr. **Dèo**). In exceptional cases the accented (stressed) vowel is denoted by a written accent, e.g. **idé** idea, **alé** alley, **depó** depot.
>
> REMARK: In the compounding of such words, that is words having the written accent, with a suffix, the accent is dropped and the word is accented (stressed) according to the general rule, e.g. **aleatr** (pronunciation **aleàtr**) alley-like.

C&L (1903/1979: 450) say the following about Universala: "L'*accent* porte sur la voyelle qui précède la dernière consonne: **línga, felíci, kavál**, à moins que la dernière syllabe ne soit un suffixe: **ábil, naziónes**. Il porte sure l'i final des radicaux substantifs: **polizí, akademí**" ('The *stress* rests on the vowel which precedes the last consonant ... unless the last syllable is a suffix ... It rests on the final **i** of nominal roots').

The general stress rule of Zakrzewski's Lingua Internacional is that the ultima is stressed if its final segment is a consonant, otherwise the penult receives the stress. This rule is slightly different from the rule of Zilengo and Idiom Neutral, as the latter allows for the possibility of the antepenult or an earlier syllable being stressed,[78] while in Lingua Internacional the choice is between the ultima and the penult. There are exceptions to Lingua Internacional's rule: words with the suffix *-ità* ("qui forme les substantifs de qualité" ('which forms nouns of quality', C&L 1907/1979: 84)) are stressed on the last syllable of this suffix, as can be seen from the grave accent which apparently is placed over its vowel to mark this, e.g. *necesità* (which we assume means 'necessity'). Also, verbs are stressed on the first syllable of their inflectional ending (or sequence of inflectional endings, if one analyzes some forms as containing more than one inflectional suffix, as seems plausible), which consist of one, two, or three syllables.

Ardano has the same basic rule as Zakrzewski's Lingua Internacional; again there are exceptions; Elhassi (2008) says:

---

[78] For example, if the last three syllables of a word were V-CV-V, the antepenult would be the stressed syllable. According to the rules of both Lingua Komun and Zilengo/Idiom Neutral the antepenult could be stressed, but under different conditions.

Remember: (Very important)
-Words are accented upon the vowel before the last if the final letter was a vowel ... [...]
But if the word ends with a constant [sic] the accent will be upon the last [vowel] [...]
Finally (') is used to accent the last vowel like in:
Hratisia' pronounced "*hratisaa*" means ***play***. [...]
(') is the only way to accent a vowel if it was the last letter. It's found only in words ending by these three suffixes (sia', mo', e') and in verbs in future tense. Other than that, it [is] maybe found in people's names.

The situation in Kotava is similar: the ultima of words whose last segment is a consonant (including semi-vowels) receives the stress, while the penult is the stressed syllable of words whose final segment is a vowel, with one class of exceptions: 1st person singular forms of verbs end in a vowel, but their ultima receives the stress (optionally marked by an acute accent, e.g. the 1st person singular present form of the verb meaning'(to) sell' is *dolé*). Fetcey and the Comité Linguistique Kotava (2009: 5) say that this is "par analogie avec les autres formes verbales conjuguées" ('by analogy with the other conjugated verb forms'), all of which end in a consonant and thus have their ultima stressed.

Romanova has a similar general stress rule, but with word-final *s* patterning with vowels in determining the stressed syllable; the webpage *Lessons for Romanova, the Auxiliary Language* (anon. n.d. g) makes the following statements: "The stress on words is similar to that of Spanish; an apostrophe after a vowel shows that it is stressed. For words without an apostrophe (the vast majority), words ending in a vowel or the letter **s** are stressed on the next-to-last syllable. Words ending in a consonant other than **s** are stressed on the last syllable."

In Novilatiin, stress can fall on the ultima, penult, or antepenult; C&L (1903/1979: 458) state, "L'*accent* (dans les mots simples) porte sur la dernière syllabe, si elle est longue (**feliic**, *heureux*); sinon, sur l'avant-dernière, si elle est longue de nature ou par position (**hoteleero**, *hôtelier*; **pauperta**, *pauvreté*); ou sinon, sur antépenultième (**konvokan**). Dans les mots composés, chaque élément garde son accent (sauf les prépositions)" ('The stress (in simple words) rests on the last syllable, if it is long ...; if not on the penult, if it is long by nature or by position ... or if not, on the antepenult. In compound words, each element keeps its stress (except prepositions)').

Like Novilatiin, Kosmos is based on Latin, and it is not surprising that it follows the Latin stress rule; C&L (1903/1979: 374) say, "L'*accent* n'est jamais sur la dernière syllabe (sauf dans les monosyllabes); il est toujours sur la pénultième ou l'antépénultième, suivant que pénultième est longue ou brève (comme en latin)" ('The *accent* is never on the last syllable (except in monosyllables); it is always on the penult or the antepenult, depending on whether the penult is long or short (as in Latin)').

Languages with Other Types of Stress Patterns

Some ALs designers are not entirely clear in their descriptions of the stress systems of their languages. Molee (1902: 109) says about Tutonish, "accent as in german [sic], or on e [= the] qualifying syllable". Concerning Alteutonik Molee (1915: 11) states, "e betonu ... is als in nordgermania, skandia n holand; namlik, an e haupt, odr beshreibande silbe; so, 'shule'haus' n 'hans'sihnle'. mit fremde worta is e betonu an e ende ov di worta ; so, 'nazion' ', ' religion' ', nsf". ('The stress is as in North Germany, Scandinavia, and Holland, namely on the main or describing syllable; thus ... With foreign words the stress is on the end of the words, thus ... and so forth').

Languages with More Complicated Stress Rules

In some languages the process of determining the stressed syllable is rather complex, sometimes surprisingly so.
    Consider the following passage about stress in Evroptal (Le Masson n.d. a):
    [1] L'accent porte – *à une exception près (cf ci-après)* – sur la syllabe qui précède la terminaison grammaticale (à savoir : -a, -at, -e, -et, -i, -it, -o, -u, -ut) [...]
    [2] Afin d'éviter toute ambiguité, l'usage veut que l'on double la voyelle supportant l'accent (cf derniers exemples) si celle-ci ne respecte pas la dernière règle.
    [3] La seule exception à la règle [1] consiste à **ne pas accentuer** la dernière syllabe d'une expression circonstancielle qui ne fait pas intervenir de préposition, ni de finale en -o; de ce fait, l'accent porte alors sur l'avant-dernière syllabe: **hoolnotj**: (pendant) toute la nuit, **kaajden**: chaque jour ...
    [1] With one exception (see below), the stress is borne by the syllable which precedes the grammatical ending (namely *-a, -at, -e, -et, -i, -it, -o, -u, -ut*) [...]
    [2] In order to avoid any ambiguity, usage requires that one double the vowel bearing the stress if the latter does not respect the above rule [i.e. if it involves the exception which is about to be mentioned].
    [3] The only exception to rule [1] is that one does not stress the last syllable of a circumstantial expression which involves neither a preposition nor the ending -o; so, the stress is then borne by the penult: : **hoolnotj**: (during) the whole night, **kaajden** every day ...

Since all the grammatical suffixes listed by Le Masson are monosyllabic, if they are present a word will have penultimate stress; we assume that a di- or polysyllabic word without a grammatical suffix will have stress on its last syllable, with the exception noted in [3] in the quotation.
    Panamane has a very complex stress pattern, although the basic rule is penultimate stress; Amador (1936: 2) states, "The predominant accentuation is the

grave. The condition of accute [sic], or *sdrugule* -- said of the word accented on the third syllable from the last -- is determined from the particular structure of words in general; in the first case, from the character of their termination, in the second from certain idyosincracies [sic] of orthography to be dealt with in due course". One group of exceptions involves words ending with <e>: "*nasione* nation, *drapote* flag, *silare* city, *strade* street, *shariote* chariot, are in practice accute, although grave theoretically, on the ground that *e* as word ending, is supposed to be mute unless preceded by another vowel or by *y*" (ibid.: 2-3). We interpret this to mean that the ultima of these words is stressed, with the orthographic <e> being silent and thus not being the nucleus of a syllable. The other words with stress on the ultima consist of "all words ending in double consonant, in *x* and in *z* ... and in mute *h*-, except such as may represent verb inflections" (ibid.: 3), e.g. *shantress* 'professional woman singer', *jenerez* 'generation', *sobrietah* 'sobriety'. Antepenultimate stress is at least sometimes marked by a silent *h* after the vowel of the antepenult, e.g. *ihnfinit* 'infinite', *Amehrika* 'America'.[79]

LdP also has a rather complex stress system; the *Lingwa de Planeta Grammar* (anon. n.d. a: 3-4) states:[80]

The main rule is: the vowel before the last consonant or «y» is stressed:
máta *mother*, suóla *sole (of footwear)*, matéria *matter*, nóve *new*, kórdia *heart*, aktór *actor*, aván *forward*, krokodíl *crocodile*, dúmi *to think*, jámi *to gather*, báya *berry*, jaopáy *signboard*.
In words of the shape (C)CVV like háo *good, well*, krái *to cry* the first vowel is stressed.
In the combination "au" "a" is stressed:[81]
áusen *outside*, áudi *to hear*, áuto *car*, máus *mouse*, káusa *cause*.
In the combinations "ai", "ei" — "i" is not stressed:
máini *to mean*, fáil *file*, bréin *brain*, méil *mail*.
There are 4 consonant endings which are never stressed. These are **-en, -us, -um, -er**: ínen *inside*, íven *even*, désnen *to the right of*, vírus *virus*, fórum *forum*, sírkum *around*; ínter *between*, kompyúter *computer*.
The endings of nouns and adjectives **-ik-, -ul-** are unstressed:

---

79 Amador (1936) usually marks stress (with an acute accent), although ordinarily this apparently would not be done; he states (p. 2), "The fix [sic] and to a certain extent fool-proof rules devised on the subject of tonicity, render absolutely unnecessary the use of a graphic sign to mark the accentuation in any case in current writing. In employing one with the persistency observed throughout this work, it has been with aforethought on the elimination of whichever uncertainty might assail the student at the start, in determining the precise tonicity of any word of more than one syllable." In this book we have preserved his indication of stress.

80 Note that while in this passage stress is marked with an acute accent, this is not ordinarily done in LdP.

81 As far as we know, none of the publicly available materials on LdP says that there are diphthongs in the language.

gramátika, pedagógika, públika, Áfrika, Amérika, polítike, lógike, únike, psikológike; stímula, ángula. This doesn't apply to compound words with -fula like handafúla *handful*.

Non-standard stress is indicated through a doubled vowel: *kwantitaa* quantity, kwalitaa *quality* (and all abstract nouns derived from adjectives via the stressed suffix **-(i)taa**); namastee *hello*, adyoo *good-bye*, bifoo *before*, malgree *in spite of*, shosee *highway*, milyoo *milieu*. The use of a doubled vowel is justified by that [sic] the stress in LdP is basically quantitative. A doubled vowel in a word with a single vowel (like in 'zoo') is not regarded to be a stress mark.

Stress and word formation.

Plural endings **-(e)s**, adverb suffix **-em** and noun suffix **-ing** do not change stress: suólas *soles*, kórdias *hearts*, naturálem *naturally* (from naturále *natural*), fishing *fishing* (from físhi *to fish*).

Compound words are stressed according to meaning: auslándajén *foreigner*.

All the suffixes beginning with a consonant are in fact one- or two-syllable semantic particles, so words formed with them may be regarded as compound ones, with the corresponding stress: pártiayuán *a party member*, sindómnik *a homeless person*, gínalík *womanly* (from gína *woman*), kúsishil *tending to bite* (from kúsi *to bite*), ófnitúl *opener*, vídibíle *visible*.

Note also the following remark on <y> (ibid.: 3): "The letters «i» and «y» denote the same sound [i]. The use of «y» basically indicates that the sound is not stressed: pyu [piú]". That is, if <i> has been written instead of <y> in this word, the penult rather than the ultima would have been stressed.

Interlingua (IALA)'s stress pattern is complicated, although again there is a simple basic rule:

> The main stress is normally on the vowel before the last consonant. The plural ending does not change the original stress of the word. Words ending in **-le**, **-ne**, and **-re** preceded by a vowel have the stress on the third syllable from the end; e.g. **fragile, ordine, tempore**. In words formed with the suffixes **-ic, -ica, -ico,** -ide, **-ido, -ula,** and **-ulo**, the stress falls on the syllable preceding the suffix. The suffixes **-ific** and **-ifico** are stressed on the first **i**.
> Deviations from this stress system are covered in the *Interlingua-English Dictionary* by respelling with stress marks. Most of these deviations might be covered by additional descriptive rules. For instance, the suffixes **-issim-, -esim-, -ifer-,** and **-olog-** are stressed on the first vowel. The suffixes **-ia** and **-eria**, in so far as they correspond to English *-y* and *-ery*, are stressed on the vowel **i**; etc. (Gode and Blair 1951: 5)

However, Gode and Blair (ibid.) have a tolerant attitude regarding stress: "The importance of stress regularity should not be exaggerated. The effort in acquiring an unfamiliar stress for an otherwise familiar word seems often inordinate. This does not, of course, imply that Interlingua words may be stressed completely at random but merely that a word like **kilometro** remains the same international word whether native habits cause a speaker to stress it on the second or on the third syllable."

Yet another language with a complex stress system is aUI; Weilgart (1979: 42) (not entirely clearly) states:

> ACCENT: 1) Most stressed are the Nasals [i.e. nasalized vowels], A̱, E̱ ... a̱, e̱, i̱, or number-elements of a word, underlined: nákiA = summer
> 2) Second stress falls on "LONG" CAPITAL VOWELS: A, E, ...: iÁ ['day'].[82]
> 3) Third stress has the "Next-to-the-Last", i.e. the syllable which starts a 2-syllable word or is in the middle of a 3-syllable: e.g. úga (house) ...
> Distinguish ío (plant), iÓ (sight) since a long vowel competes, [b]ut again first syllable stress: ÍO (hearing), as both vowels are now long. [...]
> (In verbs, the stem-vowel, even if short, keeps a melodic accent, although in Past & Future the long "-pA-" & "-tA-" endings compete: "ov" ['live'] becomes "ópAv" [past indicative/infinitive form] with a high-sung tone on the "ó". [...])
> In a struggle between LONG and nasal, the nasal wins the stress: ákiA, year, "Ezé" = Helium ...

Evidently by "Most stressed", "Second stress", and "Third stress" Weilgart does not mean 'primary', 'secondary' and 'tertiary stress', but the ranking of factors for determining where (primary) stress falls.

Languages without Stress, with Optional Stress, and/or with Choice with Respect to Stress

Some ALs are said not to have mandatory stress, or not to have any syllables with more stress than others, and some ALs allow speakers a choice about which syllables to stress.[83]

Searight (1935: 31) says of Sona, "The tonic accent is evenly distributed, as in (F[rench]), (T[urkish]), (J[apanese])".[84] With respect to Desa *Chat* Davis (1999/2000) states, "all syllables are given equal stress (emphasis)". Steiner (1885: 16) says of Pasilingua, "Die Silben sind in der Prosa gleichwertig und gleichmäßig betont" ('The syllables are equally and evenly stressed in prose'). In Konya, "Stress is even, with optional de-emphasis on 'unstressed' syllables" (Sulky

---

[82] In aUI upper and lower case vowel letters stand for different sounds: Weilgart (1979: 9) says, "Short vowels are written with small letters, and LONG vowels with CAPITALS. ... whether vowels are long or short, they keep the same pronunciation, e.g. even long 'I' sounds never [sic] as in 'fire', but as in 'police'". The latter part of this is incorrect with respect to some vowels, since for example Weilgart (ibid.) gives *off* and *pot* as examples for the pronunciation of <o> and Oh! and emotion as examples for <O>.

[83] Some works presenting an AL say nothing about stress in that language, e.g. Rosenblum (1935) on Fitusa.

[84] This statement is incorrect with respect to Turkish.

2005a).[85] C&L (1903/1979: 188) say about Balta, "Toutes les syllabes devront être à peu près également accentuées; la dernière pourra l'être en peu plus" ('All the syllables will have to be stressed roughly equally; the last syllable will be able to be stressed a little more').

In general there does not seem to be obligatory stress in Esata, as Bothi (2004) states, "Except in certain limited cases, there is no use of emphasis in pronouncing the component syllables of words in Esata, and speakers may use emphasis as desired". In the next (2006) edition of this work he says, "There are no rules concerning use of emphasis in pronouncing the component syllables of words in Esata, except that verb forms, which end with the letter -*a*, are often pronounced with emphasis on the final letter". He later (ibid.) states, "Esata verbs end in -*a*. In spoken Esata we often stress the final -*a* of verbs to distinguish them clearly from the associated noun form".

Traditional Slovianski and Naučný Slovjanský are not rigid with respect to stress; van Steenbergen (2010) states about the former of these:

> Accentuation is free. However, if you want to stay on the safe side, it would deserve recommendation to follow as guidelines:
> • when a word has two syllables, stress falls on the first syllable;
> • when a word has three syllables, stress falls on the first or second syllable;
> • when a word has four syllables, stress falls on the second or third syllable;
> • stress should not be influenced by inflection; if the adjective „*beli*" is pronounced **beli**, the genitive should be pronounced **belogo** and not **belogo**.

Algilez also has freedom concerning stress; consider the remarks below, from Giles (2010a: 16):

> There is no necessity for stress on any particular syllable in Algilez words. However it is important that individual roots are [sic] pronounced clearly and separately to avoid confusion. Root words have been chosen to avoid alternative meanings as much as possible when they are combined but it will still occur from time to time. The context should help avoid misunderstandings. Occasionally it may help with some compound words if the 'mid' root is stressed, in order to avoid confusion. Pronunciation should otherwise generally follow that of the French language where there is normally equal stress on each syllable

There is a stress rule in Spokil, but one is not required to follow it (meaning that no syllable in a word would be stressed?); Nicolas (1904: 3) says, "L'accent se place facultativement sur l'avant-dernière syllabe dans les mots terminés par un voyelle; sur la dernière dans le mots terminés par un l; dans les incorporés, l'accentuation est facultative" ('The stress is placed on the penultimate syllable in

---

85 Sulky (2005b) states, "An unstressed syllable consists of a consonant followed by **a**". The Konya letter <a> has the pronunciation of the underlined letters in the English words "father or about" (Sulky 2005a). We do not know whether Sulky thought that these letters stand for the same sound or whether one has one has a choice with respect to the pronunciation of <a>.

words ending in a vowel; on the last syllable in words ending in **l**; in incorporated [i.e. borrowed] words, the stress is optional').

With respect to UNI Wainscott (1975: 2) says, "No accents; no accentuation. Each speaker may place accent as he or she prefers. Because all words are short there will be no confusion".

Ruggles seems to allow some choice about which syllable is stressed in a word in his Universal Language, and, given the following passage, he might allow or expect more than syllable to be stressed:

> The sense of the speaker, and force with which he wishes to be understood, will, in most cases, dictate the place where accent or emphasis should be placed; and though distinctness and sense will often require the accent to be placed differently in the same word, yet the following rules may generally be observed.
> RULE I. The radical syllables are *accented*; as, *Homz*ten ['a man'] ...
> RULE II. The syllables expressing gender in nouns, adnouns and adverbs, are *accented*; as, Homz*tin* ['a man or woman', *-i-* being the marker of "Personal common" (Ruggles 1829: 21) gender] ...
> RULE III. The syllables expressing mood in verbs are *accented* ...
> RULE IV. Particles, when subjoined to other parts of speech, and adjuncts,[86] are generally *unaccented* ...
> RULE V. Syllables not specified in the above rules are *unaccented*, when distinctness or emphasis does not require them to be particularly noticed."
> (Ruggles 1829: 75-6)

Languages with More than One Stressed Syllable

In several ALs there is supposed to be more than one stressed syllable in some words, with such syllables not differing in level of stress. With respect to NOXILO Sentaro (2010a) says, "Subtle accent is set on the 1st vowel, and 3rd vowel for a long word ... Accent is set on the long vowel ... and the vowel before consecutive same consonants ... [...] The above rule is applied for the ***most*** [sic] of the NOXILO ISWs (International Standard Words)". We do not know whether there is a meant to be a difference between an "accent" and a "subtle accent" but there can be a word with only the accent referred to as "subtle", or with more than one such accent (and with no other accent), e.g. ELAFANA 'affirmative', which has a "subtle" accent on the 1st syllable and on the penultimate syllable.

Anderson's (n.d.) instructions about stress in Ande are not entirely clear, but they seems to indicate that there will often be several (equally) stressed syllables in a word. We first quote from p. 35, which will show the terminology that he uses and his view on the nature of stress: "The terms 'normally voiced' and

---

86 Ruggles (1829: 60) states, "Adjuncts are syllables subjoined to radices for the purpose of forming derivative words, having a specific relation to their primitives".

'shortly voiced', have as their standard of comparison the voice volume normal to words of one syllable. Volume, pitch or duration of spoken sound is of course comparative and arbitrary. Note that ordinary accentuation is merely that of sound volume. Expressive accentuation is to a greater extent effected by modulation of the pitch and duration of sound." That is, if we understand him correctly, "normally voiced" can be taken to mean 'stressed' and "shortly voiced" means 'unstressed'. Bearing that in mind we can look at his (ibid.: 34) instructions:

> Each syllable in a word should be clearly articulated, slurring or overstressing of any syllable should be avoided.
>
> RULE 1: Except where accordance with Rule 3 may require – all words composed of complete standard vocables have the principal syllable normally voiced, and syllables preceding and following this are alternately short and normal.
>
> RULE 2: Words having more than one syllable integral to the root, have each such syllable normally voiced.
>
> RULE 3: The final syllable preceding a period is preferably normally voiced; this may also apply with good effect to final syllables in certain other cases.
>
> In order to accord with the above rules, affixes are of various types. A shortly-voiced "A" is used as an interposed or final mollifier, in accord with Rule 1, above. [...]
>
> A suffix (when not individual [i.e. when not a separate word, if we understand correctly]) with an initial "i" (short) and the vowel "i" – when preceding another vowel – are [sic] shortly voiced.
>
> A final "i" may be short or normal, as per Rule 3.
>
> All other syllables are normally voiced.

Conclusion

There is a great variety of stress systems among ALs, going from the very simple to the quite complex, and from having no obligatory stress to having more than one stressed syllable per word. However, it seems quite rare for a language to use stress phonemically,[87] which may be due in part to the difficulties which phonemic stress can cause to non-native speakers of a language. Thus at least in this respect AL designers have generally avoided complexity in the stress systems of their languages.

---

87 Solresol appears to have phonemic stress.

Part II: Morphology and Syntax

Chapter 5: Nominal Plural Formation in Artificial Languages

In this chapter we look at how ALs indicate plurality of nouns.

Languages without Plural Marking on Nouns

Some ALs do not have plural marking for nouns. This is true of Konya, Ling, Singlish,[88] and Temenia. It is also the case in Sasxsek; Nutter (n.d. a: 15) says, "Adjectives [sic] of quantity are used to indicate number whenever necessary. There are no separate singular and plural forms". His examples include *ieni kitab* 'one book', *duvi kitab* 'two books', and *meni kitab* '(several) books'. Kupsala (n.d. b) states, "Pandunia is entirely an analytical language. Words undergo no inflection or agglutination of any kind for any purpose. Consequently nouns do not have separate forms in singular and plural. E.g. *jan* person, people; *fut* foot, feet".

Zilengo also lacks plural marking on nouns (although they are inflected for case); Lins (2001/n.d.) states, "Besonders wichtig war Oka [the designer of Zilengo] der Verzicht auf die Unterscheidung von Singular und Plural beim Substantiv" ('Especially important to Oka was the abandonment of the distinction between singular and plural in the noun'). Wilkinson and Wilkinson (2010) say about Neo Patwa, "there is no distinction between singular and plural nouns. *Pwason* can be either 'a fish' or 'more than one fish'". The same situation holds in Toki Pona; Knight (2005: 8) says:

> Another way that Toki Pona is ambiguous is that it can not specify whether a word is singular or plural. For example, jan can mean either "person" or "people". – If you've decided that Toki Pona is too arbitrary and that not having plurals is simply the final straw, don't be so hasty. Toki Pona is not

---

88 Singlish here refers to the artificial language presented in Gao (2005), which is a "simplified English" (ibid.: 1), not the variety of English spoken in Singapore. Gao (ibid.: 6) justifies the doing away with plural marking (one of the "[f]ive suggested principal rules" (ibid.: 3) of Singlish) as follows:
> The ending "s" for a plural noun carries little meaning.
> In English, one people, ten people, a million people are correct forms. If someone used ten peoples, it is considered as a mistake. You can realize that ten people equal to ten peoples, since ten means plural already. But, if someone used ten boy (omitted "s" in boys), it will be considered as a mistake. Why? Since in "ten boy" the "ten" already means plural, as it is in ten people. So that "s" is no need [sic]. Why we need treat things unfairly and to consider that ten people is correct (is right), but ten boy is incorrect. If you are wise, you will say ten boys is a wrong form. In Chinese language all the singular nouns and plural nouns are the same forms. Therefore, the "s" as a suffix after a noun adds a lot of extra work with very little value. Omit that "s" In [sic] Singlish.

the only language that doesn't specify whether a noun is plural or not. Japanese, for example, does the same thing.

In Kosmos nouns are not inflected, but the article is; in fact the article does nothing other than giving information on number, case, and gender (i.e. it does not indicate (in)definiteness, which might make one wonder whether it should be called an article, as C&L (1903/1979: 374) do, presumably following the language's designer, Eugen A. Lauda). The following table shows some of its forms (those without neuter gender marking):

	SG	PL
NOM	ta	tas
GEN	tio	tios
DAT	te	tes
ACC	tan	tans

Table 1: *Some Forms of the Kosmos Article (Couturat and Leau 1903/1979: 374)*

Thus, like several natural languages and a good number of ALs, Kosmos has -*s* as a plural suffix, but it is not a nominal plural suffix.[89]

Likewise in Chabé Abane there is no inflection on nouns and inflectional information, including number, is conveyed by the article, which again has nothing to do with (in)definiteness, and again -*s* is its plural suffix. Nouns cannot occur without this article, whose forms are below:

	M SG	M PL	F SG	F PL
NOM	a	as	e	es
GEN	ad	ads	ed	eds
DAT	af	afs	ef	efs

Table 2: *Forms of the Chabé Abane Article (after Couturat and Leau 1903/1979: 83)*

Somewhat similarly, in Universal-Sprache nouns do not bear inflectional marking but there are singular and plural forms of the definite article (*el* and *li* respectively) and a singular form of the indefinite article (*un*).[90] As one might expect under the circumstances, there are also singular and plural forms of other determiners such as demonstrative adjectives and possessive adjectives.

---

89 The article also occurs with pronouns, in a hyphenated form following the pronoun, e.g. *mi-tas* 'we'.
90 C&L (1903/1979: 257) state, "Le pluriel indéfini est marqué par l'absence d'article" ('The indefinite plural is marked by the absence of an article').

Languages with a Sole Plural Marker

We now turn to languages which do have plural marking on nouns. Below we list the plural markers of languages which have a single invariable (synthetic) plural marker (leaving aside allomorphic variation which is not mentioned by our sources).[91] Note that these are the written forms of the endings, which sometimes mask identical pronunciations, e.g. the *-y* plural suffix of Atlango is phonetically identical to Esperanto's *-j*, as Antonius (2009a) indicates:

-ci:	Pantos-Dimou-Glossa[92]
-e:	(replacing final *-a* of singular) Parla
-i:	Algilez, Ardano (e.g. *tribon* 'shark', *triboni* 'sharks'; *beso* 'coin', *besoi* 'coins'), Idiom Neutral
-I:	UNI[93]
-i:	(replacing final *-o* of singular) Arlipo, Ido
-is:	Menet's Langue Universelle
-j:	Esperanto
-n:	Olingo
-s:	Balta, Communicationssprache, Dilpok, Europal, Farlingo, Fitusa, Homidyomo, Langue Fédérale,[94] Langue Nouvelle (Faiguet), Latinesce, Lingone, Mondlingvo, Mundelingva, Pasilingua, Perio, Romániço,[95]

---

91 Later we will see languages which have some variation in plural marking, but we might note that in some ALs which have a single plural marker, nominative singular noun forms (to which the plural marker is attached) always end in the same segment; this is the case e.g. in Esperanto. In most ALs which have more than one plural marker the allomorphy is phonologically conditioned, based on the last segment of the singular form, which is not always the same. Therefore languages such as Esperanto do not have what is perhaps the most common feature causing a language to have more than one plural form, so the uniformity of plural marking follows from another property of the language.

92 The letter <c> is pronounced [s] in this language. The same suffix marks plural forms of personal pronouns and some other pronouns, e.g. *e* 'I (M)', *eci* 'we (M)'. Definite and indefinite articles agree with their nouns in number, as do adjectives; the plural forms of these words are marked by-*i*, e.g. *el eke* 'the horse (NOM)' (C&L 1903/1979: 248), *eli ekeci* 'the horses (NOM)' (ibid.: 249).

93 UNI only uses capital letters.

94 In the Langue Fédérale, adjectives agree with nouns in number, but the plural suffix for adjectives is different than that for nouns, being *-i* (which replaces the singular adjectival ending *-a*).

95 In the section on "Proper Nouns", "which include names of individual people as well as words that are exclusively national or local", Morales (n.d. b) says, "if the plural of a foreign word is generally known, it should be used as the plural in Romániço, too (e.g., **dollars**). If it is not, one should add **-(o)s** (with the hyphen) to the word, thereby helping to prevent confusion (at least in writing) with existing Romániço words".

-u: Ruggles' Universal Language, Salveto,[96] Sintezo, Ulla, Vela, Virgoranto, Weltsprache (Eichhorn)
-u: the Blue Language, John Wilkins' language
-y: Atlango, Ayola, Veltparl[97]
-yn: Unitario
-z: Delormel's language, Ro (1921) (e.g. *taf* 'day', *tafz* 'days')[98]

The word class marker of nouns in Uropa is -*a*; in writing the plural is marked by changing this to -*ā,* but apparently the spoken form of the singular and the plural can be the same, as Donisthorpe (1913: 3) says, "Plural nouns carry a bar over the final -a, thus -ā. There is nothing mysterious about this bar: it simply means that the final -a is doubled. It is shorter and neater to write Kanā than Kanaa. In speaking, the -ā can be lengthened out a little, if required. But we find no difficulty in talking about sheep without saying 'shee-eep' for the plural".

Apparently in Zakrzewski's Lingua Internacional the plural suffix -*i* is simply attached to consonant-final stems while if the stem ends in a vowel -*i* replaces it.

Arulo has a single plural marker, -*i*, which replaces the -*o* of singular forms, but there is a slight modification for certain words: "The plural of proper names, foreign words, letters, numbers, and particles is formed by **i** preceded by a hyphen: **Cato-i, pound-i, be-i, du-i, ma-i e se-i**, Catos, pounds, bes [i.e. Bs], twos, buts and ifs" (Talmey 1925: 4).

We can see that -*s* is a very popular plural marker, which will be even more evident when we look at languages with some variation in plural marking, since

---

[96] This is the plural marker in the version of Salveto described in Lorenz (2010). Lorenz (2005) gives -*i* as the plural marker. It sometimes replaces the gender markers (which are vowels) at the end of singular forms, but does not always do so; Lorenz (ibid.) states, "Normally the plural form **-i** removes the gender from the word (e.g. one man would be **un omo**, two men might be **du omi**), but in many cases the gender is needed. In these cases, instead of dropping the genderizing vowel **a** or **o**, the **-i** suffix is *added* to it. So two men would be **du omoi**; two women would be **du omai**". (However, in one section in Lorenz (2010), "Fractions", the plural marker is still indicated to be -*i*; we assume that this is an error (i.e. that Lorenz forgot to change it).)

[97] The letter <y> stands for [y] in Veltparl.

[98] Although Foster (1913) does not say anything about it, apparently Ro (1913) has the same plural marker, given the following sentences:
(ia)   Il   ap   gegar   el   360   gegad-z.
        into   a   circle   are   360   degree-PL
        'In a circle are 360 degrees.'
(iia)   At   ger   iv   Ru   Ro   el   zeg gerde-z   ur   zac   gerbi-z.
        the   price of   *Ru Ro*   is   50 cent-PL   or   two   shilling-PL
        'The price of *Ru Ro* is 50 cents or two shillings.' (Foster 1913: 37)
Words in Ro (1919) such as *hepcaz* 'winnings', *paqibaz* 'tongs', and *abz* 'we, us' (cf. *ab* 'I, me') indicate that -*z* is the plural marker in this version of the language as well (for both nouns and pronouns).

one of the variants is usually -*s* (and the other is usually -*es*). This is presumably due to the influence of English and/or one or more other major Western European languages.

Languages with More than One Plural Marker

We now turn to languages in which there is more than one plural ending. Usually there is a simple and regular rule concerning which ending appears, and this rule usually involves the final consonant of the stem to which the plural affix is to be attached. Below we give details on languages in which there is such a rule:

Amerikan: -*s* for V-final stems, -*a* for C-final stems[99]
Lingua: -*s* if the stem's last segment is not *s*, -*es* for stems whose last segment is *s*.
Romanova: -*s* for V-final, -*es* for C-final (including semivowels[100])
Meso: apparently -*s* for V-final stems, -*es* for C-final stems
Mondial: -*s* for V-final stems, -*es* for C-final stems

---

99 Molee (1888: 186-8) writes at length about plural marking in his language Amerikan and in some natural languages:

> Let us now ask, have we fulfilled all the beautiful promises as well as they can be fulfilled? The promise of making the forms Gmc., conservative, short, euphonious and in harmony with language in general? We think we have. The Anglo-Saxons formed plurals by adding *a* ... The Friesic, the oldest branch of the German tongue, did the same ... The Germans and Skandinavians [sic] form many plurals on *e*, but this sounds something like *a*, and was more often *a* in ancient times. In principle it is the same. [...] In Irish *e* or *a* is used to form the plural ... The Italians end most of their plurals on *e* or *i* ... In Latin we also have plurals on *a* ... [...] We have shown, I think, that *a* as a plural sign obtains in the Gmc., Irish, Romanic, Latin, Greek and Slavonic tongues, hence it must be in harmony with language in general, as well as with our own family. It cannot be made shorter than *a* and *s* – one letter only in each case. It cannot be made more euphonious than an open, spreading vowel. The rule can also be applied in all cases, without one exception! We need not say much about *s*, as that is retained from the old grammar. *S* is a good coalescing sound much favored by the Greeks, but we use it too much in the present English. *S* is a plural sign in English, French, Spanish, Portuguese and Volapük.
> What an easy and simple rule for forming the plural, namely, vowels take *s*, and consonants take *a*. No exceptions. Now we have a dozen ways of forming plurals, and some nouns have no plurals. That throws a doubt [sic] on all words. Each word necessitates an act of special memory.

It is perhaps unfortunate that the Amerikan alphabet contains both <a> and <ɑ>, since in some fonts the former looks like the latter when italicized, meaning that one might be confused from passages such as that above as to what the plural marker after consonants is. However, since Amerikan plural words (with consonant-final singular stems) which are not in italics end with <a>, it seems clear that this plural suffix is -*a* (i.e. not *-ɑ*).

100 Anon. (n.d. g) says "The letters **i** and **u** are semivowels (pronounced like **y** in **yes** and **w** in **win**) when followed by any vowel, or when preceded by **a, e,** or **o,** so **i** and **u** don't count as separate syllables in this case, unless they're followed by an apostrophe, which shows that they are full, stressed vowels".

Lingua Komun: -s unless stem ends with *l, n,* or *r,* in which case *-es*
Eurolang: -s unless stem ends with *ch, s, sh, x, z,* or *zh,* in which case *-es.*
Eurolengo: -s unless stem ends with *s, ch,* or *x,* in which case *-es,* e.g. *glas* 'glass', *glases* 'glasses', *branch* 'branch', *branches* 'branches' (L. Jones 1972: 3)
Voldu: *-y* for V-final stems (e.g. *fento* 'window', *fentoy* 'windows' (Stadelmann 1945: 5), *-oy* for C-final stems (e.g. *buk* 'book', *bukoy* 'books' (ibid.)).

C&L (1903/1979) sometimes make reference to euphonie (euphony) in describing the conditioning of the choice of plural markers of ALs. According to them Mundolingue has the ending -s, "or **-es** quand l'euphonie l'exige"('when euphony requires it') (ibid.: 424), e.g. *duchess* 'duchess', *duchesses.* Likewise in Universala, "Le *pluriel* est marqué par le désinence **-s** ou **-es**, suivant que l'euphonie l'exige" ('The *plural* is marked by the ending **-s** or **-es**, as euphony requires') (ibid.: 450). In Nov Latin as well nouns receive the plural suffix *-s* or *-es* "suivant les règles d'euphonie" (ibid.: 416),

Bothi's (2006) is not entirely clear or explicit about plural marking in Esata: "Plurals are formed by adding *ze* to the noun. In most cases the plural ending is abbreviated to *-z* alone, eg *bo* boy, *boz* boys. Some nouns ending in *-s -w* or *-y* can simply substitute that final consonant for *-z* in the plural." One might suspect that the intended meaning of the last sentence is 'Some nouns ending in *-s, -w,* or *-y* can simply substitute *-z* for that final consonant in the plural'.

In Afrihili the first and last segments of common nouns are vowels. In the singular these vowels are different; in the plural the vowel in initial position becomes identical to that in final position, e.g. *omulenzi* 'boy', *imulenzi* 'boys', *awande* 'groundnut', *ewande* 'groundnuts'.

In some ALs there are two plural affixes and the choice between them does not depend on a segment of the stem. A possible example of such a language is Dil, in which the plural marker is *-z,* but in the nominative case there is an *e* before this *z*.[101] We see this in the table on the following page, which shows the inflected forms of *om* 'man'.

---

101 One could say that the plural suffix is always *-z,* and that the *e* preceding it is the nominative suffix, which only shows up in the plural. This has the advantage of allowing one to posit an invariable plural marker (rather than saying that the plural marker is *-ez* in the nominative and *-z* in the other cases).
Note that not all Dil singular forms end in a consonant, and we have no evidence that vowel-final stems are any different with respect to the case and plural marking that they take, which weakens the argument that *-e-* is simply an epenthetic vowel. However, we have had to rely on a secondary source (C&L 1903/1979: 181-7) for this language, so it is possible that our information is incomplete in one respect or another.

Mundolinco has different plural markers for masculine and neuter nouns on the one hand and feminine nouns on the other.[102] The former is *-i* (replacing the *-o* of the singular) and the latter is *-u* (replacing the *-a* of the singular, e.g. *padra* 'mother', *padru* 'mothers' (C&L 1907/1979: 45)).

	SG	PL
NOM	om	omez
GEN	oma	omaz
DAT	omo	omoz
ACC	omi	omiz

Table 3: *Forms of* Om *'Man' in Dil (modified from Couturat and Leau (1903/1979: 181)*

The main plural suffix of Auxil is *-i*; it is added to consonant-final stems (e.g. *profesor* 'professor', pl. *profesori* (Rodríguez Hernández 2002: 16) and re-places the final vowel of vowel-final stems (e.g. *tablo* 'table', pl. *tabli* (ibid.)). However, "Kiam oni ne povas demeti la lastan vokalon, ĉar ĝi indikas sekson, ekz. AMICO / AMICA, oni uzas la pluralan finaĵon S: AMICOS = amikoj AMICAS = amikinoj" ('When one cannot remove the last vowel, because it indicates the sex, for example AMICO / AMICA, one uses the plural ending S: AMICOS = male friends AMICAS = female friends'; ibid.).

More Complicated Systems of Plural Marking

Most AL designers strive to make their language easy to learn. One would therefore expect plural marking to be a simple matter in an AL. However, there are languages with more complexity in this area of the grammar.

There are three plural markers in Euransi, *-n*, *-am*, and *-ho*, but to our knowledge nowhere in the publicly available materials on the language is it stated under which circumstances they are used. It appears that at least sometimes *-n* and *-ho* are in free variation, since Sztemon (2001a) indicates that they can both be attached to *dârya* 'sea'. In the table in Sztemon (ibid.) "Singular & Plural", *-am* only appears once (and *-ho* does not appear at all), attached to the word *ravân* 'spirit', i.e. *ravânam*; this is the only stem in the table that ends with a consonant, so perhaps the choice between *-am* and *-n* depends on whether the stem ends with a consonant or a vowel (*-n* is attached to e.g. *milati* 'nation' to form *milatin*).

Weltsprache (Volk and Fuchs) has case suffixes, and like Latin, upon which it is based, its case affixes also encode number marking. An additional complication is that vowel-final nominal stems do not take inflectional marking for number or

---

102 From the small amount of information that we have on this language, we would guess that it has natural rather than grammatical gender.

case; these categories are marked on their article, if present (while both the noun and the article (if present) of NPs headed by consonant-final nominal stems will have such marking).[103] The singular and plural case endings for those nominal stems that take them are below:

	SG	PL
NOM	–	-es
GEN	-is	-um
DAT	-i	-ib
ACC	-a	-as

Table 4: *Nominal Case/Number Suffixes of Weltsprache (Volk and Fuchs)* *(C&L 1903/1979: 263)*

The different forms of the definite article are given in the following table:

	SG	PL
NOM	le	les
GEN	lis	lum
DAT	li	lib
ACC	la	las

Table 5: *Forms of the Definite Article in Weltsprache (Volk and Fuchs)* *(C&L 1903/1979: 262)*

Tal has a rather complicated system of plural marking. We quote from C&L (1907/1979: 13-4):

> Les *substantifs* ont deux déclinaisons, suivant qu'ils sont déterminés ou indéterminés. Et leur radical a même deux formes: pour obtenir le sens déterminé on redouble la consonne finale: **manno** (homme) au lieu de **mano**. Voici les deux paradigmes du singulier.
>
> | | Déterminé. | Indéterminé. |
> |----|-----------|--------------|
> | N. | **manno** | **mano** |
> | G. | **manni** | **mani** |
> | D. | **mannu** | **manu** |
> | A. | **manna** | **mano**[104] |
>
> Le pluriel se forme en ajoutant, soit **s**, soit **j** aux formes du singulier (suivant que le mot suivant commence par une voyelle ou une consonne). Il peut se former en outre au moyen des deux séries de désinences suivantes:
>
> | | Déterminé. | Indéterminé. |
> |----|-----------|--------------|
> | N. | **əmo**[105] | **əno** |

---

103 Note further that the indefinite article does not have plural forms.
104 We believe that this is an error for **mana**.

G.	əmi	əni
D.	əmu	ənu
A.	əma	əna

qui sont remplacés respectivement par **əro, əri, əru, əra** quand le radical se termine par un **m** ou un **n**.

(*'Nouns* have two declensions, depending on whether they are determined or undetermined. And their root itself has two forms: to obtain the determined meaning one doubles the final consonant: **manno** (man) instead of **mano**. Here are the two paradigms of the singular. [...]
The plural is formed by adding either **s** or **j** to the forms of the singular (depending on whether the following word begins with a vowel or a consonant). In addition it can be formed by means of the following two series of grammatical endings ... which are replaced by **əro, əri, əru, əra** respectively when the root ends with an **m** or an **n**.')

Plural formation in Panamane is more complicated than in most other ALs; Amador (1936: 8-9) describes it as follows:

Terms ending in mute *e*, change this for *i*; *seéle* soul *seéli*; ...
When to [sic] the mute *e* precedes *e-t*, the consonant is duplicated; *prophéte* prophet *prophetti*; ...
If before the mute *e* comes *m* or *n* preceded by vowel, the plural is made with *n* the mute *e* recovering then its alphabetical value [i.e. it is pronounced]; *nasióne* nation, *nasionen*; ...
Terms ending in consonant, single or double, except *y*, take *i* for the plural, the single consonant in some instances being duplicated for the sake of euphony; *man* man *mánni*; *póhsor* power *póhsori*; ... *lip* lip, *líppi*; *lit* bed, *lítti*; *práhdik* practice *práhdiki*; ... *ok* eye, *ókki*; ...
But if the final consonant is *r* or *l*, preceded by *e*, this [i.e. <e>] is dropped as the *i* of the plural is added -- provided the term does not become, because of its structure, sdrugule ... *páder* father, *pádri*; *tábel* table, *tábli*; ...
Terms ending in vowel, single or double -- save mute *e* -- take *n* for the plural; *dóma* house, *dóman*; ...
When the term ends in *h*, this is dropped and *e-n* added; *resultáh* result *resultáen*;
To terms ending in *u*, is added *n*, or *i*, or *i-n* ad libitum; *grídu* shout, grídun, grídui, or gríduin;...
Terms ending in *y* take e-n, preserving the *y* its conventional *e* (eh ....) value; *bródy* brother, makes its plural *bródyen*, pronounced bróh...deh...en;...

---

105 The letter <ə> does not occur in Tal, but is used by C&L (1907/1979) instead of "une lettre russe [which occurs in Tal] qui représente l'*e* atone" (a Russian letter which represents the atonic *e*'; p. 13).

43

Analytic Plural Marking

As in natural languages, in ALs plural marking usually involves affixes. However, this is not always the case. Desa *Chat*'s plural marker is the word *ji*, which follows its noun.[106]

The basic plural marker of Hély's language internationale is the word *es*, which precedes its noun, and which is preceded by the article, if one is present, e.g. *dar es pater* 'the fathers' (C&L 1907/1979: 16), cf. *dar pater* 'the father' (ibid.). The markers of natural gender are also analytic, *o* and *a* for masculine and feminine respectively, and if both plural and natural gender are marked, the particles involved fuse into one, *os* for masculine plural and *as* for feminine plural, e.g. *dar os canis* 'the male dogs' (ibid.).[107]

Minyeva also uses a separate word to indicate plurality and this word also precedes its noun; G. Jones (2006) says:

> In Minyeva, a noun with no number stated doesn't have a number specified - it could be one or more than one.
> te pleva - the dog or the dogs
> To say that there is more than one, the plural marker 'ni' can be used:
> te ni pleva - the dogs
> To say that there is only one, simply use 'fwa' (the number 1):
> te fwa pleva - the dog (the one dog)

Dual Forms

As one might expect, ALs with dual forms of nouns are rare, but Mondi-Lingua has a dual suffix, *-u*; according to Monnerot-Dumaine (1960: 53) the dual of this language was "inspiré de l'arabe" ('inspired by Arabic').

Identical Nominal and Pronominal Plurals

In some ALs nouns and (some) pronouns form their plurals in the same way, creating greater regularity in the language. (Of course this phenomenon can also

---

[106] The distinction between synthetic and analytic markers in Desa *Chat* is obscured somewhat by the great freedom it allows with respect to writing: Davis (1999/2000) states, "Desa *Chat* can be written from left to right, or from right to left, either letter-by-letter, syllable-by-syllable, word-by-word or without any spaces between words". Given that no syllables of words are supposed to be stressed more than any others, it might also be difficult to detect word boundaries in the spoken language.

[107] One might wonder why there is no marking of masculine gender before *pater* in the first example given in this paragraph, i.e. why the plural marker there is *es* and not *os*. C&L (1907/1979: 16) say, "Naturellement, on ne les [the gender markers] emploie pas avec les noms qui sont masculins ou féminins par le sens" ('Naturally, one does not use them before nouns which are masculine or feminine by their meaning').

be found in some natural languages. e.g. French *il* 'he', *ils* 'they' (M).) For example, in Uropa *ma* is 'I' while *mā* is 'we'. Ayola has the same plural suffix (*-y*) for nouns and pronouns, e.g. *dya* 'he/him/she/her', *dyay* 'they/them' (people), but with the 1st and 2nd person personal pronouns the root is partly changed: *myo* is 'I/me' and *moy* is 'we/us'; *vu* is 'you (SG)' while *voy* is 'you (PL)'. UNI plural pronouns, like plural nouns, have the suffix *-I*, e.g. *UD* 'I', *UDI* 'we'. Like nouns, personal pronouns in Vela have plural forms in *-s*, e.g. *ji* 'I', *jis* 'we'. In Virgoranto as well *-s* is the plural marker for nouns and personal pronouns, e.g. *me* 'I', *mes* 'we'.

Order of Plural Marking and Other Inflection

Among ALs that have both case suffixes and a suffix marking plurality we find languages with both possible orders of these affixes. Among those languages in which the case suffix is before the plural suffix are Communicationssprache, Dil (e.g. *om-o-z* 'men' (DAT)), Perio (e.g. *homu-l-s* 'men' (GEN)), and Volapük (e.g. *fat-i-s* 'fathers' (ACC)). Esperanto has only one case suffix, the accusative suffix *-n*, and it follows the plural marker. Other languages with the order case-plural are Arulo: (e.g. *la kind-i-f ludo* 'the children's play' (Talmey 1925: 4)), Pasilingua (e.g. *kingo-s-bi* 'kings' (DAT)), and Voldu (e.g. *padro-y-m* 'to the fathers' (father-PL-DAT))

Euransi is the only AL that we know of which marks possession with suffixes. An example given by Sztemon (2001a) shows that in Euransi the plural suffix *-am* precedes the 1st person singular possessive suffix *-ëm*: *ravân* 'spirit', *ravânam* 'spirits', *ravânëm* 'my spirit', *ravânamëm* 'my spirits'. One might assume that the same is true of Euransi's other plural and possessive suffixes.

Non-Use of Plural Affixes

We have seen that there are ALs without plural marking. There are also ALs which have plural marking but do not (have to) use it when e.g. English would. Sona has a plural affix, but there are various circumstances in which it does not occur:

> The number of a noun is not always distinguished. In English we may speak of sheep, fruit, fish, man, tiger in both singular and plural sense, as 'man goes after tiger.' So in Sona – *ra uke taxe*. Plural number is never marked after a numeral or the radical *e* 'number' = 'many,' or when a nouns stands as predicate to a plural pronoun: e.g. *ti (zi) ra* 'they are men,' *mie (zi) pan kora* 'we are all boys.' A PLURAL, however, may be formed with the sf. [=suffix] *e* 'number,' 'many'; e.g. *mie* 'we' (from *mi* 'I'), *koraye* 'boys.' As pf. [=prefix] this radical means quantity, many, frequency, multi-; e.g. *ekora* 'many boys,' *eri* 'often,' *ena* 'every, each.' (Searight 1935: 40)

Plural marking in LFN is done in the same manner as in some other ALs (-*s* if the stem is vowel-final, -*es* if it is consonant-final), but it is not always required: Fisahn (n.d.) says, "If there are other words (such as **multe** or numbers) that indicate plurality, the **-s** *may* be dropped". LdP has the same plural suffixes as LFN, with the choice between them being determined by the same factor, and they are optional in a similar (if not the same) set of circumstances; the *Lingwa de Planeta Grammar* (anon. n.d. a: 23) says, "After any indication of plurality (numerals; quantifiers like 'mucho' *many*, *much*, 'kelke' *several*, *some*, 'shao' *little*, 'ambi' *both*, grupa de *a group of*, menga de *a lot of*, 'para' *a pair of*; plural subject, personal pronouns 'nu' *we*, 'li' *they*), as a rule, plural endings are not used". Among the examples then given are *dwa oko* 'two eyes', *mucho yar* 'many years', and *Li es may amiga* 'They are my friends'.[108]

The same general situation holds in Voldu; Stadelmann (1945: 37) states, "After words indicating the plural, substantives can omit the plural ending. Ex: Tey have muce cild ['they have many children'], tri gars ed du girl ['three boys and two girls']." With respect to Algilez, Giles (2010a) states, "If the noun is clearly plural (e.g. with a preceding number) then the 'i' [the plural suffix] can be omitted". One of his examples is *pãril* 'father', *du pãril* 'two fathers'. Mondlango's nominal plural marker is the suffix -*s*, but it is not obligatory: anon. (n.d. j) states, "The plural form is optional, for example: tri domo = tri domos ['three houses']".

This kind of non-use of plural affixes also occurs in some natural languages, for example in Turkish the plural suffix usually does not appear after cardinal numerals.

Conclusion

We have seen a fair degree of uniformity with respect to number marking in ALs: most languages discussed in this survey have either a single plural suffix (which is often -*s*) or two allomorphs whose occurrence depends on the sound immediately before them. However, other possibilities occur: a few ALs have analytical plural markers (which is unusual from the viewpoint of major Western European languages) and a small number have surprisingly complex systems of plural marking.

---

108 There is a difference between LFN and LdP: while one generally omits the plural marker in the latter, this may not be so in the former. One will have noticed that "may" in the quotation above about LFN is italicized; Fisahn (n.d.) says the following about this: "Wherever you see the word *may* in italics, it means that this option is a non-standard one which is none-the-less acceptable as a variation. You could say it's not what you would be taught in school, but no one would be surprised to hear it. The point here is that we need to combine some sort of standardization with enough flexibility to allow for natural differences among speakers of different native languages!"

Chapter 6: The Forms and Uses of Demonstratives in Artificial Languages

Demonstrative adjectives (i.e. demonstrative determiners) and pronouns are among the most frequently occurring words of natural languages; presumably the same is true of those ALs that are actually used. In this chapter we shall look at the forms that these words have and the systems into which they are organized. We are only able to look at a relatively small number of ALs but we hope to give an idea of what happens in this area of the grammar of such languages.

Apparently *A Priori* Demonstratives

As one would expect, the demonstratives of some *a priori* languages are not derived from those of natural languages, and proximal and distal demonstratives are similar in form. We see this in (1) (we assume that these words are *a priori*):

(1) Fitusa: *at-* 'this', *it-* 'that'
Ro (1913) (pronouns): *al* 'this', *am* 'that'[109]
Sona (pronouns[110]): *in* 'this', *un* 'that'

Although Anti-Volapük is not an *a priori* language, its demonstrative pronouns appear to be in an *a priori* system; they are *tscha* 'this' and *tsche* 'that'. Demonstrative systems of various other mixed and *a posteriori* languages seem either to be entirely *a priori* or, if they contain an *a posteriori* member, the other member(s) was/were created based on it in an *a priori* manner (i.e. by changing one of its sounds). We give some of these systems below:

(2) Algilez (pronouns/adjectives): *xe* 'this', *ce* 'that'[111]
Dil (pronouns): *id* 'this', *ed* 'that'
Orba (pronouns): *den* 'this', *len* 'that'
Universala (pronouns): *ta* 'this', *te* 'that'[112]
Weltsprache (Eichhorn) (pronouns): *sdo* 'this', *klo* 'that'
Weltsprache (Volk and Fuchs) (pronouns): *dic* 'this', *lic* 'that'[113]

---

109 These words are the same in Ro (1919) and Ro (1921). They also occur as demonstrative adjectives.
110 These words can also be used as demonstrative adjectives.
111 Giles (2009: 2) says, "There are no definite or indefinite articles in Algilez ... If there is a need for such words then 'xe' or 'ce' (this or that) or 'an' (one) can be used. When translating from Algilez to English use 'the' or 'a' as appropriate".
112 These pronouns are part of an *a priori* set of pronouns, the other members of which are *ti* 'the one/that (which)' (it is glossed by C&L (1903/1979: 451) as 'celui (qui)'), *to* 'the same (one)', *tu* 'exactly the same (one)'.

Demonstratives as Part of Correlative Systems

In some ALs demonstratives are part of a larger system of regularly created pronouns, the system of correlatives. The Esperanto correlatives are well-known; we show some of them below:

ie 'somewhere'	*kie* 'where?'	*tie* 'there'	*ĉie* 'everywhere'	*nenie* 'nowhere'
ies 'someone's'	*kies* 'which one's, whose?'	*ties* 'that one's'	*ĉies* 'everyone's'	*nenies* 'no one's'
io 'something'	*kio* 'what?'	*tio* 'that thing'	*ĉio* 'everything'	*nenio* 'nothing'
iu 'someone, some (person or thing)'	*kiu* 'which (one), who?'	*tiu* 'that (one)'	*ĉiu* 'every(one), each (one)'	*neniu* 'no (one)'

Table 1: *Part of the Esperanto System of Correlatives (from Butler 1965: 274, with modifications)*

Although some parts of the system are obviously *a posteriori*, the system as a whole is like some *a priori* systems of vocabulary, in which words with related meanings have similar forms.

A Posteriori Demonstratives

It is not a great surprise that Anglo-Franca has taken its demonstrative pronouns from English; they are *this* 'this' and *that* 'that', with the plural forms *these* and *those* respectively.[114] The demonstrative adjectives of Communicationssprache also come from English, but oddly enough the proximal one is based on the English singular form, while the distal is based on the English plural form (presumably this was done to give them a similar form); they are *tis* and *tos* (and are not inflected for plural or any other category). The demonstrative pronouns of this language are built from the demonstrative adjectives, and are inflected; their nominative singular forms are *tisia* 'this' and *tosia* 'that'.

Given their form, one might think that the demonstrative pronouns-adjectives of Universal-Sprache also come from or were influenced by English; they are *dit* 'this' and *dat* 'that' (the plural forms are *diti* and *dati*). One might also believe that the demonstratives of Ayola were borrowed (with changes) from English: its

---

113 These are the masculine nominative singular forms; in the feminine and neuter forms the *i* of these forms is replaced by *a* and *o* respectively.
114 In Anglo-Franca <th> stands for a voiceless dental or alveolar plosive.

basic demonstrative pronouns are *tiso* 'this (one)' and *tato* 'that (one)' (the corresponding demonstrative adjectives being *tisa* and *tata*).

The demonstrative pronominal roots of Europal are *dis-* and *yon-*, glossed by Weisbart (n.d.: 7) as 'dies-' and 'jen[-]'; they may well have come from German and/or English. Parla's *jena* 'that' clearly was borrowed from German, the origin of *ca* 'this' is less obvious.[115]

Mundolingue is largely based on Latin and so it is not unexpected that its demonstrative pronouns resemble Latin forms; they are *ist* 'this' and *il* 'that'.[116] Interlingua IALA's demonstrative adjectives *iste* 'this' and *ille* 'that' are identical to Latin forms.

The Ardano word *cues* 'this', which is both a demonstrative adjective and a demonstrative pronoun, comes from Italian; one might suspect that the same is true of *cuel* 'that'. The plural versions of these are formed with the same suffix that creates plural forms of nouns, *-i*: *cuesi* 'these', *cueli* 'those'.

The Salveto words for 'this' and 'that' are *lo* and *la* respectively. They have the same written form as, and perhaps were based on, two forms of the Italian definite article; the definite article does not exist in Salveto itself. *Lo* and *la* are demonstrative adjectives, but the former apparently can occur as a demonstrative pronoun, and one might assume that the same is true of the latter.

Formal Distinctions between Demonstrative Adjectives and Demonstrative Pronouns

We have seen that in some ALs the same words serve as both demonstrative adjectives and demonstrative pronouns, while in some others the two types of words have different forms. We shall now look at more examples of the latter situation.

Sasxsek has demonstrative pronouns which are distinct from, though similar to, its demonstrative adjectives. (However, like nouns in the language, none of them is marked for number.) The former are *co* 'this (one), these' and *to* 'that (one), those' and the latter are *ci* 'this, these' and *ti* 'that, those'.[117]

The demonstrative adjectives and pronouns of Eurolang are also formally distinct. The proximal demonstrative adjective is *da* 'this', while the pronoun is *di* 'this, this one'. The corresponding distal words are *tele-da* and *tele-di*. *Tele-di* is glossed in Hunt (1998b) as 'that, that one; **1.** "that" as opposed to "this" **2.** that

---

[115] These are the demonstrative pronouns; the corresponding demonstrative adjectives end in *-o* rather than *-a*.

[116] One can add gender suffixes to these forms. *Il* can be used as a demonstrative adjective; presumably the same is true of *ist*.

[117] The latter words can also function as adverbs, *ci* meaning 'now; here' and *ti* meaning 'then; there'. This may not be too surprising given that adverbs are generally not formally distinct from adjectives.

one far away, or at least further away than "this one"'; the gloss for *tele-da* conveys the same general idea.

Demonstrative Systems with Three Terms

Among the ALs with a tripartite system of demonstratives is Panamane (which is not surprising, since its designer was from a Spanish-speaking country, Panama). Below are what seem to be the demonstrative adjectives of this language:

(3) *sty* 'this'   *éssy/kez* 'that'   *kuéllo* 'that yon'
     sétti 'these'   *kézzi* 'those'   *kuélli* 'those yon'

Sotos Ochando, also a Spanish speaker, designed his Lengua Universal with a tripartite system as well; it is *a priori*, like the language in general. Sotos Ochando (1860: 138) glosses the pronouns *sada*, *sade*, and *sadi* as 'este (*hic* latin)', 'ese (*iste* latin)', and 'aquel (*ille* latin)' respectively.

Demonstrative Systems including a Distance-Neutral Term

Mundelingva has a distance-neutral demonstrative pronoun, *do* (glossed by C&L (1907/1979: 78) as 'celui'); its proximal and distal demonstra-tive pronouns are *ido* and *ilo* respectively (glossed as 'celui-ci' and 'celui-là' by C&L (ibid.)).

There is also a distance-neutral demonstrative pronoun in Euransi, *ar* 'this/that'. This is not surprising since Euransi's designer, Libor Sztemon, spoke Czech, which has such a pronoun. The Euransi pronouns *vehi* and *vohu* mean 'this' and 'that' respectively.

Hély's langue internationale has what C&L (1907/1979: 17) call a "générale" (general) demonstrative pronoun, *ist*; we take it to be distance neutral. It makes up part of the proximal and distal demonstrative pronouns, *ist ic* and *ist ac* respectively.

Olson (1950: 8) says of Ling, "The only demonstrative pronoun is *ek* 'this', 'that', 'these', 'those'. If necessary, the adverbs *hi* 'here' and *la* 'there' may be added: *ek libro hi es blu, ek la es red* 'this book is blue, that one is red'". Given his example sentence it appears that *ek* can be a demonstrative adjective as well as being a pronoun.

Unusual Systems of Demonstratives

In Ruggles' Universal Language the suffixes (or "pronominal letters", as Ruggles (1829: 18) calls them) -*b*- and -*g*- are equivalent to the demonstrative adjectives of e.g. English; for example, *homzben* and *homzgen* mean 'this man' and 'that man' respectively (from *hom*- 'man (in the sense of 'human'), with the positive member of the set of "letters of gradation" (ibid.) -*z*-, the "[p]ersonal masculine" (ibid.: 21) gender suffix -e-, and the nominative suffix -n-). This suffix goes in the same position as several other suffixes which are equivalent to some determiners or quantifiers in languages such as English, including -t- 'a, some' (e.g. *homzten* 'a man'), -k- 'who, which' (e.g. *homzken* 'which man'), and -v- 'every, each, all' (e.g. *homzven* 'every man').

Temenia has the demonstrative adjectives τι 'this/these' and τα 'that/those'. Unlike in many natural languages such as English and Turkish, and many or most ALs, they occur after their head noun, e.g. λυωαυπε τα 'that dog' (Brown 2007b: 5), and in fact after adjectives and numerals, if these are present, e.g.:

(4) λυωαυπε ρυξι ρεζι τα
    dog   big   three that/those
    'those three big dogs' (ibid.)

Another unusual feature of Temenia is its lack of demonstrative pronouns: Brown (ibid.: 6) says, "Demonstrative pronouns do not exist in Temenia. Instead of saying, *'I want this'*, or, *'I want those'*, it is necessary to express that which is referred to. That is, *'I want this cookie'*, or, *'I want those shoes'* (or, at least, *'I want that thing'*)".[118]

Konya is also atypical of ALs with respect to its demonstratives. The demonstrative adjective *tise* apparently is distance-neutral, as it is glossed as 'this, that' in Sulky (2005b), where the following sentence appears:

(5)   min-wi nuxu koxi nile tise
       I   need car   blue that
       'I need that blue car.'[119]

Sulky (ibid.) states, "There are no articles (*the, a, an, some*), nor plural forms. Definiteness and number are taken from context, or established with more specific words". However, *tise* can function as (something like) an anaphoric definite article:

(6)   min-wi kenu pem-neni tise
       I   know boy   the
       'I know the boy.' (ibid.)

Sulky says after this sentence, "**tise** is used not only for *this; this one here*, but also to refer to something that has already been identified in the conversation".

---

118 Apparently the word ωαθι 'one' can be the head of an NP which has one of the demonstrative adjectives as its final word, given the phrase ωαθι τεκιυφιξυε τι 'this wool one' (Brown 2007c: 3).

119 Sulky (ibid.) makes the following remark after this sentence: "Demonstrative adjectives are often last in a string of modifiers, similar to numbers. But this is up to the speaker."

As far as we know, Sulky has not provided Konya with proximal and distal demonstratives,[120] but consider the following sentence:

(7) min-wi nuxu koxi nile tise ye noli mime note
    I   need car blue this and one red other
    'I need this blue car and that red one.' (ibid.)

After this example Sulky comments, "**note** = *other; alternative* is often used where English would use a *this / that* pair".

The word *tisen-wi* means 'this (one), that (one), this thing, that thing', i.e. it is a pronominal equivalent of *tise*. The *-wi* in it is a "conversion suffix" (ibid.), which we have already seen in the above examples in the word for 'I', *min-wi*.[121] Below are some sentences containing *tisen-wi*:[122]

(8a) min-wi nuxu tisen-wi
     I   need that
     'I need that.'

(8b) tisen-wi wa Kenatya
     this   is Canada
     'This is Canada.' (ibid.)

(8c) min-wi fulu xefali wa simo   tisen-wi
     I   want horse is similar.to that.one
     'I want a horse like that one.' (ibid.)

Konya also has the word *tisi* 'this, it (abstract)', as in the following example:

---

120 However, a modified version of the language, Konya-2b (by Jim Henry III), does have such demonstratives, *ny-* 'this' and *mw-* 'that'.
121 Sulky (2005b) is not very clear or explicit about the function or use of this suffix, but pronouns generally contain it (although it apparently is not limited to being in pronouns, e.g. *kom-nutun-wi* 'swimmer' (*nutu* means '(to) swim')).
122 The following sentence may contain an error; if it does not, it indicates that *tise* can also act as a demonstrative pronoun:
   (i) tise wa Heqyam-nexi
       this is England
       'This is England.' (ibid.)
   There is also what appears to be a pronominal equivalent of *note*, *noten-wi* 'other one, other thing'; compare the following sentence with (7):
   (ii) min-wi nuxu koxi nile tise ye noten-wi mime
        I   need car   blue this and other.one red
        'I need this blue car and that red one.' (ibid.)

(9) Melanya pan-sene wa pose   naye   min-wi kenu nin-ye tisi
    Melanie sick   is past.time however I   know not   it
    'Melanie was sick, though I didn't know it.' (ibid.)

Conclusion

Demonstrative systems of ALs show considerable variation. The same words may or may not serve as both pronouns and adjectives, some systems include three degrees of proximity, and some systems include a distance-neutral term.

Chapter 7: On Case Assignment by Prepositions in Artificial Languages

Adpositions of natural languages vary widely in their case assigning behavior: some assign only one case, but that case can be different for different adpositions, sometimes even in the same language, while others can assign two or three cases, the choice depending on various factors. In this chapter we shall look at which cases prepositional objects in ALs receive. Of course this depends on the (overt) case system (if any) that an AL has, since that will constrain the possibilities. If a language has no case marking then there is nothing to say here.

Languages in which Adpositional Objects Are Always in the Same Case

Adpositional Objects Always in the Nominative

Stadelmann (1945: 17) is explicit about the case borne by objects of prepositions in Voldu, which has four morphologically distinct cases for both pronouns and nouns, nominative, genitive, dative, and accusative (although the last of these may only be marked in cases of potential ambiguity, at least with NPs headed by nouns): "All prepositions govern the nominative. Ex: Kam tu *nu*. Come to us." Weltsprache (Volk and Fuchs) has the same four cases, but prepositional objects are always in the nominative case. The same seems to be true of Dil, which again has the same set of cases.

American also has nominative, genitive, dative, and accusative cases, and prepositions take nominative objects (whether they are headed by nouns or by pronouns), e.g. *in America* 'in America (NOM)' (O'Connor 1917: 34), *dë tos tri republicos* 'about those three republics (NOM)' (ibid.: 36). Four cases (in addition to the vocative) are distinguished on personal pronouns of the Blue Language, nominative, genitive-ablative, dative, and accusative, and again prepositional objects always have nominative objects.

In pan-kel nouns are not declined, but there are nominative and dative/accusative forms of personal pronouns, e.g. *a* 'I', *as* 'me'. Objects of pan-kel prepositions are in the nominative, e.g. *it o* 'with you (NOM)' (Wald 1909: 8).

It is highly unusual among Indo-European languages (on one or more of which most *a posteriori* and some mixed ALs are largely based) for adpositions to occur with nominative objects (though it does happen in Albanian). In this way some ALs are distinctly unlike their natural language sources.

Adpositional Objects Always in the Accusative

As mentioned in chapter 5, in Kosmos case inflection is borne only by the "article" (which also occurs with pronouns); there are four cases, nominative, genitive, dative, and accusative, and prepositional objects are always in the accusative. Pantos-Dimou-Glossa has a morphological accusative case, marked on at least some types of pronoun and on definite and indefinite articles (though not on nouns), and thus there are two distinct cases, nominative and accusative; prepositional objects are always accusative.

Uropi has nominative, dative, and accusative forms of personal pronouns (as well as possessive forms), and again prepositional objects are in the accusative. Eurolengo, like English, shows case distinctions between nominative and accusative only with some pronouns (e.g. *die* 'they', *dem* 'them'), and as in English, prepositions take accusative forms of these pronouns, e.g. *for dem* 'for them' (L. Jones 1972: 16, tr. 17). In Europal 1st and 2nd person personal pronouns have distinct nominative and accusative forms; prepositional objects are always in the accusative form.

Adpositional Objects Always in the Locative (if Case Affixes Present)

Temenia has items that some might consider case suffixes; as Brown (2007b: 2) states, "The more common semantic roles are indicated by suffixes on the noun". There are such markers for agent, patient, possessive, recipient, source, beneficiary, comitative, "instrumentive" (as Brown (ibid.: 3) calls it), and locative. However, Brown (ibid.: 4) says, "The noun markings in Temenia may seem to imply that they are inflectional noun *cases*, as in Latin. This is one way to look at it. On the other hand, since the noun markings are simple agglutinative suffixes, it is equally possible to consider them postpositions that, when written, are suffixed to the noun". Further, he later (pp. 7-8) says:

> Nouns in Temenia are not marked for case (and neither are pronouns …). However, nouns and pronouns can be marked with suffixes (as described in the section on Word Order), which carry the same type of grammatical information as case markings carry. The reason that these suffixes are not considered case markings is because they are optional. If the intent is clear from the context of the sentence, then the suffix can be omitted.

Whatever these items are, it is the locative one, -ωα, that is attached to nouns when they are objects of postpositions (all adpositions in Temenia are postpositions), e.g.:

(1) θυ ξυε τυι κιμαθο-ωα μοετυο
    he put book table-LOC on
    'He put the book on the table' (ibid.: 3)

However, like Temenia's case suffixes in general, -ωα on postpositional objects "may be omitted if it is clear from context" (ibid.).[123] The choice of the locative as the postpositional case might not be surprising, since it appears that most of the postpositions of Temenia have a locational meaning (in one of their senses).

Languages Arguably with a Prepositional Case

Interlingua (IALA) has different case forms for most personal pronouns (but not for nouns); the first and second personal plural pronouns do not change form for case. Some of these pronouns have the same form when they are subjects and when they are prepositional objects, while others (all of the 3rd person pronouns) have the same form when they are prepositional objects and when they are direct objects. This is shown in the following table:

	NOM	PO	ACC
1SG	io	me	me
2SG	tu	te	te
3MSG	ille	ille	le
3FSG	illa	illa	la
3NSGN	illo/il	lo	lo
3MPL	illes	illes	les
3FPL	illas	illas	las
3NPL	illos	illos	los

Table 1: *Interlingua (IALA) Personal Pronoun Forms (after Gode and Blair 1951: 21)*

On the basis of this one could claim that Interlingua (IALA) has a prepositional case (which is assigned by all prepositions).

Languages in which Adpositional Objects Are Not Always in the Same Case

We now look at ALs in which there is variation in the case borne by adpositional objects.

The situation of Esperanto is well known: prepositional objects are in the nominative, except that certain prepositions can take accusative complements to convey the meaning of motion, e.g.:[124]

---

123 It is a little difficult to see how it could not be clear from context: either a NP is followed by a postposition or it is not.
124 Wells (1969: 15) says, "*The accusative is never used after* **al** *to,* **ĝis** *till, or* **el** *from, out of, since these prepositions show motion in any case*".

(2a) La   muso   kuris sub   la   lito
      the mouse ran   under the bed(NOM)
      'The mouse ran around under the bed'

(2b) La   muso   kuris sub   la   lito-n
      the mouse ran   under the bed-ACC
      'The mouse ran under the bed' (Wells 1969: 15)

With respect to Modern Indo-European Quiles (2009: 261) states, "Prepositions are regularly used either with the Accusative or with the Oblique cases". (Modern Indo-European apparently has nominative, vocative, genitive, dative, accusative, ablative, instrumental, and locative cases on nouns, although there is some syncretism, and four declensions.) We have not found any specification regarding which prepositions take which cases.

Conclusion

Most ALs with case systems do not have the level of complexity of adpositional case assignment as is found in Ancient Greek, Latin, or German, in which different prepositions assign different cases and the same preposition can sometimes assign different cases under different conditions. This is to be expected, given that ALs are designed to be learner-friendly.

Chapter 8: Indirect Objects in Artificial Languages

Different languages have different ways of marking indirect objects. In this chapter we are concerned with how word order is used to indicate indirect objects, and with word order restrictions on indirect objects in languages in which they are marked by some means in addition to word order.

Languages with a Dative Case Suffix

We begin with languages in which there is a dative case marker. Dil has four cases, including the dative. One might think that this would go together with relative freedom of position for the indirect object, and this may be the case, but C&L (1903/1979: 184) say that the S V DO IO is the "régulière" ('regular') order. We do not know under what conditions there can be deviations from this order.

Voldu has dative case marking on both nouns and pronouns:

(1a) Giv   hi-m   da-n.
      give   he-DAT   it-ACC
      'Give it to him.'

(1b) Send   da-n   frato-m.
      send   it-ACC   brother-DAT
      'Send it to the brother.'

(1c) Giv   da-n   girla-m
      give   it-ACC   girl-DAT
      'Give it to the girl.' (Stadelmann 1945:33)

However, one can also use the preposition *tu* 'to' to mark indirect objects; Stadelmann (ibid.) says, "English will be inclined and allowed to say: Send dan *tu* frat. Even with pronouns: Give dan *tu* hi. (English style)".[125] The order of objects is not explicitly stated in Stadelmann (ibid.), but given the examples there, it seems that when the non-prepositional indirect object is a pronoun, it precedes the direct object (whether it is a pronoun or headed by a noun), as in (1a) and the following sentences:

(2a) Fay   hi-n   giv   yu-m   teo ...
      make   he-ACC   give   you-DAT   tea
      'Make him give you tea ...' (ibid.: 53)

---

125 Earlier (p. 6), he says that the dative "can always be rendered in the English way, with *tu*".

(2b) Tel nu-m ire-vi-n!
     tell we-DAT any-something-ACC
     'Tell us anything!' (ibid.: 54)

Consider the sentences in (3), in which the non-prepositional non-pronominal indirect object precedes the direct object; the difference between them and (1b-c) (which have the reverse order of direct and indirect objects) is that the direct object is a pronoun in (1b-c) but not in the examples in (3):

(3a) Giv cildo-m de pyes of bred na tabl!
     give child-DAT the piece of bred on table
     'Give the child the piece of bread on the table!' (ibid.: 50)

(3b) Zov siro-y-m fabriko!
     show gentleman-PL-DAT factory
     'Show the gentlemen the factory!' (ibid.: 49)

(3c) Rid cild-om telo!
     read child-DAT tale
     'Read the child a tale!' (ibid.: 49)

There seem to be two rules at work in Voldu: pronouns precede other NPs, and non-prepositional indirect objects precede direct objects. The former rule overrides the latter, as shown by (1b-c): a pronominal direct object will precede an indirect object headed by a noun.

When there is a prepositional indirect object, it can follow the direct object (as in the Voldu examples in the quotation above, and as in English), or it can precede it:

(4a) Rid tu cild tel!
     read to child tale
     'Read the child a tale!' (ibid.)

We do not have enough relevant data to posit any factors determining the order in such cases, although one might note that in the examples in the quotation, the direct object is a pronoun and it precedes the prepositional indirect object, so perhaps that must be the order under those circumstances.

Temenia has a suffix marking recipients (as well as endpoints of motion), -λα, although, like other case suffixes, it is not obligatory under certain circumstances; recall that Brown (2007b: 8) says, "If the intent is clear from the context of the sentence, then the suffix can be omitted". He then gives the following example:

(5a)   πακο ηυπι ψοηο ζελεηα-λα
       Paco give gift Selena-DAT
       'Paco gave the gift to Selena'

(5b)   πακο ηυπι ψοηο ζελεηα
       (same meaning)

Brown (ibid.) comments, "The recipient suffix (-λα) is omitted from the second sentence. This is permissible in Temenia if Selena's role as the recipient of the gift is clear from the conversational context".

Regarding word order in Temenia, Brown (ibid.: 2) states, "The basic word order in Temenia is Agent-Verb-Patient" and later (p. 3) says, "In the basic word order, nouns in other than the agent or patient role follow the patient in the sentence ... When there are multiple non-agent, non-patient roles in the sentence, their order, after the patient, is not relevant". On freedom in word order he says (ibid.: 6), "To provide *focus* in a sentence it is possible to utilize a word order other than the basic word order shown above. [...] ... it is permissible to permute the words to change the focus of the sentence. In Temenia, the focus of the sentence falls on the *first* word in the sentence". One of his examples is:

(6)   πακο-λα   ζαξα-κα   ηυρι ζερι-πυ
       Paco-DAT Sasha-AG   give pig-PAT
       'To Paco, Sasha gave a pig' (ibid.: 7)

Brown (ibid.) cautions against the overuse of such orders: "These non-standard word orders are used sparingly in Temenia. Just as one does not often say, in English, 'To Paco, Sasha gave a pig', one should not deviate frequently from the normal agent-verb-patient word order in Temenia unless the intent is to change the focus of the sentence from the agent and to emphasize some other constituent of the sentence."[126]

Languages with a Prepositional Indirect Object (and without a Dative Case)

We now turn to languages in which there is no dative case affix but there is a preposition which marks indirect objects.

In Sasxsek indirect objects generally involve both a preposition (*fu* 'to, towards') and a particular position in the clause: Nutter (n.d. a: 43) says, "A basic sentence occurs as subject, verb, [direct] object (SVO). Any indirect objects

---

126 Temenia has optional *wh*-movement in *wh*-questions, and thus indirect objects can appear *in situ* or in clause-initial position.

follow afterwards each introduced by appropriate prepositions".[127] An example is below:

(7) mo don   kitab fu lo.
     I   give book   to he
     'I gave him a book/ I gave a book to him.' (ibid.: 15)

Wh-movement can, but does not have to, occur in *wh*-questions; if an indirect object undergoes *wh*-movement then of course it will occur in a different position, namely before the subject, e.g.:

(8) fu ho   fo   don   kitab.
     to who you give book
     'Whom did you give the book to?' (ibid.: 44)

Nutter (n.d. a) does not mention any other situation in which an indirect object occurs outside of its usual place.[128]

Weltsprache (Eichhorn) is similar in that there is a (presumably obligatory) NP-initial particle equivalent to a dative case suffix, *a*, but there is also a particular position for the indirect object: the order of a clause's main constituents is S V DO IO. We do not know whether or when different orders can appear. Lingua has a (mandatory?) dative preposition, *u* 'to, for', and a "normal" (C&L 1903/1979: 385) order of S V DO IO.[129]

In Konya, in which there is also a preposition which precedes indirect objects, the position of the indirect object is not fixed with respect to that of the direct object; Sulky (2005b) says, "Konya isn't very fussy about the order of a verb's objects". Below is a sentence in which the indirect object occurs before the direct object:

(9) min-wi tonu tun-yo koti saseti
     I   give to   cat   basket
     'I give a basket to the cat' (ibid.)

---

127 Nutter has a broader notion than usual of *indirect object*.
128 An apparent exception is a *wh*-question in which the direct object has undergone *wh*-movement; in this case the indirect object would not occur immediately after the direct object, but one could say that it is still in its usual position and that it is the direct object that is not in its typical place.
129 This may be a reflection of the fact that "La *syntaxe* est imitée des langue modernes, surtout de l'anglais" ('The *syntax* is imitated from modern languages, especially from English', (C&L 1903/1979: 385).

The preposition *ua* 'to' obligatorily marks indirect objects in Ande (in which neither nouns nor pronouns are inflected for case). Indirect objects, like subjects and direct objects, are not restricted to a single position, although some word orders are seen as better than others. We quote two passages from Anderson (n.d.):[130]

> The subject and [direct] object are indicated solely by sentential position. Where subject and object both precede the verb, or both follow it, then the subject stands nearest to the verb; otherwise, the subject precedes the verb and the object follows the verb. The object preferably stands nearer the verb than the indirect object, in a sentence where both precede the verb, or both follow it. (pp. 39-40)
>
> Eight different arrangements of a simple form of sentence are given under; each being within the compass of approved word order.
>
> | | | |
> |---|---|---|
> | 1 : A yvi tu ua qu | translated | I send this to you. |
> | 2 : A ua qu yvi tu | translated | I to you send this |
> | 3 : Ua qu a yvi tu | translated | To you I send this |
> | 4 : Ua qu yvi nu[131] tu | translated | To you send I this |
> | 5 : Tu a yvi ua qu | translated | This I send to you |
> | 6 : Tu a ua qu yvi | translated | This I to you send |
> | 7 : Tu ua qu a yvi | translated | This to you I send |
> | 8 : Yvi nu tu ua qu | translated | Send I this to you (p. 96) |

Anderson (ibid.: 97) refers to version 1 as "the standard rendering" and calls version 6 as the "probably least desirable arrangement".

LdP has no dative suffix and an obligatory dative preposition, *a*, and the *Lingwa de Planeta Lernikursa* (anon. n.d. d.: 5) indicates that the order of major clausal components is S V DO IO, giving the following example:

(10)   Me dai   kitaba a   boy.
       I   give   book   to   boy
       'I give the book to the boy.' (OT)

However, immediately after this the following two sentences are given, showing that at least when the indirect object is a pronoun and the direct object is headed by a noun either one can precede the other (a similar pair of sentences appears on the preceding page):

(11a) Me dai   kitaba a   lu.
       I   give   book   to   he
       'I give the book to him.' (OT)

---

130 Anderson seems to have a very broad notion of 'indirect object', perhaps including any prepositional object.
131 The words *a* and *nu* both mean 'I'; Anderson (ibid.: 47) says, "'A' may be used before verbs, instead of 'Nu'".

(11b) Me dai a lu kitaba.
       (same meaning)

We see from the following example that when both the direct and indirect objects are pronouns, the former can precede the latter:

(12) Dai   it   a   me
      give it   to   me
      'Give it to me' (*Rikki-Tikki-Tavi* (anon. n.d. e))

Given the lack of explicit relevant statements in English sources on LdP, we cannot fully determine what is possible with respect to the position of pronominal indirect objects. Below is one more example containing a direct and an indirect object:

(13) li   dai   a   gayar to   ke   ta   yao
      they give to   guy   that that he   want
      'they gave to the guy what he wants' (anon. n.d. f: 6)

Ayola has a preposition for indirect objects (which also serves an allative function), *alu* 'to'; although to our knowledge it is not stated in materials for learning Ayola that it is required with direct objects, we believe that it is; if so, all indirect objects will be in PPs. Ayola Research Group (2007: sec. 2.3.5) states, "The usual order in Ayola is subject-verb-object (SVO) except in interrogative sentences ... While the direct object usually immediately follows the transitive verb, it may sometimes be preceded by a prepositional phrase". That is, Ayola has a basic order of S V DO IO, as shown in the following sentence:

(14) Dya donits carpo alu dyaza sestro.
      she gave   scarf to   her   sister
      'She gave a scarf to her sister.' (ibid.)

Below is a sentence in which the indirect object precedes the direct object:

(15) Plea   donaw alu myo libro jvonu lingoy.
      please give   to   I   book   about languages
      'Please give me a book about languages.' (ibid.: sec. 2.5.2)

Ayola Research Group (ibid.: sec. 2.4) also says, "Prepositional phrases can move freely within a sentence". They then give an example containing *alu*, but in an allative sense, not an indirect object sense:

(16a) Dya kondwirits alu la butiko.
      she drove   to the store
      'She drove to the store.'

(16b) Alu la butiko dya kondwirits.
      to the store she drove
      'To the store she drove.'

However, if we take this statement at face value, and assuming that indirect objects are always PPs, then we would expect indirect objects to be able to "move freely" and appear e.g. in clause-initial position.

Ayola has what we believe to be a rare feature among ALs: there are two different passive verbal affixes, *ge-* and *gye-*, the choice between them determined by whether the direct object or the indirect objects is raised to subject position:

(17a) Libro ge-don-its   alu la femo   byu amiko.
      book PASS-give-PST to   the woman   by   friend
      'A book was given to the woman by a friend.'

(17b) La femo   gye-don-its   libro byu amiko.
      the woman PASS-give-PST book by   friend
      'The woman was given a book by a friend.' (ibid.: sec. 2.3.6)

Algilez, which has the obligatory indirect object preposition *u* 'to', has considerable freedom with respect to the placement of indirect objects (and other sentence constituents); Giles (2010a: 10) says:

> There are many different ways in which sentences can be ordered which still give the same meaning. Only two ways should normally be used. The remainder, although grammatically possible, should only be used for 'poetic' reasons or reasons of emphasis. [...]
>
> **3.2 Normal word order, Subject-Verb-Object, 'Active' Subject:**
> The old woman quickly gave   a big fish to her two little cats
> peel ajoma   gevoz spidoma piskis ema u   du filis eta avel
>   S   Va   D-O   P   I-O
> [...]
> **3.3 Alternative word order, 'Passive' Subject.**
> Modify verb with 'ad' prefix :
> a big fish was quickly given   <u>by</u> the old woman to her two little cats
> piskis ema <u>ad</u>gevoz spidoma   peel ajoma   u du filis eta avel

It might thus seem that the standard position for indirect objects is after the direct object in active sentences and after the agent phrase in passive sentences (the agent in this example is not preceded by a preposition for a reason which will become clear). However, on p. 62 Giles has a passive sentence with the indirect object before the agent phrase and this sentence is supposed to illustrate one of the two "preferred alternatives" (ibid.) out of "13 variations" (ibid.) of word order in Algilez (the other being S V DO IO as in the passage above):

(18) an piskis fata adgevoz   u tri   filis blaka ad du   peil ajoma
      one fish fat   was.given to three cat black by two man old
      'one fat fish was given to three black cats by two old men'

Giles (ibid.) makes the following remark about this sentence: "Since the people doing the action (two old men) do not immediately follow the verb, 'ad' is required as a preposition." If the agent phrase in a passive sentence (i.e. a sentence in which the verb has passive morphology) is not separated from the verb by another constituent, the agentive preposition *ad* (which is homonymous with the verbal passive affix),[132] does not (have to) occur, although *u* must always precede recipients. The order S V Agent IO in a passive sentence (as in 3.3 in the above quotation) does not occur among the "13 variations" by Giles (ibid.: 62-3), i.e. it is not given as either one of the "preferred alternatives" or the one of the non-preferred ones. It is possible that Giles was not concerned with the linear relation between indirect object and agentive phrase when thinking of "preferred alternatives", i.e. that with the "preferred" order for passive sentences the subject precedes the verb, which is followed by the indirect object and the agentive phrase, with either of the last two constituents occurring before the other.

Giles does not say that the "13 variations" are the only ones permissible; his words are, "Just about any combination of word orders is grammatically possible in Algilez. Here are 13 variations of the same sentence. The first two examples, 21.1 [= S V DO IO] and 21.2 [= (Y)] are the preferred alternatives. The others examples are grammatically correct but should only be used in exceptional cases (e.g. for 'poetic' reasons)" (ibid.: 62).

The order S V IO DO occurs in a sentence (ibid.) illustrating one of the non-preferred "alternatives":

(19) du   peil ajoma gevoz u tri   filis blaka, an piskis fata
      two   man old   gave to three cat   black   one fish fat
      'Two old men gave to three black cats, one fat fish'

Giles (ibid.) comments, "note the comma after blaka. This serves as a grammatical 'break' in the sentence".

On p. 11 Giles gives the following sentence:

---

132 *Ad* apparently can be replaced by the nominal suffix -*da*.

(20)   u   il   adgevoz   bøl   ad   An
       to   he   was.given ball by   Ann
       'To him was given the ball by Ann' (i.e. 'He was given the ball by Ann')

He says of it (ibid.), "This form is 'grammatically correct' but its use is not recommended".[133] Several sentences with the indirect object first are among the sentences illustrating Giles' 11 non-preferred possibilities, including the one below:

(21)   u   tri   filis blaka, an   piskis fata adgevoz   du   peil ajoma
       to   three   cat   black   one fish   fat   was.given two man   old
       'to three black cats, one fat fish was given by two old men' (ibid.: 63)

The following non-preferred "alternative" shows that the indirect object can appear between the subject and the verb in an active sentence:

(22)   du   peil ajoma u   tri   filis   blaka gevoz an   piskis fata
       two man   old   to three cat   black gave   one fish   fat
       'Two old men to three black cats gave one fat fish' (ibid.: 62)

It appears that in Algilez the indirect object can occur anywhere in relation to other major clausal constituents, although non-standard orders are not encouraged.

L. Jones (1972: 4) says concerning Eurolengo, "In the case of a direct and an indirect object, as in other languages, the direct precedes the indirect. e.g. ... dona it mi = give it to me". However, he does not seem to follow this rule:

(23a) Aur if vos donara mi le karte, nos studiara it
       'Now if you will give me the menu, we will study it'
       (L. Jones 1972: 28, tr. 29)

(23b) El ofrara vos un opsion de voyajar per air, per mar and per tren o per bus, akordant a voster gusto.'
       'He will offer you a choice of travelling by air, by sea and by train or by bus, according to your taste.'
       (ibid.: 28, tr. 29)

(23c) Kano vos rekomendar mi un otro hotel?
       'Can you recommend me another hotel?' (ibid.: 36, tr. 37)

---

133 In fact, this sentence might not be grammatical given a later (p. 63) remark by Giles (about one of the 11 non-preferred word order possibilities): "'adgevoz' is not used since the thing given (an piskis fata) follows the verb". One might think that Giles has made an error in one place or the other.

In all of these sentences the direct object is a NP headed by a noun (and it is after the indirect object, which is a pronoun), so perhaps Jones only had in mind clauses in which both objects are (personal) pronouns. We do not know of any clauses in Eurolengo in which the direct object is pronominal and the indirect object is not. When both objects are NPs headed by nouns, it seems that the direct object is before the indirect object, which is introduced by the preposition *a* 'to':

(24a)   Vos donara dis karte a le portor in le buro a kote
'You will give this card to the porter in the office next door'
(ibid.: 32, tr. 33)

(24b)   Nos sendo mucho marchandise a Amerika and a mucho lands in Europe – Alemania, Franse, Espania, Italia and Portugal
'We send a lot of goods to America and to many countries in Europe – Germany, France, Spain, Italy and Portugal.' (ibid.: 22, tr. 23)

We have not found any examples Eurolengo of a pronominal indirect object occurring with *a*. Eurolengo may have a fixed word order (in statements) with respect to indirect objects, but the rule is not as simple as Jones has indicated.

The situation in Interlingua (IALA) is complex. There is the preposition *a* 'to' (and the form *al*, from a + the definite article *le*), which (obligatorily?) introduces indirect objects headed by nouns, e.g.:

(25)   Ille invia flores a   su   matre
        he   sends flowers to his mother
'He sends his mother flowers/He sends flowers to his mother'
(Gode and Blair 1951: 11)

We would think that such indirect objects generally (if not always) follow direct objects. Gode and Blair (ibid.: 26) make the following statement with respect to objects which are personal pronouns:

> In a combination of two personal pronouns that one precedes whose relation to the verb is more indirect or remote.
>
> **Illa me lo dice** 'She tells (it to) me'
> **Illa me lo ha dicite** *or* **Illa ha dicite me lo** 'She has told (it to) me'
> **Pro dicer me lo illa debeva telephonar** 'To tell (it to) me, she had to telephone'[134]

---

134 Another statement (ibid.) conflicts in part with this: "In a combination of two pronouns, one personal and one reflexive, the latter precedes." The example then given indicates that this rule overrides the other rule if the direct object is a reflexive pronoun, as in this example it is before the pronominal indirect object:
(i)   Illa se   nos monstra
      she   herself us   shows
      'She shows to us'

However, later on the same page they say, "The place of pronouns in the sentence is not rigidly fixed. The preceding paragraphs describe the norm from which deviations are justified by considerations of rhythm or emphasis". As can be seen from the examples in the last quotation, *a* need not occur with indirect objects which are personal pronouns, although it can appear with them; Gode and Blair (ibid.) state:

> There is no distinction between accusative and dative forms of the pronouns like that which appears in some other languages. Parallel to English usage the dative idea is clarified for differentiation or emphasis by the preposition **a**.
> **Io inviava un telegramma a mi granpatre** 'I sent a wire to my grandfather'
> **Io lo inviava a mi granpatre** 'I sent it to my grandfather'
> **Io le inviava un telegramma** 'I sent him a wire'
> **Io le lo inviava** *or* Io lo inviava a ille 'I sent him it' or 'I sent it to him'

In Esata words can sometimes be written together; this is true of *to* 'to', which marks indirect objects, and so its status as a separate word may not be entirely obvious. It is a short form of **tohe* (which as the asterisk indicates, is a form that we have never seen, though the root *toh-* 'to' is listed in Bothi (2006)). Bothi (ibid.) says:

> An indirect object pronoun may be introduced by *-to* eg. **tomi** to me, **tohi** to him, but this is optional, unless there are both direct and indirect object pronouns, then it must be signaled with *-to* eg. **yogidahe toxi** I gave it to her. An indirect or direct object pronoun may be written together with a subject pronoun, **yoxisi** I see her instead of **yosixi**. This word order is not present in English, but is commonplace in other languages.[135]

Other than what is said in this quotation, no instructions about word order in indirect object constructions are given by Bothi (ibid.).[136] However, we can get some idea of it from examples such as the following:

Concerning the position of personal and reflexive pronominal objects in relation to that of verbs, Gode and Blair (ibid.: 25-26) say, "PERSONAL AND REFLEXIVE PRONOUNS (except in prepositional constructions) precede the simple tense forms of the verb but follow the participles and the infinitive. [...] In the compound tenses which consist of an auxiliary tense form plus an infinitive or past participle, the personal or reflexive pronouns may precede the auxiliary or follow the participle or infinitive".

135 In Esata under some circumstances (at least in the written language) one can form a longer "run-on word" (ibid.) out of two or more words. *To* is also an allative preposition in Esata.

136 However, there is the general remark, "We retain a close relationship in word sounds and order with the English language, to make it easy for English speakers learning Esata, and also to facilitate learning of English for those who start with Esata" (ibid.). Most (but not all) of the examples given below are consistent with this, as they do not have an order that English would not have.

(26a) gi-de-cu-to-da-bo
give-the-eat-to-that-boy
'Give the food to that boy.'

(26b) Du-no speka mi-gi-yu pat fa-yode sifud platr
do-not expect I-give-you part of-my seafood platter
'Don't expect me to give you part of my seafood platter'

(26c) da-xu brina-ze gu-luk
that-should bring-they good-luck
'that should bring them good luck'

(26d) wi-go-xo-yu-da
we-go-show-you-that
'we're going to show you that'

(26e) Den wi-ke-xo hico va-wi bayda
then we-can-show each.other what-we bought
'Then we can show each other what we bought'

(26f) va-mi-xi-go-se?
what-I-she-go-say
'what am I going to say to her?'

(26a) is the only example that we know of where both the direct object and the indirect object are NPs headed by nouns (though *cu* is supposed to be a verb meaning '(to) eat'; twice in Bothi (ibid.) it seems to behave as a noun meaning 'food'), and the direct object precedes the prepositional indirect object. To our knowledge, in all examples in Bothi (ibid.) in which the indirect object is a pronoun and the direct object is a NP headed by a noun, the order is as in (26b) and (26c), with the indirect object (without a preposition) being before the direct object.

When both the direct and indirect objects are pronouns, more than one order is found. The example *yogidahe toxi* 'I gave it to her' in the quotation above has the order DO prepositional IO. In (26d) we see the order IO DO. This example seems to violate the rule given by Bothi that *to* 'to' is required when the indirect object and direct object are pronouns. It is possible that Bothi does not realize that *da* is a pronoun in this example, since he lists it among the "articles", and sometimes in the texts in Bothi (ibid.) it does act as a demonstrative adjective/determiner, though not here. However, this cannot be the explanation for the absence of *to* in (26f), which has the type of word order mentioned in the quotation above (specifically S IO V), since Bothi (ibid.) lists *va* 'what' among the interrogative pronouns. Perhaps the requirement for the presence of *to* is only meant to apply when the indirect and direct objects are personal pronouns (although Bothi does not say this).

Languages in Which the Indirect Object is Marked Neither by a Case Affix nor by an Adposition

We shall now examine an AL which has neither a dative case affix nor a preposition for indirect objects. Tacchi (n.d.: sec. 79) indicates that in Eurasto (which is a modified version of English) the indirect object precedes the direct object:

> The i-verb expresses Transitive acts and in all its forms governs an Immediate Object ... But many of the I-verbs are doubly transitive, i.e. they contain two transitive verbs each; e.g., the verb *give* means cause to receive, and consequently governs two objects. The first transitive verb in every Doubly transitive verb is to cause, therefore its Object must be the Immediate Object leaving the other to take 2nd place. Strict rule, e.g.,
> yo′ givAz mo′ plum,   *You gave me (made me receive) a plum.*
> yo′ tilAz wo′ d′u nwiz, *You told him (made him hear) the news.*
> yo′ digigAz mo′ gra′nd   *You made me dig ground*

Note that in Tacchi's examples the indirect object or causee is a pronoun and the direct object is an NP headed by a noun. Tacchi has one example of a ditransitive construction in which both indirect and direct objects are pronominal, although the direct object is a demonstrative pronoun, not a personal one:

(27) giv   mo′   t′as   E′nj   d′as
      give   me   that   in.exchange.for   this
      'Give me that for this' (sec. 96)

He does not give any sentences in which both objects are NPs headed by nouns or in which the direct object is pronominal and the indirect object is not. Although Tacchi speaks of a "strict rule", he may allow for it to be broken, as he says (ibid.: sec. 80), "But my Strict Rule is as declared above, and all departures are certainly poetic". We do not know whether such "departures" would involve word order (although the rule concerns word order): immediately before this sentence he discusses the possibility of a ditransitive verb appearing without an (overt) indirect object:

> If you say "We must each give mother something, I will give plums and you should give cake," in the last two clauses you are speaking pronominally and ellipsing the Immediate Object. But if you prefer to say "I will give plums," w can be inserted before the Time syllable to avoid ambiguity, e.g.
> wi givwuz plumi, *They will give plums.*

It thus appears that the "strict rule" is that ditransitive verbs are to be accompanied by indirect objects and direct objects, appearing in that order. As far as we can determine, indirect objects in Eurasto are indicated only by word order.

Unclear Situations

In some natural languages the distinction between case affixes and adpositions is not always clear. This can also be true of ALs, but in the case of ALs it may be due to a confusing description by the language designer.

With respect to Sona Searight (1935: 48-9) says, "As in I[talian] direct and indirect object pronouns follow, or are suffixed to, the verb in this order; e.g. *xo en mi* or *xoyenmi* show it to me, *ka mi on* or *kamion* lead me to him; but to avoid an ugly sound *li* 'to' may precede indirect *on, an, en* ['he', she', 'it']; e.g. *xo inye li on* show these to him". As this quotation indicates, Sona sometimes allows separate words to be written as one word (and it is reminiscent of Esata, discussed above). A possibly related point is that the morphological status of *li* is not entirely obvious: in the last Sona sentence in the quotation it looks like a separate word, but the following passage (ibid.: 54) makes the situation appear less clear (since in it Searight calls *li* a prefix but writes it as a separate word):

> Movement towards, direction is indicated by:– *li* to, toward cf. A[rabic] *li*. As pf. [= prefix] it signifies 'to' (Dative):– *li mi* to me, *li kan* to the house; As sf. [=suffix] it means 'towards', -wards; e.g. *inli* hither, *unli* thither, *keli* whither? *neinli* hence, *nekeli* whence, *kanli* home-wards. Note the form *dili* for; cf. R[ussian] *dlya*. The same radical forms adverbs of motion; e.g. *akali* up, *anili* down, combined *akaliani* up and down; *fuli* out, *lifu* to and fro.[137]

On p. 61 Searight lists *li* among the case markers, as the marker of the dative case, but without a hyphen after it (apparently indicating that it is a word, not an affix), and has it as a separate word in his example for it: *li mi* 'to me'.[138] (On the same page Searight gives *-li* as the "directive" case marker, with the example *mili* 'for me'.) In Sona words and sentences in Searight (1935) *li* with the meaning 'to' in a dative (or allative) sense is not attached to the beginning of a root, i.e. it is written as a separate word, except in the word *liua*, which Searight (1935: 54) glosses as 'to it, F[rench] y'. The word *ua* by itself does not mean 'it', it is an "emphatic"

---

137 The words *neinli* and *nekeli* appear odd because they contain both *-li* and the ablative marker *ne-*; the former might seem redundant given the presence of the latter.
138 The same is true of the marker of the ablative case, *ne*, as in *ne me* 'from me' (ibid.) and of most of what we are calling "case markers" here; our use of this term should have no implication that something is an affix as opposed to being an adposition. Searight himself does not use this term.

(ibid.: 53) particle meaning 'for, as for, in order to', as in *tu ua* ' for you, as for you' (ibid.: 54).[139]

Whatever the morphological status of *li*, since, as we have seen, Searight (ibid.: 49) says that it "may precede indirect *on, an, en*", we take it that it is not required with 3rd person singular pronominal indirect objects, at least when there is also a pronominal direct object. Given his examples *xo en mi* 'show it to me' and *li mi* 'to me' we can say that *li* sometimes does and sometimes does not occur before 1st person singular indirect objects, but we do not know whether there are any circumstances in which it must be used before such objects, or in which it must not be used before them. The following example indicates that *li* is not required before 3rd person plural pronominal objects (at least when they are attached to the verb):

(28) xo-ti anye uene
 show-them(CN) their(F) duty
 'Show them their duty' (ibid.: 48)

It is not clear to us whether *li* is required with other pronominal indirect objects, or with non-pronominal indirect objects. Searight does not give any specifications about the relative order of direct object and indirect object when one or both of them are NPs headed by a noun, although (28) shows that the order V IO DO is possible when the indirect object is a pronominal NP and the direct object is a NP headed by a noun and the example below indicates that the order V DO IO is possible when both objects are NPs headed by nouns (although the presence and position of the PP starting with *so* 'with' confuses the matter somewhat):

(29) ...da vaka hani-tu li un idadi, so tu leni
 to forward name-your to that department with your letter
 ge jidiubizamelen.
 and record.of.personal.services
 '...to forward your name to that department, together with your letter and record of personal services' (ibid.: 86)

Conclusion

Having examined indirect object constructions in a fair number of ALs one generalization that we could make is that it seems rare for an AL to have an absolutely rigid order of constituents in these constructions, at least when non-prepositional indirect objects are involved (even in Eurasto the possibility of alternative word orders may not be entirely ruled out), but it may also be

---

139 Other words apparently containing *ua* include *neua* 'from it', *soua* 'with it'.

uncommon for there to be complete equality of word orders, with all possibilities regarded equally highly or with one order not being "standard" or "basic".

In addition, we may note that in some ALs possibilities for the relative order of direct and indirect objects are (or seem to be) sensitive to whether they are pronouns or NPs headed by nouns. We also sometimes find when a language has a preposition for marking indirect objects, this preposition does not always have to be present. Thus indirect objects in ALs can behave in a rather complex way, both with respect to their position and with respect to their marking.

Chapter 9: Comitative and Instrumental Marking in Artificial Languages

In this chapter we shall look at how comitative and instrumental NPs are marked in some ALs, and particularly at whether they are formally distinct from each other. The idea for the chapter came as a result of one of us (Libert) writing a review of Stolz et al. (2006), a very detailed work about comitative and instrumental marking in the world's languages. Like natural languages, ALs differ in whether comitatives and instrumentals are marked differently (although it is often difficult to determine this as language designers are frequently not explicit about such matters).

Languages Not Distinguishing between Comitatives and Instruments

Uropi may not distinguish between comitatives and instrumentals, as the preposition *ki* 'with' is used to mark both functions (and there do not seem to be any prepositions which mark only one of them).[140]

Languages (at Least) Partly Distinguishing between Comitatives and Instruments

We shall now examine some languages in which there is at least one marking which is restricted to one of the two functions discussed here.

The Eurolengo word *kon* 'with' apparently serves both comitative and instrumental functions:

(1a) Vos habito in London kon voster familie.
'You live in London with your family.' (L. Jones 1972: 10, tr. 11)

(1b) Le haus isto chofado kon un sentral kalefaksion.
'The house is heated with a central-heating system.' (ibid.: 14, tr. 15)

(1c) Dis folgo sel jeneralik kon un puding de Noél and minse patés.
'This is generally followed by a Christmas pudding and mince pies.' (ibid.: 18, tr. 19)

---

140 Means of transport are indicated with the preposition *in*, but one could argue that this is simply a locative preposition (and not sometimes some kind of instrumental(-like) preposition), since it (also) means 'in' in the usual sense.

(1d)　　Dis part of le malen istan akompaniado kon le proper vins
　　　　'This part of the meal has been accompanied by the appropriate wines'
　　　　(ibid.: 26, tr. 27)

(1c) is interesting since the Eurolengo *kon* is translated not by *with*, but by *by*; note also that although *kon* there may seem to convey the meaning of accompaniment, it is not exactly the same meaning, since the Christmas pudding and mince pies do not appear at the same time as what is referred to by *dis* (the main part of the dinner), i.e. not together with it, but after it.[141] Likewise *kon* in (1d), which contains a form of the verb meaning 'to accompany', is translated as *by*; in English it seems more common to say "accompanied by" than "accompanied with".[142] Eurolengo also has a way of saying 'by means of', *per medium de*, so one can clearly mark an instrument.

In Uropa one can use the same word, *kum*, to mark both accompaniment and instruments, but there is also a word with only an instrumental meaning, as Donisthorpe (1913: 33) states in the following passage (which also shows his view on the semantic closeness of the concepts):

> It is often said that the English word "with" has two different meanings: – "together with" and "by means of." But in truth, the two meanings run into one another. [...] Fila, kum glada mortyri ursa, = the boy, together with (or, by means of) a sword, slew the bear. But it is frequently less ambiguous to use the word "usyr." Fila usyr glada mortyri ursa. But, Fila kum lay frata mortyri ursa. ['The boy with his brother slew the bear']

Usyr is perhaps composed of -*us*- 'tool, instrument' (as in e.g. *fosusa* 'spade') and *yr*, which is the causative suffix and as a separate word means 'in order that'. In (2a) below we see *kum* used with the meaning of accompaniment; this word can be incorporated into a verb, as in (2b), and can itself take a tense ending, like other prepositions in Uropa, as in (2c):

(2a)　　Ma　　sper-e　　　　a-m　　　va　　　cen-u　　　　kum　　ma
　　　　I　　　hope-PRES　NN-ACC　you　　dine-FUT　　with　　me
　　　　'I hope you will dine with me' (ibid.: 6)

141　Cf. the following example:
　　(i)　It konsisto de frut-jus, flakons de korn o poraje ... folgado de tost and marmalade
　　　　'It consists of fruit juice, corn flakes or porrige ... followed by toast and marmalade'
　　　　(ibid.: 26, tr. 27)
　　There are three other instances of *folgado de* in L. Jones (1972) (on pp. 26, 30, and 54), and so perhaps (1c) is anomalous or contains an error.
142　Cf. the example below, in which Eurolengo *kon* also corresponds to English *by*:
　　(i)　le frutemp-flors isto replasado kon tulips and le blosom on le frutarbs
　　　　'the spring flowers are replaced by flowers and the blossom on the fruit trees'
　　　　(ibid.: 54, tr. 55)

(2b) Ma spere va kumcenu ma
(same meaning) (ibid.)

(2c) Gilma   kum-e   lay   sister
     William   with-PRES   his   sister
     'William is with his sister' (ibid.: 32)

Donisthorpe apparently regards *kum* (and English *with*, for that matter) as neutral with respect to the distinction between being accompanee-oriented and companion-oriented (using terms in Stolz et al. 2006), and in fact similar to a coordinating conjunction. This is shown by the fact that he also gives (p. 32) 'His sister is with William' as a possible translation of (2c), and by the following remark: "If Harry is with Tom, clearly Tom is with Harry. Hence it is unnecessary to use the relation-mark 'ym' [the accusative marker] [with *kum*]. The same is true of the words 'et' ['and'] and 'net'[143] " (1913: 33).

Suma has the prepositions *ona* 'with' and *fone* 'with (by means of)', the latter occurring in e.g. *ma oki ma fone oko* 'I see with my eyes' (Russell 1966: 71). *Ona* can have a comitative meaning, as in "SUP ona ma" 'sup with me' (Russell 1967: 5),[144] but it also apparently can have an instrumental meaning, or something like it:

(3) ... sio   sia kami to   sami ona   MONEY sio   sia   RECEIVE
         which she can to   buy   with   money which she   receive
     mote bane
     for milk
     'which she can buy with the money which she receives for the milk'
     (Russell 1967: 10, OT).

Desa *Chat* has the words *kutu* 'with' and *kuya* 'by means of', but Davis (1999/2000) does not contain instructions on when they are used or examples of them in use, so we are not sure that instrumental and comitative marking are always distinct in this language. This also holds for Ro (1913): it has the word *ip* 'by means of', but we do not know the semantic range of its word *ir* 'with'. With respect to such languages we can at least say that there is marking which is unambiguously instrumental. Likewise pan-kel seems to at least partly distinguish comitative and instrumental functions, since it has the prepositions *it* and *pre*, which are glossed in the pan-kel-German dictionary part of Wald (1909) as 'mit'

---

143 We do not know the meaning of this word; perhaps it is a mistake for *noet*, which means "*without* in the sense of un-added-to" (Donisthorpe 1913: 55), or a contracted form of it.

144 The first ten stories in Russell (1967) are written in a mixture of Suma and English words, the English words (such as *sup*) being all in upper case letters.

(p. 24) and 'vermittels' (p. 34) respectively. The same is true of Germando, with its prepositions *met* 'with' and *door* 'by means of'.

Temenia has comitative and instrumental case suffixes, -ωι and -ρο respectively, although they are sometimes not obligatory, so comitative and instrumental NPs will not always be formally distinguished from each other (or from NPs bearing other semantic roles).

Languages (Apparently) Completely Distinguishing between Comitatives and Instruments

Here we look at languages in which there seems to be no overlap of marking of comitatives and instrumentals.

The formal distinctness of comitative and instrumental marking in Sasxsek is clear, since Nutter (n.d. a: 26) gives more complete glosses for the two prepositions involved, *ku* and *ju*: the former means 'with, included, accompanied by' while the latter means 'using, with, by means of'. The same is true of Eurolang, which has the prepositions *con* 'with (accompanied by)' and *par-us* 'with (an instrument), by using'. Voksigid distinguishes between comitatives and instrumentals, as it has the words *kum* and *wid*, which are glossed by Gilson (2009b) as 'with (comitative)' and 'with (instrumental)' respectively.

Romániço appears to make a distinction between comitative and instrumental functions, since it has the two prepositions *cun* 'with' and *per* 'by, by means of', with the former not being used with an instrumental meaning. The following phrases and expressions (from Morales 2010a) will give some idea of the contexts in which *cun* occurs: *café cun lacto* 'coffee with milk', *facer afaros cun* '(to) do business with', *poner si/cader en conflicto cun álichi* '(to) run afoul of someone', *confuser la inocentos cun la culpintos* '(to) confuse the innocent with the guilty', *personos cun bona gusto* 'people of taste', *atender cun nepacientitio* 'to look forward to'. *Per* occurs in a somewhat different range of contexts than English *with* in an instrumental sense and *by* (*means of*), as can be seen from the following phrases (also from Morales 2010a): *absenta per congedo* 'absent on leave', *carichizer carito per merços* '(to) load a cart with wares', *distanta per tri km* 'three kilometers off', and *luder gigo per violino* '(to) play a jig on the fiddle'.

In Ruggles' Universal Language there also seems to be a separation of accompaniment and instrument, since there are the two suffixes (which can also be separate words, if *h-* is added to them) *-et* 'by, with, by means of' and *-ut* 'with, together with, including'.

Neo Patwa has "verbs that function as prepositions" (Wilkinson and Wilkinson 2010) and there are different ones for accompaniment and instruments, *tomo* '(to) accompany; with' and *pakai* '(to) use; with' respectively.[145] Below is a sentence containing the latter:

(4) Yu   pakai   kata-ada, kata nyama.
     you use   cut-tool cut   meat
     'You cut meat using a knife.' (ibid.)

In Ande comitative and instrument functions are separated. Anderson (n.d.: 78) lists several prepositions of Ande which can translate the English word *with*, including *sua* 'with, in the company of', *pra* 'by means of', *lo* 'for (the benefit/purpose of)', and *iuli* 'becoming, by, with'.[146] Examples of their use are below:

(5a) Naya   sua   nu
      come   with   me
      'Come with me' (ibid.: 80)

(5b) To   uv   sekm   pra   tu
      it   was   cut   with   this
      'It was cut with this' (ibid.)

(5c) Qo   uv   lo   nu
      he   was   for   me
      'He was with me (on my side)' (ibid.)

(5d) Iuli   iv   qo   uv   yol
      with   that [= that state]   he   did[147] leave
      'With that he left' (ibid.)

More Complicated Situations

Finally, we see some languages in which are more complex for one reason or another.

Minyeva distinguishes comitative and instrumental functions, and in fact has more words for 'with' in various senses than most natural or artificial languages; these words are: *nwa* 'with, using, by (*transportation*)', *ble* 'with (accompaniment)', *nye* 'with (*instrument*), using, by (*sense*)', *bao* 'with, having

---

145 There is also the word *tene* '(to) have; (to) exist; with'.
146 Anderson (ibid.) speaks of '[t]he loose manner in which certain prepositions are employed in English".
147 *Uv* is used as an past auxiliary in both active and passive constructions, and so we have, based on Anderson (n.d.: 56), glossed it as 'was' or as 'did', depending on the context.

(*temporary possession*)', **mlo** 'with, having (*inalienable possession*)', **slu** 'with, having (*alienable possession*)', and *pye* 'with (together with)'.

Ayola also has several words equivalent to *with* in various meanings, although one of these words, *ecu*, sometimes corresponds to other words of English and other languages. Ayola Research Group (2007: sec. 2.4.1) calls *ecu* (which it glosses as 'with/from/etc.') one of the 'built-in-joint-argument prepositions". (The other preposition of this type is *acu* 'to/for/etc.'.) Ayola Research Group (ibid.) says the following about *ecu*:

> **ecu** ... and **acu** ... are used with a small but important group of verbs such as 'combine', 'mix', 'join', 'separate', 'converse', 'prefer', 'substitute', etc. which require at least two arguments of the same type, i.e. joint arguments, to complete their meaning.
> **ecu** is used when the joint arguments are symmetric; that is, they can be interchanged without a change in meaning, and the two arguments occur on opposite sides of the verb.
>
> **Active Forms**
> La hidrogeno kombinats ecu la oksigeno. — *The hydrogen combines with the oxygen.*
> La unta strado djuntats ecu la dusto. — *The first street joins to the second.*
> La latma pado seprihats ecu la streto. — *The wide path separates from the narrow one.*
> [...]
> Note the simplicity of the Ayola sentences in using only the one preposition **ecu**. Different prepositions are not needed because the meaning of the action is fully expressed by the verb.

In some sentences *ecu* may have a comitative meaning; the preposition *kunu* 'with' only has a comitative meaning, and these two prepositions are not interchangeable:

> Although the prepositions **ecu** and **kunu** both translate as 'with' in English, they function differently in Ayola. Consider the two sentences:
>
> Dik konversits vonu politiko ecu Djim. *Dick conversed about politics with Jim.*
> Dik ganits alu Nu York kunu Djim. *Dick went to New York with Jim.*
>
> One might ask why Ayola cannot use **kunu** in the first sentence as well as the second. The answer lies in the contrast between the two verbs. **konversare** requires a joint subject denoting at least two persons whereas with **ganare** the jointness of the subject is optional. (ibid.: sec. 2.4.3)[148]

---

[148] This distinction between required and optional co-participants extends into the set of conjunctions, or rather, that of *connectives*: Ayola Research Group (2007: sec. 3.3) states, "A connective is a word that connects words, phrases or clauses within a sentence or a sentence to a previous discourse. When it connects clauses to form a longer sentence, a connective acts in the same manner as a conjunction", while a conjunction, as defined by Ayola Research Group (ibid.: sect. 3.4) "conjoins clauses within a sentence". *Cwe* is the connective

In Ayola the instrumental function is distinguished from the comitative function, as there is a preposition for the former, *medu* 'with (by means of)'. There is also a preposition meaning 'without (not by means of), *nonmedu*, and there is a negative version of the comitative preposition, *nonkunu* 'without (unaccompanied by)'. Another preposition of Ayola is *avu* 'with (having)'; it is listed among the prepositions having to do with "Feature" (ibid.: sec. 2.4.2). Below is an example containing it:

(6) Tom ludits teniso kunu Dik avu hoca energenso.
    Tom played tennis with Dick with great energy.
    'Tom played tennis with Dick with great energy.' (ibid.: sec. 2.4.2)[149]

There is a corresponding negative preposition, *nevu* 'without (not having)'. The preposition *smeru* means 'with (in the same direction as)'; *veku* is a preposition involved with "Transferal" (ibid.: 2.4.2) and means 'with, of', as in the following sentences:

(7a) Dya plenizits la balono veku heliumo.
     he filled the balloon with helium
     'He filled the balloon with helium.'

(7b) Dya pustizits la glaso veku vino.
     she emptied the glass of wine
     'She emptied the glass of wine.' (ibid.)

Thus whether *veku* means 'with' or 'of' depends on the verb of the clause.

The term *preposition* as used in Ayola Research Group (2007) does not refer to heads of preposition phrases occurring inside noun phrases (such as *with* in *the man with blue eyes*); such words are called *links*.[150] The fine distinctions existing

---

corresponding to *ecu*, used for co-participants required for the action of the clause, and *ceyu* is the connective equivalent of *kunu*, as can be seen in the following examples:
(ia) Dik cwe Djim konversits vonu politiko.
    'Dick and Jim conversed about politics.'
(ib) Dik ceyu Djim ganits alu Nu York.
    'Dick and Jim went to New York.' (ibid.: sec. 2.4.3)
149 It is not clear to us why this sentence has *kunu* rather than *ecu*, given that one has to play tennis with someone else. One can of course practice by hitting a tennis ball against a wall, but perhaps this is not properly described as "playing tennis". (For that matter, conceivably one could have a conversation with oneself, but perhaps what happens then is that one person is taking on two or more conversational roles, and more than one role is necessary for a conversation.)
150 The head of a PP in a clause contained in a NP (e.g. *with* in *his claim that he waited with great patience*) would be a preposition rather than a link.

among Ayola prepositions (including that between comitative and instrumental prepositions) carry over to links, as each preposition has a corresponding link (as far as we know). The following table shows the link counterparts of some of the Ayola prepositions that were mentioned above:

Preposition	Link
ecu 'with/from/etc.'	jyecu
kunu 'with (accompanied by)'	ckunu
avu 'with (having)'	jyavu
smeru 'with (in the same direction as)'	cmeru

Table 1: *Some Ayola Prepositions and Corresponding Links (based partly on Ayola Research Group (2007: sections 2.5.1, 2.5.2)*

Below are examples containing two of these links:

(8a) La dusta strado djunta jyecu la unto estats longa.
 the second street joined to the first is long
 'The second street joined to the first street is long.' (ibid.: sec. 2.5.1)

(8b) bambino jyavu kwina anyoy
 child of five years
 'a child of five years' (ibid.: sec. 2.5.3)[151]

Among the prepositions of Voldu are *pri* 'near, by, with' and *so* 'with'. Given the following examples, it is not entirely clear to us what determines the choice between them:

(9a) Pri kio fila?
 with who daughter
 'With whom is the daughter?' (Stadelmann 1945: 40)

(9b) Karla pri drug-a-y, ze nebr-a
 Caroline with friend-F-PL, in.the.house.of neighbor-F
 'Caroline is with the (girl)-friends at the (woman) neighbor's.' (ibid.)

(9c) Buko-y fro kusn-a bo, pri vas.
 book-PL from cousin-F there near vase
 'The books from the (female) cousin are (over) there, near the vase.' (ibid.)

---

151 The section is which this example occurs is labelled 2.5.2, but since the preceding section was also labelled 2.5.2, it should be 2.5.3.

(9d) Skólero-y   so   ticer   tu stasyón.
     pupil-PL   with   teacher to station
     'The pupils have gone to the station with the teacher.' (ibid.: 41)

(9e) Von   yu   not   kam   so   nu?
     want you   not   come   with   us
     'Do you not wish to come with us?' (ibid.: 42)

(9f) Nu   bring-a   bred   so   nu.
     we   bring-PST   bread   with us
     'We brought some bread with us.' (ibid.: 52)

(9g) Nu   el-a   so   tey   na   monto-y.
     we   be-PST   with   them   on   mountain-PL
     'We were with them on the mountains.' (ibid.: 42)

(9h) Tey   vork   so   tey   for   tey-e   (si-e)   madra.
     they   work   with   they   for   they-POSS   (REFL-POSS)   mother
     'They work with them for their (own) mother.' (ibid.: 52)

(9i) Vu   spik   so   ci.
     you   speak   with   each.other
     'You speak with each other.' (ibid.: 10)

(9j) Yu   vaz   yu-n   so   mi-e   vaz-il.
     you   wash   you-ACC   with   I-POSS   wash-means
     'You wash yourself with my cloth.' (ibid.: 53)

(9k) Linde   Maria   lud   so   blu-e   bal.
     pretty   Mary   play   with   blue-ATT   ball
     'Pretty Mary plays with a blue ball. (ibid.: 45)

All of the relevant sentences in the exercises in Stadelmann (1945) involving movement ((9d-f) and another one on p. 43) have *so*, and so perhaps this is the preposition to use to indicate accompaniment of someone in motion. However, both *pri* and *so* are used to mean being with stationary people, and this and nearness to an object (in (9c)) are the only meanings that *pri* has in the sentences in Stadelmann (1945).[152] (9h-i) involve accompaniment of action, not simply location with, and it contains *so*, as do (9j-k), which involve an instrumental meaning, or something like it. There is a sentence in Stadelmann (ibid.: 16) in

---

152 In Stadelmann (ibid.: 19) there is an example of an adverbial use of this word (which therefore is stressed); again it has a meaning of proximity: *Tu stand pri* 'To stand near by'.

83

which the preposition *per* arguably has an instrumental type meaning, although it is glossed by him (p. 17) as 'by (passive)':

(10) Per   studing   se   lern.
      by   studying   one   learns
      'One learns by studying.'

Conclusion

Almost all of the languages discussed have at least a partial formal distinction between comitatives and instrumentals and some seem to have a complete distinction, with no overlap of marking. Minyeva and Ayola have complex systems of prepositions (or similar words) corresponding (partly) to English *with*.

Part III: Lexicon

In this part of the book we look at vocabulary in various semantic fields. In each of the following chapters we have separate sections for *a priori* languages on the one hand and *a posteriori* and mixed languages on the other. However, some languages are difficult to classify into these groups, e.g. Spokil and Ande, and others might place them into the other group.

With respect to the *a priori* language that he designed Brown (2007a: 3) states, "Most of the lexicon ... for Temenia was generated randomly". Given this, one might say that there is no point in including words from this language in our topical vocabulary tables or discussions here. However, there are some words from this language that are *a posteriori* and it might be interesting to see which ones they are (which should be fairly clear in many or most cases). The creation of the words of Desa *Chat* was an (almost) entirely random process but we have also included them in the chapters of this part; even with such languages there might be intriguing questions such as how much polysemy exists, to what extent there is overlapping in meaning, and the composition of compounds (if there are any) in the semantic fields that we examine.

A question that one might ask when examining terms with the same meaning from *a posteriori* and mixed languages is how much variation there is in form, e.g. do words for 'blue' seem to have the same general form or do significant numbers of them follow different models? Of course if there is a lack of variation in terms, this is probably due to the spread of one cognate through most or all major (Western) European languages; if one wants to borrow a word for 'metal' from a major European language, one does not have much choice in its form, and therefore the terms for 'metal' in most *a posteriori* languages will be the same or similar. Where one has a significant choice, i.e. where words for the same concept from major European languages are not all similar (as with terms for some colors), it is more likely that there will be a greater degree of variation among words in *a posteriori* and mixed ALs for this concept.[153] (One should bear in mind that we are not claiming any kind of statistical validity for any statements we make, since we have not surveyed all ALs and since some ALs are derived from, and thus heavily influenced by, other ALs, and it would be difficult to know what counts as a separate AL.)

Obviously to a large extent the appearance of one general form rather than another in an AL depends on the natural language(s) drawn upon by that AL, thus for example we would expect a Latin-based AL to choose something like **blank* as the word for 'white' and a English-based one to borrow the English word

---

153 Naturally such remarks apply only to ALs based on major (Western) Indo-European languages, as most *a posteriori* languages are, but the same general phenomenon would be seen if one were looking at ALs based on languages of other families or areas.

white. However, we still believe that it is worth investigating which forms are chosen by ALs, since many ALs do not limit themselves to using a single natural language as a source, and even among languages based mainly on one language we still find some surprises (i.e. words coming from a different language).

In looking at such matters one will want to know where the terms of an AL come from, but such information frequently is not provided by designers/ describers of ALs. When we have such information, we often give it.[154,155] Note that we give what the language designer/describer says is the source, which conceiv-ably could differ from the actual source.

There are some gaps in our tables of terms from languages. There are several causes of this: frequently our sources do not give a term for the meaning in question, and often a term may be provided but is problematic for one reason or another, such as that we cannot be certain that it has the meaning that we are interested in.

Chapter 10: Color Terminology of Artificial Languages

Color terms of natural languages have been much investigated by linguists and anthropologists. In this chapter we look at systems of color terms of ALs.

A Priori **Languages**

In Sona color terms contain *ro*, which is the radical meaning 'color'. The list of "simple colors" given in Searight (1935: 47) is: *naro* 'black', *jero* 'grey', *jenaro* 'slate', *suro* 'blue', *huro* 'azure', *usuro* 'silver', *viro* 'opal', *puro* 'yellow', *urro* 'gold', *puvero* 'yellow green', *vero* 'green', *vemero* 'olive', *muro* 'brown', *jemuro* 'dun', *garo* 'pink', *boro* 'carmine', *zoro* 'red', *umoro* 'cream', *bero* 'white'. By "simple colors" Searight does not mean something like "basic color term" as in e.g. Berlin and Kay (1969), since some of his terms are clearly morphologically complex, e.g. *puvero*, from *puro* and *vero*. However, Searight (ibid.) also gives a list of "compounds": *suzoro* 'bluish-purple', *zosuro* 'reddish purple', *suvero*

---

154 With respect to Lingwa de Planeta, the *LdP-English Dictionary* (anon. 2010b) says the following: "Word etymologies are currently given sparingly, and usually only one source language is indicated. However you should bear in mind that we have often adopted roots that are widely spread across languages. For example, the word 'kitaba' is originally from Arabic, but the root is also present in Turkish, Hindi, and many other languages." The same seems to be true of etymological information on LdP in Ivanov and Lysenko (2007). Note also that what one or both of these works give as the source for a word may clearly not be the original source for it; for example, in Ivanov and Lysenko (2007) the source for the LdP word *adres* 'address' is said to be Turkish (the Turkish word being *adres*), although the Turkish word itself is a borrowing.

155 Bollen (n.d. b) often gives the source of a Lingone word as "sort of PIE [Proto-Indo-European]".

bluish green', *vesuro* 'greenish blue'. It is unclear to us how these are different from *puvero* or *jenaro*. Sona has affixes to indicate "shades of color" (ibid.): *ta-* bright, *-ta* 'deep', *-van* 'dark', *-ko* 'light', *-fi* 'pale', *-ki* 'slightly', *-nan* 'dull'.

The color term system of Ygyde is able to describe a large number of shades with short words:

> Colors are defined as intensities of their red, green, and blue components. Names of colors are three letters long. The first letter of all color names is **u**. The second letter is a consonant, and the last letter is a vowel. (The leading letter **h** is ignored because it is used in spoken Ygyde only.) The red green blue table provides rules that help memorize the color names listed in the color table. The red green blue table uses three new terms: dominant color, second color, and third color. The dominant color is the color component (red, green, or blue) that has greater intensity than the remaining color components. If blue is not the dominant color, it is the third color. Red is the third color only if green and blue (cyan) are the dominant colors.
>
> If the second letter (ignore **h**) of the color name is **b**, there is no dominant color, so red, green, and blue components have the same intensities. There are four such colors: **uba** (white), **ubo** (gray), **ubu** (dark gray), and **ubi** (black).
>
> If the second letter (ignore **h**) is not **b**, the last letter describes dominant color(s) and the second letter describes the remaining color components. **If you cannot memorize the entire red green blue table, try to memorize vowels associated with the dominant colors and the fact that light colors are associated with consonants listed in the beginning of the alphabet table.** (anon. 2010a)

Examples of the terms of this system are *hupa*, which means a shade in which red is the dominant color, with an intensity of 100%, and in which green and blue each have an intensity of 67%, in other words, 'pink', and *ujy*, which means a shade in which blue is the dominant color, with an intensity of 67% and in which red and green each have an intensity of 33%.

The table below contains color terms of some other *a priori* languages.

	'white'	'yellow'	'orange'
Desa *Chat* (adjs.)	mumexe	pinoke	hatiki[156]
Kotava (adjs.)	batakaf	blafotaf	kramtukaf
Minyeva (adjs.)	meva	vaki	qato[157]
Ro (1913)	bodac	bofaf	bofad[158]
Ro (1919)	bodoc	bofof	
Ro (1921) (adjs.)	bodaco	bofafo	

---

156 Cf. the noun for the fruit 'orange', *xafugu*.
157 Cf. the noun *kwijo* 'orange (the fruit)'.
158 Cf. the word for the fruit 'orange', *lufsan*.

Ro (1931)	bodoc	bofof	
Suma (adjs.)	pana	kusa	kisa[159]
Temenia	πευπαυ	τοαφε	ξοαθα[160]

	'red'	'pink'	'purple'
Desa *Chat* (adjs.)	haxuca		
Kotava (adjs.)	keraf	raltukaf	rolmukaf
Minyeva (adjs.)	funa		tijo
Ro (1913)	bofac		
Ro (1919)	bofoc		bofoq
Ro (1921) (adjs.)	bofaco		
Ro (1931)	bofac		
Suma (adjs.)	kasa	rosa (Eng.)	vula[161]
Temenia	κουφορε	ψαεχοζο	

	'blue'	'green'	'brown'	'grey'	'black'
Desa *Chat* (adjs.)	cadetu	wuduxo	muhowa	halili	piluyo
Kotava (adjs.)	faltaf	kusaf[162]	bertraf, lerkaf[163]	lukoptaf	ebeltaf
Minyeva (adjs.)	lice	nula	zuki	deju	sotu
Ro (1913)	bofal	bofag	bodal	bodag	bodam
Ro (1919)	bofol	bofog	bodol	bodog	bodom
Ro (1921) (adjs.)	bofalo	bofago			bodamo
Ro (1931)					bodom
Suma (adjs.)	vila	vala	topa	tepa	pina
Temenia	θιαφυηε	λαυφε	λολαηαεφυ	θοφυξυξυ	πυεκετο

Table 1: *Color Terms in Some* A Priori *Languages*

Desa *Chat* also has the color adjectives *hahexo* 'cream' and *bukika* 'violet'.

In addition to the words in the above table Kotava has the adjectives *flemaf* 'beige', *jemakaf* 'tawny', *kadulaf* 'violet',[164] and *tcubraf* 'bistre'. One will notice that all of the Kotava color terms given end in *-af*, and several end in *-ukaf*. The word-class marker for qualificative adjectives in Kotava is *-(a)f*, and *-ukaf* (which

---

159 The word for 'orange (the fruit)' is *kisa belo* (*belo* means 'fruit'); here therefore is the unusual situation of the word for the fruit 'orange' being based on the color word rather than the other way around.
160 Cf. *ψιρι* 'orange (the fruit)'.
161 This word also means 'violet'.
162 *Kusaf* also means 'acidulous'.
163 *Bertraf* is glossed in anon. (2007a: 24) as 'brun, marron', while *lerkaf* is glossed (p. 146) as 'marron, de couleur marron'.
164 Cf. *minsa* 'violet (the flower)'.

contains -*af* [165]) derives an adjectival color term from a noun meaning something typically or canonically of that color. Thus the adjectives for 'orange' and 'pink' are built from the nouns *kramta* 'orange (the fruit)' and *ralta* 'rose' (the final *a* of the root is deleted). Anon. (2007a) has many other Kotava color terms formed with -*ukaf*, some of which are given in the following table:

Kotava	English	Root
aktukaf	'milky-white'	*akt* 'milk'
azilukaf	'iron-colored'	*azil* 'iron'
drelgeukaf	'of changing color'	*drelge* 'chameleon'
eribukaf	'amber-colored'	*eriba* 'amber'
forteyukaf	'blood-red'	*fortey* 'blood'
frolgukaf	'turquoise-colored'	*frolga* 'turquoise'
glordukaf	'peach-colored'	*glorda* 'peach'
jagilukaf	'strawberry-colored'	*jagila* 'strawberry'
keltukaf	'sky-blue'	*kelt* 'sky'
kolotukaf	'apricot-colored'	*kolot* 'apricot'
krubukaf	'olive-green'	*kruba* 'olive'
mardukaf	'pearl-colored'	*mard* 'pearl'
muvudukaf	'jonquil-colored'	*muvuda* 'jonquil'
noldukaf	'snow-white'	*nolda* 'snow'
varkukaf	'ochre-colored'	*varka* 'ochre'

Table 2: *Some Color Adjectives of Kotava Containing* -ukaf

The Kotava adjective *rolmukaf* 'purple' is problematic: there is a noun *rolm* meaning 'purple', but one might think that it does not have this meaning in the sense of 'the color purple', even though that is the most common sense of the English word *purple*, since, as we have just seen (and as is indicated by Fetcey and the Comité Linguistique Kotava (2009: 44)), -*ukaf* attaches to a noun meaning some thing (and thus not to a noun naming a color). Also, all the (other) nouns denoting colors that we know of in Kotava end in -*e*: *kuse* 'green', *lerke* 'brown', and *lukopte* 'grey'. Therefore, either *rolm* means 'purple' in some other sense than the color (e.g. 'cloth which is purple'), or *rolm* and *rolmukaf* are anomalous (or an error has been made in their creation).

Another problematic adjective is *kerukaf* 'scarlet'. The *Lexique Kotava* → *Francais* (anon. n.d. i) indicates that *kerukaf* is etymologically related to *keraf* 'red'. If *kerukaf* is derived from the root *ker-* (the root of *keraf*, i.e. what remains when we remove the adjectival ending -*af* from it), and if this root means 'red' (as it apparently does and as we would expect), then *kerukaf* is anomalous in the same

---

165 Fetcey and the Comité Linguistique Kotava (2009) consider -*ukaf* a suffix, but one could argue that it is two suffixes, -*uk*- and -*af*.

way as *rolmukaf* may be: it is formed by attaching *-ukaf* to a root that already means a color (rather than to a root meaning something that has a certain color associated with it). In some sources, e.g. anon. (2007b), there is a word *kera*, but it means 'expectation', and so *kerukaf* could not plausibly be derived from it. Among other problematic color adjectives ending in *-ukaf* is *geblitukaf* 'mauve': there is no word **geblit* in Kotava, or if there is, it is not given in the publicly available materials on the language, as far as we know.[166]

The color terms of Ro (1913) all begin with *bo*, which are the characteristic initial segments of words whose meaning involves "[p]roperty of matter" (Foster 1913: 21). More specifically, most of the Ro words in the table above begin with *bof*, and *bof* is the word that means 'prismatic color'. The other Ro (1913) words which have *bof* as their first segments are *bofam* 'indigo', *bofaq* 'violet', and *bofax* 'variegated'. The other Ro (1913) color terms in the table have *bod* as their first segments (there is no word **bod* listed in Foster (1913)); the other words of this language which begin with *bod* are *bodaf* 'pearly' and *bodaj* 'russet'.

The Ro (1919) color terms are the same as those of Ro (1913), except that there is a somewhat different range of colors covered, and the next to last segment is *o* rather than *a*.[167] Although it is not explicitly stated by Foster (1919), it appears that this *o* is the marker of adjectives in this version of Ro (e.g. *matof* 'old'), and thus that these words are adjectives. One cannot make an analogous statement about Ro (1913): while many adjectives have *a* as their penultimate segment (e.g. *bokal* 'musical'), quite a few do not (e.g. *rebeb* 'thoughtful'), and there is no lack of words which have *a* in this position but which are not adjectives (e.g. *bipad* 'umbrella').

The color terms that are given by Foster (1921) are similar to the corresponding color terms of the 1913 and 1919 versions of the language, differing from those of the 1913 version only in having an *o* at the end; Foster (1921: 3) states that *-o* is the marker for adjectives.[168] Foster (1931) only gives four names of colors, and three of them have been changed back to those of Ro (1919), the exception being *bofac* 'red', which is the same as the Ro (1913) form.

The Suma word for 'azure' is *boto vila* (*boto* means 'sky').

A Posteriori and Mixed Languages

The Balta words for the prismatic colors were formed in an unusual way: they contain the roots for the cardinal numerals from 'one' to 'seven' and *kol* 'color',

---

166 Note also that there are adjectives ending in *-ukaf* whose meaning does not involve color, e.g. *mialukaf* 'average' (apparently derived from the noun *miala* 'half') and *lizukaf* 'local, regional' (apparently derived from the noun *liz* 'place').
167 Ro (1919) also has the words *bofab* 'color' and *bofnob* 'achromatic'.
168 Ro (1921) also has the words *bofab* 'color' and *bofnabo* 'colorlessness'. The word-final *o* in the latter word is surprising since it is a noun; perhaps there is an error here and it was meant to be an adjective, or the *o* should not be present..

e.g. *balkol* 'violet' (from *ba* 'one'), *belkol* 'indigo' (from *be* 'two'), *jalkol* 'orange' (from *ja* 'six'), *jelkol* 'red' (from *je* 'seven').

Some, but not all, of the Neo Patwa words for colors are compounds containing the word *tinta* 'color, paint':

Neo Patwa	English	other words contained or source of word
safi	'white, bright, clear'	Swahili
yelo	'yellow'	English
damu-tinta	'red'	*damu* 'blood'
tyen-tinta	'blue'	*tyen* 'sky'
lapa-tinta	'green'	*lapa* 'lapa'
bun-tinta	'brown'	*bun* 'mud'
nube-tinta	'grey'	*nube* 'cloud'
siya	'black, dark'	Persian

Table 3: *Neo Patwa Color Terms*

Most of the Ande words for colors seem to be compounds, but unlike those of Neo Patwa, they are apparently composed of (sometimes modified) roots for other colors. The Ande color terms which are not compounds are *uin* 'white', *iel* 'yellow', *roi* 'red', *uvn* 'blue', and *nu'* 'black'.[169] *Iel* appears to be *a posteriori* (from English), and *roi* may be as well, but the other words are either *a priori* or of less obvious origin (at least to us). The following table shows what we believe to be the composition of some compound words for colors:

Ande	'English'	roots contained (before modification, if any)
elro	'orange'	*iel* 'yellow' + *roi* 'red'
vnel	'green'	*uvn* 'blue' + *iel* 'yellow'
roivn	'purple'	*roi* 'red' + *uvn* 'blue'
nu'ro	'maroon'	*nu'* 'black' + *roi* 'red'
uinro	'pink'	*uin* 'white' + *roi* 'red'
nu'el	'brown'	*nu'* 'black' + *iel* 'yellow'
uinel	'straw'	*uin* 'white' + *iel* 'yellow'
uinu'	'grey'	*uin* 'white' + *nu'* 'black'

Table 4: *Some Ande Compound Color Terms*

We shall now present color terms from some other *a posteriori* and mixed languages, starting with terms for 'white':

---

169 In Ande <v> stands for a vowel; Anderson, who probably was a speaker of Australian English, gives the following words (among others) to illustrate its pronunciation: *all, ought, or, was, want*. Recall that the apostrophe stands for the velar nasal.

	'white'		'white'
Afrihili (adjs.)	pongo	LFN	blanca
Algilez (nouns)	wot[170]	LdP (adjs.)	blan
American (adjs.)	blanc-	Mondlango (adjs.)	wayta
Ardano (nouns)	sanan (Manchu)	Neo (adjs.)	alba
Arlipo (adjs.)	blanka	Olingo (adjs.)	blanqa
Arulo (adjs.)	blanka	Omnial (adjs.)	albe
Atlango (adjs.)	blanka	Panamane	biánkos
Auxil	blanc	Panamerikan	blanki
Ayola (adjs.)	alba (Lat.)	pan-kel (adjs.)	ak
Dil	vit (Eng.)	Perio (adjs.)	vita
Esata	wayt-, blan- (Fr.)	Romániço (adjs.)	blanca
Esperanto (adjs.)	blanka	Romanova	blanco
Eurolengo	blank	Rug.	halb-[171]
Evroptal	wit (Dutch)	Salveto (adjs.)	blanc
Farlingo (adjs.)	blanke	Sasxsek (nouns)	saf
Fremdu (adjs.)	blanke	Sermo (adjs.)	albo, blanco
Glosa	leuko (Gk),[172] aspro (Gk.), blanka, albi[173]	Sintezo (adjs.)	blanka
		UNI	USE
		Uropi (adjs.)	bij
Id. Neut. (adjs.)	blank	Vela (adjs.)	vit
Ido (adjs.)	blanka	Virgoranto (adjs.)	blanka
Int. IALA	blanc, albe[174]	Voksigid (verbs)[175]	blanka
Ling	vit	Volapük (adjs.)	vietik
Lingone (adjs.)	wayte (Gmc.)	Voldu	blank

Table 5: *'White' in Some* A Posteriori *and Mixed Languages*

Although these words come from a variety of apparent sources, the most popular general form is **blan(k)*, accounting for about half of the total.

The table on the following page contains terms for 'yellow'. Again the terms come from several different apparent sources and hence show much variation. Glosa also has the terms *helvo* 'pale yellow' and *kroko* 'saffron yellow' (both from Greek).:

---

170 This word also means 'whiteness'.
171 This root is glossed by Ruggles (1829: 115) as 'whiteness, white colour'.
172 This word also means 'bleach'.
173 Concerning *albi* Springer et al. (2009: 20) say, "prefer leuko".
174 These words are adjectives; the noun meaing 'white' is *blanco*.
175 Voksigid has no underived nouns or adjectives; the Voksigid words that we give in this table, and in other tables in the book, are verbs. Thus, for example, *blanka* means 'be white'.

	'yellow'
Afrihili (adjs.)	dozimi
Algilez (nouns)	yel[176]
American (adjs.)	iël-
Ardano (nouns)	nirimug (Bambara)
Arlipo (adjs.)	flava
Atlango (adjs.)	amaryela, yela
Ayola (adjs.)	flava (Lat.)
Esata	yelo, jalo (It.)[177]
Esperanto (adjs.)	flava
Eurolengo	gilt
Evroptal	gel (Low German)
Farlingo (adjs.)	yelove
Fremdu (adjs.)	yelowe
Glosa	xanto (Gk.),[178] flavo, galbino, safro
Id. Neut. (adjs.)	yelb
Ido (adjs.)	flava
Int. IALA	jalne
Interlingue	yelb
Konya (adjs.)	xele
Ling	jel
Lingone (adjs.)	yele (Eng.)
LFN	jala

	'yellow'
LdP (adjs.)	hwan (Mandarin)
Mondlango (adjs.)	flava
Neo (adjs.)	jala
Olingo (adjs.)	flava
Omnial (adjs.)	flave, iktere, xante
Panamane	jáunos
Panamerikan	yelo
pan-kel (adjs.)	gul
Romániço (adjs.)	flava
Romanova	amarilo
Rug.	fulv-, flav-
Salveto (adjs.)	flav (Lat.)
Sasxsek (nouns)	nolan
Sermo (adjs.)	jalo
Sintezo (adjs.)	flava
UNI	LEM
Unitario (adjs.)	amarija
Uropa (adjs.)	flav
Uropi (adjs.)	ʒel
Vela (adjs.)	yel
Virgoranto (adjs.)	gelba
Voksigid (verbs.)	gelo
Volapük (adjs.)	yelibik
Voldu	gelv

Table 6: *'Yellow' in Some A Posteriori and Mixed Languages*

Below we see terms for 'orange':

	'orange'
Algilez (nouns)	oran[179]
Arlipo (adjs.)	oranzhala

	'orange'
LdP (adjs.)	oranje[180]
Mondlango (adjs.)	oranja

---

176 This word also means 'yellowness'.
177 These words apparently are nouns, as their final segment is *o* (the final segment of Esata adjectives is *i*).
178 This word also means 'blond; yolk'.
179 Cf. *ranj* 'orange (the fruit)'.
180 The noun meaning 'orange (the fruit)' is *oranja* (in LdP word-final *e* usually is found in adjectives, while *a* is one of the final segments of nouns).

93

Ayola (adjs.)	orandja[181]	Neo (adjs.)	oranja[182]
Esperanto (adjs.)	oranĝa[183]	Panamerikan	oranja(kolor)[184]
Eurolengo	oranje	Romanova	aranjado (noun and adj.)[185]
Fremdu (adjs.)	oranje		
Glosa	rubi-xanto, orange (Fr.),[186] rubi-flavo[187]	Salveto (adjs.)	orang
		Sasxsek (nouns)	nolanxkiz, naranxlaun[188]
Id. Neut. (adjs.)	oranj-kolorik[189]	Sintezo (adjs.)	oranja[190]
Ido (adjs.)	oranjea[191]	Uropi (adjs.)	aranӡi
Int. IALA	orange (adj.)[192]	Vela (adjs.)	rag
Lingone (adjs.)	oranje (Eng.)	Virgoranto (adjs.)	oranga
LFN	orania (noun and adj.)[193]	Voksigid (verbs.)	oranja
		Volapük (adjs.)	linyelibik

Table 7: *'Orange' in Some* A *Posteriori and Mixed Languages*

Here there is not much variation and there is often an (apparent) etymological relation with the term for 'orange (the fruit)', or the same term is used for both meanings. For example, the Arlipo adjective *oranzhala* 'orange' (i.e. having that color)' apparently is derived from the noun *oranzho* 'orange (the fruit)' by means of the suffix *-al-* 'similarity, relatedness', and the Uropi adjective *aranӡi* 'orange' seems to be derived from the word *arànӡ* 'orange (the fruit)'. In contrast the Volapük word *linyelibik* 'orange colored' has no etymological relation to the word 'orange (the fruit)', which is *boan*, but it does apparently contain *yelib* 'yellow'.

---

181 Cf. the noun *orango* 'orange (the fruit)'.
182 Cf. *oranjo* 'orange (the fruit)'
183 Cf. *oranĝo* 'orange (the fruit)'. *Oranĝa* also means "konsistanta el [oranĝ]o(j)" ('consisting of oranges' (Waringhien 1970: 769), as in [*oranĝa*] *marmelado* 'orange marmelade' (ibid.).
184 *Oranja* also means 'orange (the fruit)'.
185 Cf. the noun *aranja* 'orange (the fruit)'.
186 This word also means 'orange (the fruit)'.
187 Springer et al. (2009: 59) say about this word, "prefer rubi-xanto".
188 Nutter (n.d. a: 38) says, "it is possible to create names for colors by relating to something of the same, or similar color [sic] such as **naranxlauni** (*orange-colored*)". *Naran* means 'orange (the fruit)', *laun* means 'color, hue, tint', and *-i* is the adjectival/adverbial ending; thus Nutter is using an adjective as an example of the result of the process, but he (ibid.) also has the noun *naranxlaun* in a list of color terms. As for the *-x-* which appears in this word (<x> has the phonetic value [ə]), Nutter (ibid.: 42) states, "Whenever compounding results in two consonants together, the letter **X x** is inserted between them for euphony".
189 The noun meaning 'orange (the fruit)' is *oranj*.
190 The Sintezo word for 'orange (the fruit)' is *oranjo*.
191 Cf. *oranjo* 'orange (the fruit)'.
192 This word can also be a noun meaning 'orange (the fruit)'.
193 This word also means 'orange (the fruit)'.

Similarly, terms for 'pink' frequently contain the sequence *ros*, indicating an etymological relationship with the word for 'rose' in the AL and/or in the natural language source. However, a fair proportion of forms are based on the English word *pink*:

	'pink'
Algilez (nouns)	pink
Ardano (nouns)	rosa (Asturian)
Ayola (adjs.)	pinka
Evroptal	pink
Fremdu (adjs.)	pinke
Glosa	rosa,[195] rodo (Gk.)[196]
Ido (adjs.)	rozea
Ling	rosi
LFN	ros

	'pink'
Neo (adjs.)	roza
Olingo (adjs.)	rozqola
Panamane	pínkos
Romániço (adjs.)	rosea
Romanova	rosado[194]
Salveto (adjs.)	ros
Sasxsek (nouns)	safxkiz
Uropi (adjs.)	rozi[197]
Vela (adjs.)	pik

Table 8: *'Pink' in Some* A Posteriori *and Mixed Languages*

The Olingo word for 'pink' apparently contains the roots for 'rose', *roz-*, and 'color', *qol-*. The Sasxsek term is a compound of *saf* 'white' and *kiz* 'red'.

We shall now look at terms for 'red' and for two shades of red:

	'red'
Afrihili (adjs.)	ja
Algilez (nouns)	red[198]
American (adjs.)	ruź-
Ardano (nouns)	roz
Arlipo (adjs.)	ruzha
Atlango (adjs.)	ruja
Auxil	red
Ayola (adjs.)	ruja (Fr.)[200]
Esata	red-, ruj- (Fr.)
Esperanto (adjs.)	ruĝa
Eurolengo	red

	'red'
LdP (adjs.)	rude (Slavic)
Mondlango (adjs.)	reda
Neo (adjs.)	ruba
Olingo (adjs.)	ruja
Omnial	eritre, rubie[199]
Panamane	rújos
Panamerikan	roje
Romániço (adjs.)	rúbea
Romanova	rojo
Rug.	rzb-[201]
Salveto (adjs.)	rub (Lat.)

---

194 *Rosado* and *purpurio* are labelled as adjectives in anon. (n.d. h); the word class of the other Romanova words in this table is not specified there.
195 This word is glossed as 'rose; pink' in Springer et al. (2009: 59).
196 This word is glossed as 'rose; rose color, pink' in Springer et al. (2009: 59).
197 This word apparently was derived from *roz* 'rose (the flower)'.
198 This word also means 'redness'.
199 *Eritre* is an adjective. We believe that *rubie* is also an adjective but are not certain about this.
200 Ayola also has the adjective *rufa* 'red (hair color)'.
201 Ruggles (1829: 139) glosses this root as "red colour, redness".

Evroptal	ruj (Fr.)	Sasxsek (nouns)	kiz
Farlingo (adjs.)	rede	Sermo (adjs.)	rubio, rubro, rube[202]
Fremdu (adjs.)	rede		
Glosa	rubi,[203] eritro (Gk.), rubri, rufi, rutilo	Sintezo (adjs.)	ruja
		UNI	UKA
Id. Neut. (adjs.)	rub	Unitario (adjs.)	rubra
Ido (adjs.)	reda	Uropi (adjs.)	roj
Int. IALA	rubie	Vela (adjs.)	red
Konya (adjs.)	mime	Virgoranto (adjs.)	reda
Ling	red	Voksigid (verbs)	rojo
Lingone (adjs.)	rode ("sort of PIE")	Volapük (adjs.)	ledik[204]
LFN	roja	Voldu	red

	'crimson'		'crimson'
Atlango (adjs.)	karmesina	Neo (adjs.)	krama
Esperanto (adjs.)	karmezina	Olingo (adjs.)	punqa
Glosa	fo-rubi[205]	Panamane	krímsos
Ido (adjs.)	karmezina[206]	Sintezo (adjs.)	karmezina
LFN	carmesi	Vela (adjs.)	zafat

	'scarlet'		'scarlet'
Esperanto (adjs.)	skarlata	Mondlango (adjs.)	skarla
Glosa	skarleto, fo rubi	Neo (adjs.)	skarla
Id. Neut. (adjs.)	skarlat	Olingo (adjs.)	sqarla
Ido (adjs.)	skarlata	Rug.	rzt-
Int. IALA	scarlatin (adj.), scarlato (noun)	Sermo	scarlatino (adj.), scarlato (noun)[207]
Ling	skarlat		
LFN	scarlata	Sintezo (adjs.)	eskarlata

Table 9: *'Red', 'Crimson', and 'Scarlet' in Some* A Posteriori *and Mixed Languages*

There is little significant variation among terms for 'scarlet', while half of the terms for 'crimson' have the general form **karmes/z(in)*. Terms for 'red' show

---

202 This word means 'red, reddish'. Sermo also has the word *rubido* '(dark) red'.
203 This word also means 'blush; ruby; ruddy'.
204 *Ledik* is glossed as 'red, scarlet' in Wood (1889: 169).
205 *Fo*(-) means 'intense, strong, vivid'. The term *fo rubi* (i.e. with the two elements written as separate words) means 'scarlet'.
206 De Beaufront and Couturat (1908: 64) give *redega* as the Ido equivalent of *crimson*.
207 This word also means 'scarlet cloth or clothes'.

more variation, although the vast majority begin with *r*, with English word *red*, French *rouge*, and Latin *ruber* all serving as models. (Spanish *rojo* also apparently was a model, but perhaps more from an orthographic than a phonetic point of view, since few ALs have the voiceless velar or uvular fricative which the Spanish letter <j> stands for.) The Arlipo word *reda* means 'dark red'. Glosa also has the *atro-rubi* 'dark-red' (recall that *atro* means 'black') and *punice* 'purplish red'.

We have only found a small number of terms for 'magenta', some of which are in the table below:

	'magenta'		'magenta'
LFN	majenta	Vela (adjs.)	kolog
Panamerikan	majenta	Voksigid (verbs)	majenta
Sasxsek (nouns)	bluvxkiz		

Table 10: *'Magenta' in Some* A Posteriori *and Mixed Languages*

The following table contains terms for 'purple' and 'violet':

	'purple'		'purple'
Algilez (nouns)	pāp	Mondlango (adjs.)	purpla
Arlipo (adjs.)	viola	Neo (adjs.)	purpa
Atlango (adjs.)	purpura	Olingo (adjs.)	purpura
Ayola (adjs.)	purpla	Panamane	púhrpuros
Esperanto (adjs.)	purpura	Panamerikan	purpura
Eurolengo	purpur	Romániço (adjs.)	púrpura
Farlingo (adjs.)	violete	Romanova	purpurio
Fremdu (adjs.)	purpure	Salveto (adjs.)	purpur
Glosa	blu-rubi, iodeo (Gk.), porfiro (Gk.), purpura	Sasxsek (nouns)	kizxbluv[208]
		Sermo (adjs.)	purpure[209]
Id. Neut.	purpur[210]	Sintezo (adjs.)	purpura
Ido (adjs.)	purpura	Uropa (adjs.)	purp
Int. IALA	purpura	Uropi (adjs.)	violen
Ling	purpur	Vela (adjs.)	purep
LFN	purpur[211]	Voksigid (verbs)	purpura
LdP (adjs.)	violete	Volapük (adjs.)	püpunik

---

208 Cf. *bluvxkiz* 'magenta' (recall that *kiz* means 'red'); Nutter (n.d. a: 42) says, "Compound words are formed by using two or more existing words to create a new word, the significant word appearing last".
209 This adjective also means 'purpurate'.
210 For some reason, although most color terms given in Holmes (1903) are adjectives, the word for 'purple', *purpur*, is labelled as a noun.
211 This word also means 'livid'.

	'violet'
Afrihili (adjs.)	banazegi
Arlipo (adjs.)	viola
Esperanto (adjs.)	viola
Fremdu (adjs.)	viole
Glosa	iodeo
Id. Neut.	violet[213]
Neo (adjs.)	velka

	'violet'
Olingo (adjs.)	viola[212]
Panamane	violáne
Salveto (adjs.)	violet
Sasxsek (nouns)	mov
Sintezo (adjs.)	violea
Volapük (adjs.)	violetik[214]

Table 11: *'Purple' and 'Violet' in Some* A Posteriori *and Mixed Languages*

Most terms for 'purple' have the general form **purpur* or a form resembling it (e.g. Mondlango's *purpla*), while most terms for 'violet' contain the sequence *viol*. There is thus not a large degree of variation among these words.

The following table contains terms for 'blue' and one shade of blue:

	'blue'
Afrihili (adjs.)	shudi
Algilez	[215]
Algon	bluv
American (adjs.)	bl-
Ardano (nouns)	nil (Hindi)
Arlipo (adjs.)	blua
Arulo (adjs.)	blua
Atlango (adjs.)	blua, lazura[216]
Auxil	blu
Ayola (adjs.)	blua
Esata	zur- (It.), bluw-, blaw- (Dutch, Ger.)
Esperanto	blua
Eurolengo	blu
Evroptal	blaw (Ger.)[217]

	'blue'
Lingone (adjs.)	blue ("sort of PIE")
LdP (adjs.)	blu (Bislama)
Mondlango (adjs.)	blua
Neo (adjs.)	blua
Olingo (adjs.)	blua
Omnial (adjs.)	blue
Panamane	bláwy, bláu
Panamerikan	blu
Pandunia	nili (noun)
pan-kel (adjs.)	bla
Romániço (adjs.)	blava
Romanova	asur
Salveto (adjs.)	blu
Sasxsek (nouns)	bluv
Sermo (adjs.)	blau

---

212 Cf. *violo* 'violet' (the flower)'.
213 This word is an adjective. The noun *violet* means 'violet (the flower)'.
214 This adjective is derived from the noun *violet* 'violet color', which in turn is derived from *viol* 'violet (the flower)'.
215 Giles (2010b) does not give an Algilez noun equivalent to the English noun *blue*, but *blu* is given as the equivalent of English *blueness*, and one might guess that it could also mean 'blue', since e.g. the noun *yel* means both 'yellow' and 'yellowness'.
216 Both of these words are given as equivalents of English *blue* in Antonius (2009b). Although it is not explicitly stated, one might suspect that *lazura* means something like 'sky blue' (the noun *lazuro* is given (ibid.) as the equivalent of *azure*) and perhaps *blua* means 'dark blue' (or perhaps it is just a general term for blue of all shades).

Fremdu (adjs.)	blue
Glosa	ciano (Gk.),[218] azur,[219] blu
Id. Neut. (adjs.)	blu
Ido (adjs.)	blua
Int. IALA	blau
Interlingue	blu
Konya (adjs.)	nile
Ling	blu

Sintezo (adjs.)	blua
UNI	UZA
Unitario (adjs.)	aŝule, blua[220]
Uropi (adjs.)	blu
Vela (adjs.)	zul
Virgoranto (adjs.)	blua
Voksigid (verbs)	blue
Volapük (adjs.)	yulibik[221]
Voldu	blu

	'azure'
Esperanto (adjs.)	lazura
Interlingue	azur
Mondlango (adjs.)	azura
Olingo (adjs.)	azura (It.)

	'azure'
Panamane	asiúre
Romániço (adjs.)	azura[222]
Sermo	azur (adj.),[223] azurato (noun)[224]

Table 12: *'Blue' and 'Azure' in Some* A Posteriori *and Mixed Languages*

Most terms for 'blue' have the general form **blu* (and a few others begin with *bl*, but have another vowel), although several other forms occur. There is no significant variation among terms for 'azure'. Eurolengo has the term *marine blu* 'navy blue' and Glosa has the word *cerule* 'sky blue, blue', which also means 'celestial, heavenly'.

There is also no significant variation among the following words for 'cyan':

	'cyan'
Ayola (adjs.)	tciana
LFN	sian
Omnial (adjs.)	ciane

	'cyan'
Panamerikan	sian
Romániço (adjs.)	ciánea
Voksigid (verbs)	siano

Table 13: *'Cyan' in Some* A Posteriori *and Mixed Languages*

---

217 In the entry for this word, the Evroptal-French dictionary (Le Masson n.d. b) says, "Prononcer Blaou, et blavi" ('Pronounce "blaou", and blavi'). This could mean that *blavi* is another word for 'blue' (a more probable interpretation than the next one, in our view), or that *blaw* could also be pronounced "blavi", or something else.
218 This word is glossed as 'blue, cyanic (blue), sky blue; celestial, heavenly' in Springer et al. (2009: 6).
219 One might suspect that this word means 'azure' but it is simply glossed as 'blue' in Springer et al. (2009: 23).
220 We do not know whether there is any difference in meaning between these two words, i.e. whether they mean different shades of blue. They are both given as equivalents of English *blue* in Pleyer (1990: 67).
221 This word is glossed as 'blue, azure' in Wood (1889: 381).
222 Morales (2010a) gives *azura* the English gloss 'azure, sky-blue'.
223 Anon. (n.d. l) gives this word the gloss "azure; also: blue, blau de cobalt cobalt blue".
224 This word is glossed as 'azure (= color of the clear sky)' in anon. (n.d. l).

Next we see terms for 'green':

	'green'
Afrihili (adjs.)	kore
Algilez	grin[225]
American (adjs.)	verd-
Ardano (nouns)	comer (Quechua)
Arulo (adjs.)	grina
Atlango (adjs.)	verda
Ayola (adjs.)	verda (Rom.)
Esata	grin-, verd- (Fr., It., Sp.)
Esperanto	verda
Eurolengo	verd
Evroptal	grun (Dutch)
Farlingo (adjs.)	grine
Fremdu (adjs.)	verde
Glosa	kloro (Gk.),[226] verdi,[227] viridi[228]
Id. Neut. (adjs.)	verd
Ido (adjs.)	verda
Int. IALA	verde
Konya (adjs.)	kalune
Ling	verd
Lingone (adjs.)	grene (Gmc.)
LFN	verde

	'green'
LdP (adjs.)	grin (Bislama)
Mondlango (adjs.)	verda
Neo (adjs.)	verda
Olingo (adjs.)	verda
Omnial (adjs.)	verde
Panamane	grúnos
Panamerikan	verde
pan-kel (adjs.)	gri
Romániço (adjs.)	vírida
Romanova	verde
Rug.	vird-
Salveto (adjs.)	verd
Sasxsek (nouns)	ian
Sermo (adjs.)	verde
Sintezo (adjs.)	verda
UNI	GAF[229]
Unitario (adjs.)	werda
Uropa (adjs.)	vird
Uropi (adjs.)	glen
Vela (adjs.)	nep
Virgoranto (adjs.)	grena
Voksigid (verbs)	verde
Volapük (adjs.)	glünik
Voldu	gren

Table 14: *'Green' in Some* A Posteriori *and Mixed Languages*

There is a large amount of variation here, but the most popular general form by far is *ve/ird. A fair number of words seem to be based on the English word *green*.

There is a high degree of uniformity among terms for 'brown', the vast majority of them having the general form *brun, or something similar:

---

225 This word also means 'greenness'.
226 This word is glossed in Springer et al. (2009: 10) as 'green, chloro-, verdant; verdure'.
227 *Verdi* is glossed as 'green, verdant; verdure' in Springer et al. (2009: 69).
228 This word is glossed by Springer et al. (2009: 70) as 'green, verdant; verdure'; they say (ibid.) about it, "prefer kloro".
229 This word also means 'grass'.

	'brown'		'brown'
Afrihili (adjs.)	samra	Mondlango (adjs.)	bruna
Algilez	brun[230]	Neo (adjs.)	bruna
American (adjs.)	brun-	Olingo (adjs.)	bruna
Ardano (nouns)	brun	Omnial (adjs.)	brune
Arlipo (adjs.)	bruna	Panamane	bráun
Atlango (adjs.)	bruna	Panamerikan	braun
Ayola (adjs.)	bruna	pan-kel (adjs.)	bra
Esata	brun-	Romániço (adjs.)	bruna
Esperanto	bruna	Romanova	bruno
Eurolengo	braun	Salveto (adjs.)	brun
Farlingo (adjs.)	brune	Sasxsek (nouns)	brun
Fremdu (adjs.)	brune	Sermo (adjs.)	bruno
Glosa	bruno,[231] badi, faeo (Gk.)	Sintezo (adjs.)	bruna[232]
		UNI	UMA
Id. Neut. (adjs.)	brun	Unitario (adjs.)	marona
Ido (adjs.)	bruna	Uropi (adjs.)	bran
Int. IALA	brun	Vela (adjs.)	mar
Ling	brun	Virgoranto (adjs.)	bruna
Lingone (adjs.)	brune (Gmc.)	Voksigid (verbs)	bruno
		Volapük (adjs.)	blonik
LFN	brun	Voldu	brawn
LdP (adjs.)	brun		

Table 15: *'Brown' in Some* A Posteriori *and Mixed Languages*

The following table shows terms for 'grey':

	'grey'		'grey'
Afrihili (adjs.)	nzonle	LFN	gris
Algilez	gre	LdP (adjs.)	grey
American (adjs.)	griz-	Mondlango (adjs.)	griza
Arlipo (adjs.)	griza	Neo (adjs.)	griza
Atlango (adjs.)	grisa	Olingo (adjs.)	gra
Ayola (adjs.)	griza (Fr.)	Omnial (adjs.)	gris
Esata	grey-, gris- (Fr., It., Sp.)	Panamane	gráwy
		Panamerikan	gris
Esperanto	griza	pan-kel (adjs.)	gra

---

230 This word also means 'brownness'.
231 This word is glossed as 'brown; scorch; tan' in Springer et al. (2009: 6).
232 Dehée (2006) glosses this adjective as 'brown; dusky, swarthy; dark-haired, brunette'.

Euransi	cayisi (Bengali)	Perio (adjs.)	vuta
Eurolengo	gris	Romániço (adjs.)	grisa
Evroptal	hal (Estonian)	Romanova	grise
Farlingo (adjs.)	grize	Salveto (adjs.)	gris
Fremdu (adjs.)	grize	Sasxsek (nouns)	gris
Glosa	polio (Gk.), cinera,[233] gri, kanesce,[234] kanuto[235]	Sermo (adjs.)	gris[236]
		Sintezo (adjs.)	griza
		UNI	UVO
		Unitario (adjs.)	cana
Id. Neut. (adjs.)	gris	Uropi (adjs.)	gris
Ido (adjs.)	griza	Vela (adjs.)	rej
Int. IALA	gris	Voksigid (verbs)	griza
Ling	gri	Volapük (adjs.)	gedik[237]
Lingone (adjs.)	grise (Gmc.)	Voldu	grey

Table 16: *'Grey' in Some* A Posteriori *and Mixed Languages*

The most popular general form by far is *gris/z*, though various other forms occur. Glosa alone is responsible for much of the variation, since it has 5 different terms.

In the table below are terms for 'black':

	'black'		'black'
Afrihili (adjs.)	gini	LdP (adjs.)	swate (Arabic)
Algilez	[238]	Mondlango (adjs.)	blaka
American (adjs.)	negr-	Neo (adjs.)	nera
Ardano (nouns)	cal (Assamese)	Olingo (adjs.)	nigra
Arlipo (adjs.)	nigra	Omnial (adjs.)	nigre, melane
Atlango (adjs.)	nigra	Panamane	noáros
Auxil	nigre	Panamerikan	negri
Ayola (adjs.)	nera	Pandunia	kala[239]
Dil	viet	pan-kel (adjs.)	nig
Esata	ner- (It.),	Perio (adjs.)	vata

---

233 This word is glossed as 'ash, ashes, cinder; gray, grey' in Springer et al. (2009: 6).
234 *Kanesce* is glossed in Springer et al. (2009: 38) as 'gray, grey, hoary, becoming gray'.
235 This word is glossed as 'ashy, hoary, gray, grey' in Springer et al. (2009: 38).
236 This word is also a noun.
237 Wood (1889: 124) gives *gedik* and *zenakölik* as equivalents of *gray*, but on p. 383 he glosses *zenakölik* as 'ashen, ash-colored, gray, drab' (*zen* means 'ashes'). On p. 115 *gedik* is simply glossed as 'gray'.
238 Giles (2010b) does not give an Algilez noun equivalent to the English noun *black*, but *blak* is given as the equivalent of English *blackness*, and one might think that it could also mean 'black', since e.g. the noun *grin* means both 'green' and 'greenness'.
239 This word is both a noun and an adjective.

	blak-, negr- (Fr., Sp.)	Romániço (adjs.)	nigra
		Romanova	negro
Esperanto	nigra	Rug.	nig-[240]
Eurolengo	neger	Salveto (adjs.)	neger
Evroptal	jav (Georgian)	Sasxsek (nouns)	kal
Farlingo (adjs.)	nigre	Sermo (adjs.)	nigro
Fremdu (adjs.)	negre	Sintezo (adjs.)	nigra
Glosa	melano (Gk.),[241] atro, nigra	Tutonish	svart (Ger.)
		UNI	UPA
Id. Neut. (adjs.)	negr	Unitario (adjs.)	nigra
Ido (adjs.)	nigra	Uropi (adjs.)	nar
Int. IALA	nigre	Vela (adjs.)	meg
Interlingue	nigri	Virgoranto (adjs.)	nigra
Ling	ner	Voksigid (verbs)	negro
Lingone (adjs.)	swarte (Gmc.)	Volapük (adjs.)	blägik
		Voldu	corn
LFN	negra	Welt. (E.) (adjs.)	nikrile

Table 17: *'Black' in Some* A Posteriori *and Mixed Languages*

The general form *ne/g(r) is clearly the most common here. Although there are other forms, none of them is found much; for example, only a very small number of languages have borrowed English *black*.

Other color terms of *a posteriori* and mixed languages include the following:

Afrihili:	*bambi* 'rose', *tindi* 'cream', *jivu* 'ash', *wolu* 'ochre', *boni* 'coffee' (cf. *εkawa* 'coffee (the beverage)')
Ayola (adjs.):	*argentea* 'silvery (having the color of silver)', *aurea* 'golden (having the color of gold)' (from Latin), *goldena* 'golden orange-yellow)', *indiga* 'blue-violet, indigo', *kuprea* 'coppery (having the color of copper)', *limea* 'lime, yellow-green', *turkisea* 'green-blue, turquoise', *vermilyona* 'orange-red, vermilion'
Esperanto (adj.):	*karmina* 'carmine'
Eurolengo:	*bronze* 'bronze', *krem* 'cream', *falb* 'fawn', *jinjer* 'ginger', *gold* 'gold', *indigo* 'indigo', and *turquos* 'turquoise'
Glosa:	*lutea* 'yellow; brownish', *glauko* 'blue-green' (from Greek), *fo-kloro* 'emerald' (*fo*(-) means intense, strong, vivid')[242]
Id. Neut.:	*falb* 'fawn-colored, tawny' (adj.), *ultramarin* 'ultramarine

---

240 Ruggles (1829: 141) glosses this root as 'blackness, black colour'.
241 This word is glossed by Springer et al. (2009: 11) as 'black, dark'.
242 Cf. *smaragdo* 'emerald (the gemstone)'.

	(color)' (noun)
Ido (adj.):	*nakarata* 'nacarat'
Int. IALA:	*mauve* 'mauve'
LFN:	*malva* 'mauve'
Neo:	*malva* 'mauve', *vermilya* 'vermilion'
Panamane:	*marúner* 'maroon'
Romániço (adj.):	*fucsia* 'fuchsia'
Rug.:	*ruf-* 'fox or chestnut colour'
Salveto (adjs.):	*argent* 'silver', *dor* 'gold'
Sermo (adjs.):	adjectives *glauco* 'blue-green, sea-green, glaucous', *verdemar* 'sea green'
Sintezo (adjs.):	*beja* 'beige', *karmina* 'carmine', and *nakarata* 'nacarat: (bright) orange-red'

We shall finish with some general remarks about some of the languages whose terms we have seen. Most of the Algilez words in the above tables are close or identical in pronunciation to their English equivalents, which is not surprising since English was the source for most of the lexicon of Algilez.

It can be seen from the tables above that Glosa is well-supplied with synonyms for color-terms.

Two of the Ido color terms in the above tables contain the suffix *-e-*, which means '-colored, having the color of' (ApGawain et al. 2008: 239).

The Perio word *vita* 'white' appears to be *a posteriori*; however, the words for *vuta* 'grey' and *vata* 'black' make up an *a priori* set with it.[243] Similarly, the Dil words *viet* 'black' and *vit* 'white' form an *a priori* pair, although the latter is *a posteriori*.[244]

Most of the color terms of Vela appear to be *a posteriori*, but a small number seem *a priori*, or at least their origin is not obvious, e.g. the words for 'black' and 'crimson'.

---

243 By "make up an *a priori* set" we mean 'make up a set in which words with related meanings are similar in form' (we will use this phrase, or similar ones, elsewhere in this book). Such sets are typical of, but not limited to, *a priori* ALs.

244 There are various pairs of opposites of this type in Dil, e.g. *nor* 'north', *noar* 'south'.

Chapter 11: Terms for Metals in Artificial Languages

Metals are common to most human cultures and most AL designers have provided their languages with words for at least a few metals. We shall generally avoid discussing obscure metals such as vanadium; if mixed and a posteriori ALs have words for them, we would not expect them to differ much from one another or from the words for them in major European languages.

A Priori Languages

We start with *a priori* languages. Rosenblum (1935) lists more than 200 Fitusa roots, but none for metals.

Like most words of Ygyde, all of its words for metals are compounds. The noun meaning 'metal' is *ysiky*, which contains the roots *-si* 'electric' and *-ky* 'rigid solid'.[245] The nouns for elemental metals end with the root *-lo* 'atom' (as do words for other elements). In the following table we see these words and what other roots they contain:

English	Ygyde	other roots contained
'iron'	yzalo	*-za* 'strong'
'lead'	ykilo	*-ki* 'massive'
'aluminum'	ozalo	*-za* 'container'
'copper'	ysilo	*-si* 'electric'
'silver'	ytusilo	*-tu* 'rich, expensive', *-si* 'electric'
'gold'	ytulo	*-tu* 'rich, expensive'
'platinum'	yzetulo	*-ze* 'idle', *-tu* 'rich, expensive'

Table 1: *Some Ygyde Nouns for Elemental Metals*

The Ygyde noun meaning 'alloy' is *osimoky*; the roots found in it are *-si* 'electric', *-mo* 'fusion', and *-ky* 'rigid solid'. Words for particular alloys are given in the following table; all of them also contain *-ky*:

English	Ygyde	other roots contained
'brass'	ocumoky	*-cu* 'new', *-mo* 'fusion'
'bronze'	otymoky	*-ty* 'old', *-mo* 'fusion'
'steel'	yzaky	*-za* 'strong'
'stainless steel'	yzezaky, (SY) yzeaky	*-ze* 'idle', *-za* 'strong'

Table 2: *Ygyde Nouns for Alloys*

---

245 The first segment of Ygyde nouns is *o-* or *y-*. The former appears when the noun contains two nominal roots (which may be preceded by an adjectival root), the latter occurs otherwise (i.e. when the noun contains only a single root, which is a nominal root, or one adjectival and one nominal root, or two adjectival roots and one nominal root).

The aUI words for metals are also compounds, as are the vast majority of words in the language, and the word for 'metal' itself, *rE*, is a compound, composed of *r* 'positive value, good' and *E* 'matter'. Weilgart (1979: 85) explains this as follows: "'rE' = metal = 'positive-matter': metals in electrolysis settle at the positive pole; metals are 'good, positive' value, used for money ... & coins." The table below shows the meanings underlying some aUI words for metals, as given by Weilgart (ibid.):

English	aUI	meaning
'iron'	wrE	power-metal
'tin'	birE	white-metal
'copper'	eirE	yellow-metal
'silver'	bikrE	white-high (grade)-metal
'gold'	eikrE	yellow-high (precious)-metal

Table 3: *Some aUI Words for Metals*

Many Sona words for metals are compounds of which one part is the word *jen* 'metal':

English	Sona	other part
'iron'	irajen	*ira* 'strength'[246]
'lead'	ponjen	*pon* 'heavy'
'nickel'	abejen	*abe* 'clear'
'zinc'	idujen	*idu* 'brittle'
'copper'	murojen	*muro* 'brown'
'brass'	purojen	*puro* 'yellow'

Table 4: *Some Sona Compounds Words for Metals*

The Sona word for "steel', *iraxin*, is also a compound, the second element of which is the radical *xin* 'gloss, glaze, sheen'. Words for metals which are not compounds include *usu* 'silver', *uro* 'gold',[247] and the "foreign words" (Searight 1935: 30) *Alumin*[248] and *Al*, both of which mean 'aluminum', and *Ni* 'nickel'.

The Latejami word for 'metal' is *cejavi*; its "etymology" is "electric/shock/strike + other natural substance" (Morneau 2006). Morneau (ibid.) says, "this etymology was chosen because metals are good conductors of electricity". The words for elemental metals, and other elements, consist of root morphemes of cardinal numerals followed by the classifier *-civ-* 'element,

---

246 The Sona items in the first 4 rows of this table are "radicals" as Searight (1935) calls them and we do not know whether, when they are separate words, they can have the meanings given here without affixes.
247 The radical *uro* also means 'glory; splendor'.
248 "Foreign words" in Sona are capitalized.

compound' and the word-class suffix for non-open[249] nouns, -i. Thus for example the word for 'iron' is *xezacivi*, as *xeza-* means '26'. The Latejami word for 'alloy' is *kucecapi* and its etymology is "number/count/group + METAL + other artificial substance" (ibid.). The word for 'steel' is *capi*.

The written forms of words for elemental metals in Suma, like those for other elements, are their chemical symbols. Their spoken versions apparently consist of the name(s) of the letter(s) in the symbol, e.g. the word for 'silver' is *Ag*, and Russell (1966: 15) gives its pronunciation as "a gi". The word for 'metal' is *mine*, while 'alloy' is *besi mine* (the verb *besi* means 'mix'). The words for alloys are compound words: *kusa Cu* 'brass' (from *kusa* 'yellow'), *topa Cu* 'bronze' (from *topa* 'brown'), *gide Fe* 'cast iron' (from *gide* 'shape, form'), and *vola Fe* 'steel' (from *vola* 'hard').

Below we see words for metals in several other *a priori* languages:

	'metal'	'aluminum'	'cobalt'	'iron'
Babm	dpap			dapg
Desa Chat	yecaqa	dewaro		mufode
Kotava	yanta	nedel	jil	azil
Minyeva				
Ro (1913)		batal	bawc	bawf
Ro (1919)	balab	babjad		babvaf
Ro (1921)	balab	babjad	babyaf	babvaf
Ro (1931)	balab			babvaf
Temenia	μεταλο	λυμιημιυ		ωυξιρεμι

	'lead'	'nickel'	'tin'	'zinc'
Babm	dpen		depk	
Desa Chat	volami		filoje	
Kotava	dig	rumel	vopel	zingel
Minyeva	lesta			
Ro (1913)	bayp	bawn	bays	
Ro (1919)	bablas	babzaf	bablam	
Ro (1921)	bablas	babzaf	bablam	babhak
Temenia	φυρε			

Table 5: *Words for 'Metal' and Words for Elemental Non-Precious Metals in Some* A Priori *Languages*

---

249 "Open" here refers to the argument structure of the word.

	'copper'	'silver'	'gold'	'platinum'
Babm	dopd	depj	dopj	
Desa *Chat*	mudoja	qobuyi	lotefo	
Kotava	lut	dilgava	moava	blentel
Minyeva			floje	
Ro (1913)	bask	basp	bast	bazapt
Ro (1919)	babgak	babgam	babgas	babzar
Ro (1921)	babgak	babgam	babgas	babzar
Ro (1931)		babgam	babgas	
Temenia	φαιζυαπι	ζοψορα	θεαπιε	

Table 6: *Words for Elemental Precious Metals in Some* A Priori *Languages*

	'alloy'	'brass'	'bronze'	'pewter'	'steel'
Babm		fucznq			gagx
Desa *Chat*		qovive			vojici
Kotava	vangluyaks[250]		iyekot		azaka
Ro (1919)	balac	balad		balam	balak
Ro (1921)		balad			balak
Ro (1931)		balad			
Temenia		λεωα			ξαπικο

Table 7: *Words for Alloys in Some* A Priori *Languages*

Most of the Babm words in the above tables contain the letters *d* and *p*, one of the two characteristic pairs of letters marking nouns which mean "Natural Solid Bodies" (Okamoto 1962: 58); some other words with them are *dpec* 'sand' and *dpis* 'a meteorite'. In addition to those words for metals, there are also words for elements, including *fagj* 'silver', *falj* 'aluminum', *fauj* 'gold', *fcuj* 'copper', *fnlj* 'nickel', *fpej* 'lead', and *fslj* 'tin'. It will be seen that most of these contain the chemical symbol for the element (with the first letter not capitalized), preceded by *f* and followed by *j*. However, this is not always the case; Okamoto (1962: xi) states, "To avoid confusion in any case, the second letter in the original symbols of elements is frequently changed adequately [sic]". There are thus two words for metals which are elements.

The Babm word for 'steel' contains the letters *g* and *x*, which is the characteristic pair of letters for nouns for "Industrial Materials" (ibid: 69); among the other words containing these letters are *gixg* 'cement', *gxom* 'linoleum', and *gexn* 'a roofing tile'. Okamoto (ibid.: xii) says that "A noun of an alloy may be coined in a similar way to the noun of [chemical] compounds, changing only the ending letter *j* into *q* as *fcuznq* (brass)". (On the previous page he states, "A noun

---

250 This word is derived from the radical of the verb *vangluyá* 'alloy'.

of chemical compounds [sic] may be coined by connecting the above-mentioned symbols of the elements which are contained in the compound, beginning with the conducting letter *f*, and mediated by *è* if there is any fear of confusion. In this case the ending letter *j* of the final element may not be omitted".)

The Kotava words for 'aluminum', 'nickel', 'platinum', 'tin', and 'zinc' end in *el*, as do words for many other elements. If there is a rule for which names of elements have this final sequence, it is not obvious: both words for metals and non-metals do; examples of the latter are *cogdel* 'arsenic' and *kriel* 'krypton'. This sequence *el* appears *a posteriori*, probably from the French word *élément* 'element'. (The word for 'element' is *ra* and thus seems *a priori*.) Although Kotava is supposed to be, and to a large extent is, an a priori language, some of the words for elemental metals seem to be *a posteriori* even leaving aside the sequence *el*, e.g. *zingel* 'zinc', *blendel* 'platinum' *paldel* 'palladium', and *magnel* 'magnesium'.

The Ro (1913) words for metals begin with *ba-*, which is the characteristic initial sequence of words whose meaning has to do with "matter" (Foster 1913: 17). Most of them seem to be partly *a posteriori*, since their last segment(s) are the same as the initial segment(s) of the English or Latin words for the same metal, or the same as its chemical symbol, e.g. the *al* of *batal* 'aluminum', the *f* of *bawf* 'iron', and the *pt* of *bazapt* 'platinum'.

In Ro (1919) no words for metals are the same as those of Ro (1913), though they still all have *ba* as their initial segments. The words for metals in the 1919 and 1921 versions of Ro are the same, except that Foster (1921) has some that are lacking in Foster (1919), e.g. *babyaf* 'cobalt' (since Foster (1921: 25-26) gives a list for words for the elements), and Foster (1921) does not have a word for 'pewter'. Foster (1921: 25) explains the system of words for elements as follows:

> The Ro word "ba" means substance, and "bab" elementary substance. The elemental substances of chemistry are named by Ro according to Mendelejeff's table of atomic weights. These names, therefore, carry in themselves an accurate description of the substances, a summary of all that science can tell concerning them. The first consonant after the initial "bab" denotes the group, and the second consonant the series in the group.

Foster (1931) provides fewer words for metals, but those which he gives are the same as those in Ro (1919) and Ro (1921).

The words for elements, and thus for elemental metals, in Oz, were constructed in the same type of way as those of Ro (1919, 1921, 1931): they all begin with *Qt*,[251] the remaining segments being determined by the place of the element in the periodic table. The words for 'iron' and 'silver' are *QtgQ* and *QtspO* respectively.

---

251 The letter <Q> stands for the vowel [ɔ].

A Posteriori and Mixed Languages

We now examine words for metals in *a posteriori* and mixed languages, starting with words meaning 'metal' (see Table 8 on the next page).

There is not much variation here; almost all of the terms seem to be based on English *metal* or a cognate word from another Indo-European language, Neo Patwa's *altai* being an exception. One might guess that Vela's *mevo* is derived from English *metal* though it has no dental/alveolar stop and introduces a new consonant. Algilez drops the first two segments of *metal* or one of its cognates and UNI omits the initial consonant. The NOXILO word has the *m* and *t* of the source word; the initial *RyO* seems to be a radical (it also is found in e.g. *RyOA* 'acid' and *RyOMNE* 'mineral') but we have not found its meaning in the publicly available sources on the language.

	'metal'
Algilez	tøl
Algon	metal
Arlipo	metalo
Atlango	metalo
Ayola	metalo
BL	madl
Ceqli	temal (anagram of *metal*)
Esata	met-, metl-
Esperanto	metalo
Eurolang	metal
Fremdu	metalu
Glosa	metali (Gk.)
Hom-id.	metalo
Id. Neut.	metal
Ido	metalo
Int. IALA	metallo
Interlingue	metalle
LFN	metal
LdP	metal
Loglan	metli

	'metal'
Mondlango	metalo
Neo	metal
Neo Patwa	altai (Mongolian)[252]
NOXILO	RyOMT
Omnial	metale
Panamane	metáll
Pandunia	metal
pan-kel	metal
Romániço	metalo
Romanova	metal
Rug.	met-
Sasxsek	metal
Sermo	metalo
Sintezo	metalo
Slovio	metal
UNI	ETL
Unitario	metalo
Vela	mevo
Volapük	metal
Voldu	metál

Table 8: *Terms for 'Metal' in Some* A Posteriori *and Mixed Languages*

---

252 Note that this word also means 'gold'; such polysemy is not surprising given Neo Patwa's small lexicon.

Below we see terms for elemental non-precious metals:

	'aluminum'
Algon	alumin
Ayola	aluminiumo
Ceqli	haluminum (Eng.)
Esperanto	aluminio
Eurolang	aluminium
Glosa	aluminium
Guosa	samfolo (Hausa)
Hom-id.	aluminyo
Id. Neut.	aluminium
Ido	aluminio
Int. IALA	aluminium
Interlingue	aluminium
Ling	alumin

	'aluminum'
LFN	aluminio
Loglan	alhumio
Mondlango	alumino
Neo	aluminyo
Omnial	aluminium
pan-kel	alum
Romániço	aluminio
Sasxsek	haluminum
Sermo	aluminium
Sintezo	aluminio
Vela	sabago
Volapük	lümin, almin[253]

	'cobalt'
Ayola	kobaltumo
Esperanto	kobalto
Eurolang	cobalt
Hom-id.	kobalto
Ido	kobalto
Loglan	coblo
Mondlango	kobalto

	'cobalt'
Neo	kobalt
Romániço	cobalto
Sermo	cobalto
Sintezo	kobalto
Spokil	cois
Vela	kobalo

	'iron'
Algilez	feris
American	yrn
Arlipo	fero
Ardano	ahin (Brahui)
Arulo	fero
Atlango	fyero
Ayola	ferumo
BL	fer
Ceqli	fero (It.)

	'iron'
LFN	fero[254]
LdP	fer
Loglan	ferno
Mondlango	fero
Neo	fir
NOXILO	WEIR
Omnial	fere, sidere
Panamane	férro
pan-kel	voj

---

[253] Wood (1889: 6) marks *almin* as one of the Volapük words which "have been replaced by others ... but are found in earlier writings" (ibid.: vii).

[254] This word also means 'iron (for clothes)'.

Esata	fer- (Fr., It., Sp.)
Esperanto	fero
Eurolang	fer
Eurolengo	fer
Fremdu	feru
Glosa	feru, sideri
Hom-id.	fero
Id. Neut.	fer
Ido	fero
Int. IALA	ferro
Interlingue	ferre
Ling	fer
Lingone	ferro

Romániço	fero
Romanova	ferro
Rug.	ferm-
Sasxsek	feron
Sermo	fero
Sintezo	fero[255]
Spokil	fis
Unitario	ferro
Vela	faharo[256]
Virgoranto	fero
Volapük	lel, lelin
Voldu	fyer
Welt. (E.)	vereo

	'lead'
Algilez	plom
American	plumbu
Arlipo	plumbo
Atlango	plumbo
Ayola	plumbumo
BL	plomb
Ceqli	blay (Ger.)
Esperanto	plumbo
Eurolang	plumbum
Glosa	molibdo (Gk.), plumba
Hom-id.	plombo
Id. Neut.	plomb
Ido	plombo[258]
Int. IALA	plumbo
Interlingue	plumbe

	'lead'
Ling	plomb
LFN	plomo
LdP	plumbum
Loglan	pubmo
Mondlango	plumbo
Neo	plombo
Panamane	plom
pan-kel	bly
Romániço	plumbo
Romanova	plombo
Rug.	plzm-
Sasxsek	plom
Sermo	plumbo[257]
Vela	ledo
Volapük	plum, plumin

255 The word *fero* is given in Dehée (2006) but not glossed; however, presumably it means 'iron', as do the Esperanto word *fero* and the Ido word *fero*.
256 Given the form of this word one might assume that it means 'the metal iron' rather than 'iron for clothes', but we are not certain about this.
257 This word also means 'lead' in the sense of 'bullets, shot'.
258 De Beaufront and Couturat (1908: 137) have *plumbo*, but later sources such as Dyer (1924a: 271) and Dyer (1924b: 196) have *plombo*.

	'nickel'
Ayola	nikelumo
Esperanto	nikelo
Eurolang	nickel
Glosa	nikel
Hom-id.	nikelo
Id. Neut.	nikl
Ido	nikelo
Int. IALA	nickel
LFN	nicel
Loglan	niklo

	'nickel'
Mondlango	nikelo
Neo	nikel
pan-kel	nikl
Romániço	níchelo
Sasxsek	nikelum[259]
Sermo	niquel[260]
Sintezo	nikelo
Spokil	niis, nilis
Vela	nikelo
Volapük	nieg, niegin

	'tin'
Algilez	stanis
Arlipo	stano
Ayola	stanumo
BL	tin
Ceqli	tsin (Ger.)
Esata	tihn-
Esperanto	stano
Eurolang	stanum
Glosa	stani
Hom-id.	estaño
Id. Neut.	stan
Ido	stano
Int. IALA	stanno
Interlingue	stanno
Ling	stan

	'tin'
LFN	stanio
LdP	tin
Loglan	stino
Mondlango	stano
pan-kel	tins
Romániço	stano
Rug.	stan-
Sasxsek	timah
Sermo	stano
Sintezo	[261]
Spokil	snis
Unitario	stano[262]
Vela	zacaho
Volapük	tin[263]

---

259 We do not know whether this word means the metal, the coin, or both.
260 This word also means 'nickel' in the sense 'a nickel coin'.
261 The word *estano* is given but not glossed in Dehée (2006), although the indication "< stano" is provided. We would think that it means 'tin'.
262 For some reason this word is in parentheses on p. 92 of the lexicon of Pleyer (1990).
263 Wood (1889: 343) gives four equivalents of the English noun *tin*: *tin*, *tün*, *lelatün*, and *vietün*. However, while he glosses the Volapük word *tin* simply as 'tin' (p. 344), he glosses *tün* as 'sheet-tin, tinned iron, tin-plate' (p. 350), *lelatün* as 'sheet-tin, tinned-iron' (p. 173), and *vietün* as 'tinned sheet iron' (p. 365). Further, on p. 350 he glosses the adjective *tünik* as 'tin, of tin (*i.e.* of sheet-tin)'. On p. 344 there also appears the Volapük noun *tinin*, which is glossed as 'Stannum, Sn. (chem.)'; v. the discussion below for forms ending in *in*.

	'zinc'
Algilez	zink
Ayola	zinkumo
BL	tsink
Esperanto	zinko
Euransi	zingu (Maltese)
Eurolang	zinc
Glosa	zink (Gk.)
Guosa	tùtíya (Hausa)
Id. Neut.	sink
Ido	zinko
Int. IALA	zinc
Ling	tsink
LFN	zinco
Loglan	zinko

	'zinc'
Mondlango	zinko
Neo	zinko
Olingo	zenqo
Omnial	zinke
Panamane	zinn
pan-kel	sink
Romániço	zinco
Sasxsek	ziqka
Sermo	zinco
Sintezo	zinko
Unitario	sink
Vela	pelico
Volapük	zik, zikin

Table 9: Terms for Elemental Non-precious Metals in Some *A Posteriori* and Mixed Languages

In some cases there is a large degree of uniformity; for example all of the words for 'cobalt' and 'nickel' and almost all of those for 'aluminum' and 'zinc' seem to be based on the same source words (or rather on one of the same set of close cognates, or on an atomic symbol derived from such a word). The exceptions in the case of 'aluminum' are Guosa's *samfolo*, which is not surprising since Guosa is based largely on African languages, and Vela's *sabago*, also not surprising since Vela has a largely *a priori* vocabulary (but note that some Vela words, e.g. *nikelo*, are *a posteriori*). The same two languages represent the only two exceptions with respect to words for 'zinc'.

On the other hand, although terms for 'iron' usually have the form **fer* or something close to it, some have other sources, thus NOXILO's *WEIR*[264] and American's *yrn* seem to be based on English 'iron', and Glosa and Omnial have words with the general form **sider*, i.e. apparently from Ancient Greek. A large majority of terms for 'lead' are based on a form of the type **plumb*, the German word *Blei* has also been a source, and Vela seems to have used the English word *lead*. Most terms for 'tin' are of the form **stan*, or something close to it, but some languages have borrowed a Gmc. (i.e. English or German) form, as in the case of the Blue Language's *tin*. The Spokil word *snis* appears to come from the atomic symbol for tin, *Sn* and the sequence *-is* (which also ends most of the other Spokil words for elemental metals given in this chapter); since *Sn* is derived from Latin

---

[264] The *WE* in this word and other NOXILO words for metals appears to be a radical, but again we do not know its meaning. It is also found in e.g. *WEHEL* 'helium', *WEA* 'atom', and *WEM* 'substance'.

stannum, one could say that *snis* is (indirectly) based on the same set of close cognates as most of the other words for 'tin' here. Vela's word for 'tin', *zacaho*, appears *a priori*, and the origin of Sasxsek's *timah* is unclear to us.

Let us turn to terms for precious metals, given below:

	'copper'
Algilez	kup
American	cupru
Arlipo	kupro
Atlango	kupro
Ayola	kuprumo
BL	kivr
Ceqli	toq (Mandarin)
Esata	kopr-
Esperanto	kupro
Euransi	kuprun
Eurolang	cuprum
Glosa	kalko (Gk.), kupra
Hom-id.	kopro
Id. Neut.	kupr
Ido	kupro
Int. IALA	cupro
Interlingue	cupre
Ling	kuper
LFN	cupre

	'copper'
LdP	kuprum
Loglan	cupro
Mondlango	kupro
Neo	kupro
NOXILO	WEPA
Olingo	tamro (Sanskrit)
Panamane	kupróne
Pandunia	kopa
pan-kel	kup
Romániço	cupro
Sasxsek	koprum
Sermo	cupro[265]
Sintezo	kupro
Spokil	cuis, cuprum
Unitario	cupro
Uropa	kupra
Vela	zadago
Volapük	koped, kupin

	'silver'
Algilez	plat
Algon	silva
American	argentu
Arlipo	arzhento
Arulo	arjento
Atlango	arjento
Ayola	argentumo
BL	silv

	'silver'
Mondlango	arjento
Neo	arjent
Neo Patwa	feda (Swahili)[266]
NOXILO	WES
Olingo	arjento
Omnial	argente
Panamane	arjéntu
Pandunia	palata

---

265 This word also means 'brass-wind instrument'.
266 This word also means 'money'.

Esata	silv-	pan-kel	plat
Esperanto	arĝento	Romániço	argento
Eurolang	argentum	Romanova	arjento
Fremdu	silveru	Rug.	hqrg-
Glosa	argenti, argiro (Gk.)	Sasxsek	serab
Hom-id.	argento	Sermo	argento
Id. Neut.	argent	Sintezo	arjento
Ido	arjento	Spokil	agis
Int. IALA	argento	UNI	GIN
Interlingue	argente	Unitario	argento
Ling	argent	Uropa	arga
Lingone	argo (Lat.)	Uropi	sirven
LFN	arjento[267]	Vela	silo
LdP	argentum	Volapük	silef, silin
Loglan	argo (Lat.)		

	'gold'		'gold'
Afrihili	uwura	Loglan	aurmo (Lat.)
Algilez	gold	Mondlango	goldo
Algon	gold	Neo	auro, gold
American	ûru	Neo Patwa	altai (Mongolian)
Ardano	soma (Waama)	NOXILO	WEG
Arlipo	oro	Olingo	oro (Sp.)
Arulo	oro	Omnial	aure
Atlango	guldo	Panamane	gold
Ayola	aurumo	pan-kel	gold
BL	lor	Romániço	auro
Ceqli	kin (Japanese)	Romanova	oro
Communia	auro	Sasxsek	goram
Esata	horo (Fr., It., Sp.), gold-	Sermo	auro
Esperanto	oro	Sintezo	oro
Eurolang	aurum	Spokil	auris
Glosa	kriso (Gk.), aureo	UNI	GUZ
Hom-id.	oro	Unitario	avro
Id. Neut.	aur	Uropa	aura

---

267 This word also means 'silver (the color)'.

Ido	oro		Uropi	gor
Int. IALA	auro		Vela	golo
Interlingue	aure		Volapük	golin, golüd
Ling	aur		Voldu	gold
Lingone	goldo (Eng.)		Welt. (E.)	naureo
LFN	oro[268]		Welt. (V+F)	oron
LdP	golda			

	'platinum'			'platinum'
Arlipo	plateno		Mondlango	platino
Arulo	platino		Neo	platin
Ayola	platinumo		pan-kel	platin
Esperanto	plateno		Romániço	platino
Eurolang	platinum		Sasxsek	platinam
Glosa	platinum		Sermo	platino
Id. Neut.	platin		Sintezo	platino
Ido	platino		Spokil	ptis
Int. IALA	platino		Uropa	platna
Interlingue	platine		Vela	patino
LFN	platino		Volapük	platin
Loglan	platino			

Table 10: *Terms for Elemental Precious Metals in Some* A Posteriori *and Mixed Languages*

There is no significant variation among the words for 'platinum' (the Spokil word appears different, since it seems to be based on the atomic symbol, but that in turn comes from the same set of close cognates as the other terms here). The degree of resemblance among words for 'copper' is not as high, though the vast majority of them have a form of the general shape *cupr*. Words for 'silver' and 'gold' show more variation, though in each case there is a dominant general form, *argent* and *aur* respectively;[269] some words for each metal seem to be based on Gmc. forms such as English *silver* and *gold* (this includes NOXILO's *WES* and *WEG*, as their final S and G presumably come from the English words), and some words for 'silver' appear to be borrowings of Spanish *plata* 'silver'. A few words for 'silver' and 'gold' come from other languages or have an origin which is difficult to

---

268 This word also means 'gold (the color)'.
269 The letter <q> is Ruggles' Universal Language stands for the diphthong [ɔɪ], so its root for 'silver', *hqrg-*, is not as different from *argent-* as might appear, though it is not clear that it is based on such a form.

determine (Sasxsek's *goram* and UNI's *GUZ* may be based on or influenced by English *gold*, but it is not obvious).

We shall now examine alloys, starting with words for 'alloy' itself (see Table 11 on the next page). The most popular form is something like **aliga(t)*, though Esperanto and Ido seem to be based on the English word *alloy* while *Volapük's metalamig* is a compound of metal 'metal' and *mig* 'mixture, compound'. Although Dehée (2006) does not give a Sintezo word for 'alloy', he does provide the word *permaloyo* 'permalloy'.

	'alloy'
Esperanto	alojo
Glosa	aligato
Hom-id.	aligo
Ido	aloyo
Int. IALA	alligato
Neo	aligayo

	'alloy'
Panamane	aliágu
Romániço	aligajo
Sermo	aligato
Vela	jabago
Volapük	metalamig

Table 11: *Terms for 'Alloy' in Some* A *Posteriori and Mixed Languages*

Below are terms for particular alloys:

	'brass'
Algilez	bras
Arlipo	latuno
Atlango	mesinjo[270]
Ayola	laytono (Fr.)
Ceqli	tsuyi (Cherokee)
Esata	bres-
Esperanto	latuno
Glosa	kupra-zink(a)
Id. Neut.	latun
Ido	latuno
Int. IALA	laton
Interlingue	latune
Ling	laton
LFN	laton

	'brass'
LdP	latun
Loglan	rasto
Mondlango	braso
Neo	oton
pan-kel	bras
Romániço	latono
Rug.	hqs-
Sermo	laton
Sintezo	latuno
Unitario	lätono
Vela	bacaco
Volapük	läten
Voldu	bras .

---

270 Antonius (2009b) gives both *mesinjo* and *bronzo* as Atlango equivalents of *brass*, while the English word *bronze* does not appear, i.e. it has no entry in this dictionary.

	'bronze'
BL	prons
Esperanto	bronzo
Glosa	kupra-stana
Id. Neut.	brons
Ido	bronzo
Int. IALA	bronzo
LFN	bronze[271]

	'bronze'
Mondlango	bronzo
Neo	bronzo
Romániço	bronzo
Sasxsek	bronza
Sermo	bronzo
Sintezo	bronzo
Vela	bacado

	'pewter'
Esperanto	stanalojo
Hom-id.	peltro
Int. IALA	peltro
Sermo	peltro
Vela	mevoco

	'steel'
Algilez	stil
Arlipo	asiero
Atlango	stalo
BL	stils
Esata	stil-
Esperanto	ŝtalo
Eurolengo	steel
Farlingo	stalo
Fremdu	aceru
Glosa	dura feru, aciera[272]
Hom-id.	acyero
Id. Neut.	asier
Ido	stalo
Int. IALA	aciero
Interlingue	stal
Ling	stal
LFN	aser
LdP	stal

	'steel'
Loglan	gasti
Mondlango	stalo
Neo	stal
NOXILO	WEIRST
Olingo	ferevo
Omnial	aciere
Panamane	asiére
pan-kel	vas
Romániço	aciario
Romanova	asiero
Rug.	kalb-
Sasxsek	polad
Sermo	aciero
Sintezo	aciero
Unitario	atsero
Vela	zakapo
Volapük	dülin
Voldu	stal

Table 12: *Terms for Alloys in Some* A Posteriori *and Mixed Languages*

---

271 This word also means 'tan, suntan'.
272 Glosa also has the word *kaliba* 'hut; steel, iron' (from Greek).

Most of the terms for 'brass' have a form something like *laton, but several languages have borrowed the English word *brass*.[273] The Glosa word for 'brass' is a compound meaning 'copper zinc'; the origin of *hqs-* in Ruggles' Universal Language is not obvious. There is more uniformity among terms for 'bronze', the only languages not following a **bronz* type model being Glosa, which again uses a compound, and Vela, whose *bacado* may be in an *a priori* type pattern with its word for brass, *bacaco*. The most popular form among the few words for 'pewter' listed here is peltr- or something close to it; Esperanto has a compound meaning 'tin alloy' and Vela's word appears to be a priori.

Terms for 'steel' may show the most variation among those discussed here; the most common form is along the lines of **asier*, but there is a substantial number of terms apparently based on German *Stahl* and a few apparently based on English *steel*. One might think that the Olingo word for 'steel', *ferevo*, contains a root **fer-* 'iron' and the suffix *-ev-* which has the meaning of "augmentation" (Jaque 1944: 34), except that Jaque (1944) does not contain a root **fer-* or a word meaning 'iron'.[274] There are also some words meaning 'steel' whose origin is not clear, e.g. Sasxsek's *polad*; Vela's *zakapo* seems to be *a priori*.

The Arlipo word for 'cast iron' is *gisfero* (the verb *gison* means 'to cast'). Volapük's word for 'cast iron', *gifalel*, was constructed in the same sort of way: *gif* means 'pouring, casting, founding' and recall that *lel* means 'iron'. Vela has what appears to be an *a priori* word for 'cast iron' (and one that is not etymologically related to its word for 'iron'), *rokebo*.

Now we shall make some more general remarks. Unlike many or most of the words of Algilez, some of its words for metals do not seem to have been taken from English. As we have seen, some of the Vela words for metals appear to come from English, e.g. *ledo*, but others seem to be *a priori*, e.g. *sabago*, so at least within this small semantic field Vela has the aspect of a mixed AL.

To our knowledge Ardano has been provided with only two words for metals, *ahin* 'iron' and *soma* 'gold'. This is in contrast to many *a posteriori* and mixed languages, which, as we have seen, have words for most or all commonly used metals.

L. Jones (1972) has the Eurolengo words *bronze* 'bronze', *gold* 'gold', and *silver* 'silver' listed among the color terms (pp. 80-1), and one might assume that they also serve as names of metals.

It will be noticed that there are two Volapük words for most of the elemental metals listed in the tables above, one ending in *in*, and one not. Given that there is

---

273 Vela may be among the languages which have borrowed the English word *brass* or at least had their choice of term for 'brass' influenced by it: the letter <c> apparently is pronounced [s], so *bacaco* is not that different from it.
274 It is interesting that words for 'metal' and 'iron' are not given by Jaque (ibid.), but that there is a word for 'zinc'. Of course Jaque may well have had created an Olingo word for 'iron' but not mentioned it in his work.

a suffix *-in* which Wood (1889: 395) says is "generally used for the chemical elements, and other elementary substances", we would guess that the difference between the members of such pairs is that the one ending in *in* means the metal in the sense of the element, while the one not ending in *in* means the metal in its every day use. This may be supported by relevant glosses in Wood (1889); for example, he glosses *koped* as 'copper' (p. 159) and *kupin* as 'cuprum, Cu. (chem.), copper' (p. 162). Perhaps the reason why there is only one word for 'platinum' is that this metal's everyday uses are limited; Wood (1889) gives only one word, ending in *in*, for other metals which rarely or never come up in everyday conversation, e.g. *tütin* 'titanium', *palin* 'palladium'.[275]

In Weltsprache (Eichhorn) *-eo* is the suffix of nouns denoting "les elements, pierres, métaux" ('elements, stones, metals', C&L 1903/1979: 296); we see it in the words *vereo* 'iron' and *naureo* 'gold'.

---

[275] The application of *in* varies, and in some cases it may not be correct to call it a suffix. In the case of e.g. *lel* and *lelin* we can say that it is attached to the word with the everyday meaning to yield the word with the more technical meaning. However, this does not hold for *silef* and *silin*, because not only is *in* not attached to the everyday word (i.e. we do not have **silefin*), but also it is not entirely clear that it is attached to any root or stem here: there is a root (and word) *sil*, but it does not have an obvious connection with 'silver', as it means 'sky, canopy of heaven'. The pair of words meaning 'copper' is still more problematic, since the vowel of the first syllable differs. The fact that the word for 'steel', *dülin*, also ends in *in* is not problematic from the point of view of its meaning, since *in* can occur with names of "other elementary substances" (Wood 1889: 83), taking "elementary" in a non-technical sense (i.e. not just involving chemical elements), but one might again hesitate to call *in* a suffix here; surely there is no semantic connection between 'steel' and the root *dül*, which means 'idyl, short pastoral poem'. A way out of this dilemma is to say that there is a bound root *sil-* 'silver', homophonous with *sil* 'sky'; likewise, there is a homophonous root *dül-*. However, this will not completely solve the problem of the words for 'copper'.

Chapter 12: Terms for Beverages in Artificial Languages

Most human societies have a variety of beverages, with words in their language(s) for them. Many ALs have also been given a fair-sized vocabulary in this semantic field.

A Priori Languages

Starting again with *a priori* languages, let us first look at words for beverages in Ygyge:

English	Ygyde	roots contained
'beverage, drink'	oguby	-*gu* 'liquid', -*by* 'food'
'milk'	yfigu	-*fi* 'feminine', -*gu* 'liquid'
'tea'	oneguby	-*ne* 'medical', -*gu* 'liquid', -*by* 'food'
'herbal tea, herbal medicine'	onebegu	-*ne* 'medical', -*be* 'plant', -*gu* 'liquid'
'coffee'	opaguby	-*pa* 'alive', -*gu* 'liquid', -*by* 'food'
'juice'	ogubeby, (SY) ogubey	-*gu* 'wet',[276] -*be* 'plant', -*by* 'food'
'alcoholic beverage'	ymigu	-*mi* 'mental', -*gu* 'liquid'[277]
'beer'	omifygu	-*mi* 'mental', -*fy* 'foam', -*gu* 'liquid'
'wine'	ytymigu	-*ty* 'old', -*mi* 'mental', -*gu* 'liquid'
'vodka'	yzamigu	-*za* 'strong', -*mi* 'mental', -*gu* 'liquid'
'aperitif'	ydamigu	-*da* 'front', -*mi* 'mental', -*gu* 'liquid'

Table 1: *Ygyde Words for Beverages*

All of these words are compounds, and all contain the root -*gu* 'liquid; wet', though it does not always occur in the same position. Some words for non-alcoholic beverages, but no words for alcoholic beverages, contain the root -*by* 'food', while all words of the latter group have the root -*mi* 'mental' as one of their components.

Now we shall see words for beverages in Latejami, which are also compounds (see Table 2 on the next page).

The Latejami word for 'coffee' is one of the few (partly) *a posteriori* words in the language. Note that although all the Latejami words for kinds of beverages consist of more than one morpheme, none of them contains the sequence of morphemes that means 'beverage'.

---

276 We assume that -*gu* 'wet' and -*gu* 'liquid' are the same root.
277 The word for 'alcohol' is *ykumigu*, in which the roots meaning 'mental' and 'liquid' are preceded by the root -*ku* 'burning'.

English	Latejami	eytmology
'beverage'	bojosi	fish/water/liquid/swim + food item
'milk'	bazopi	one/unity/harmony/child/offspring + plant/animal substance
'juice'	boybofupi	plant/green/growth/leaf + fish/water/liquid/swim + processed food substance[278]
'tea'	boyfupi	plant/green/growth/leaf + processed food substance
'soda (pop), pop, non-alcoholic carbonated beverage'	dwebofupi	play/sport/leisure + fish/water/liquid/swim + processed food substance
'coffee'	kafefupi	sound mnemonic + processed food substance
'alcohol, spirits, booze, liquor'	zoyfupi	enjoy/friend + processed food substance
'beer'	zuzoyfupi	minimal polarity + ALCOHOL/SPIRITS
'ale'	fozoyfupi	small/low polarity + ALCOHOL/SPIRITS
'wine'	canzoyfupi	average polarity + ALCOHOL/SPIRITS
'liqueur'	kezoyfupi	big/high polarity + ALCOHOL/SPIRITS
'liquor, hard liquor, booze, distilled liquor'	bizoyfupi	maximal polarity + ALCOHOL/SPIRITS

Table 2: *Latejami Words for Beverages*

Table 3 (on the next page) shows terms for non-alcoholic beverages in some other *a priori* languages.

The Fitusa word for 'mother' is *mamo*, which (although it is *a posteriori*) may be in an *a priori* type pattern with *mimo* (given the relation between mothers and milk); *momo* 'butter' and *mumo* 'cheese' are part of such a pattern with it.

The Kotava word for 'beverage' is *uliks*.

The Ro (1913) words for beverages begin with *po*, the characteristic initial segments of words whose meaning involves food, and most of them begin with *pof*, which as a word by itself means 'drink'. The word for 'milk' begins with the sequence *por*, the word *por* meaning 'diary product'. The Ro (1919) words in the above table are similar to or the same as those of 1913, the exception being the word for 'milk' which also has the three initial segments *pof* (words for other diary products still begin with *por*). Ro (1921) has the same words for 'milk', 'cocoa', 'tea', and 'coffee' as Ro (1919). Foster (1931) only gives a word for the first of these, and again it is *pofam*.

---

[278] Latejami has a different word for 'sap, juice of a plant', *boyzopi*.

	'milk'	'cocoa'	'tea'	'coffee'	'juice'	'lemonade'
Desa *Chat*	jeyusu		bifuju	caxife		
Fitusa	mimo		pofo	pufo		
Kotava	vrod		yel	fad	kratela, jaxipa[279]	
Minyeva	zema		nwacki	grefka		
Ro (1913)	porab	pofak	pofat	pofac		
Ro (1919)	pofam	pofag	pofad	pofac		pofal
Sci. Dial	ajad		ahat, amel	ahal, amek		ajag
Sona	umo, umosu[280]		Te, Cai	Kafe		
Suma	bane		tiko	tako	sapo (Eng.)[281]	kusa belo teki demo
Temenia	ζυχοε		τει	καφε		

Table 3: *Terms for Non-Alcoholic Beverages in* Some A Priori *Languages*

In addition to its words for 'coffee' and 'tea' the Scientific Dial System has the following words:

aham	'Java coffee'
ahan	'mocha coffee'
ahap	'green coffee'
ahaq	'roasted coffee'
ahar	'blended coffee'
ahas	'ground coffee'

ahav	'Ceylon tea'
ahaw	'Japan tea'
ahax	'Paraguay tea'
ahay	'kafta tea'
amhab	'Hyson tea'
amhac	'gunpowder tea'
amhad	'green tea'
amhaf	'black tea'
amhag	'Chinese tea'

Table 4: *Words of the Scientific Dial System for Types of Coffee and Tea*

Other Scientific Dial words for beverages include *ajal* 'root beer' and *ajam* 'juniper ale'.

---

279 Anon. (2007a), the Kotava-French dictionary, glosses *kratela* as 'jus' (p. 136) and *jaxipa* as 'sève' (p. 105). The existence of the word *jaxipak*, glossed (ibid.) as 'gobelet, flacon à sève', may indicate that *jaxipa* is meant to have the sense of a beverage. Anon. (2007b), the English-Kotava dictionary, gives *jaxipa* as the Kotava equivalent of *juice* (p. 66), and anon. (2007c), the Kotava-English dictionary, glosses *jaxipa* as 'juice' (p. 41). *Kratela* as a separate word does not appear in either of these sources, but anon. (2007c) contains the word *ksagokratela* 'pineapple juice' (p. 51).

280 The radical *umo* is glossed by Searight (1935:94) as 'breast; milk; suckle'; *umosu* apparently consists of it and the radical *su* 'water; liquid; flow'.

281 This word also means 'sap'.

Although the vocabulary of Temenia is *a priori* to a very large extent, its words for 'tea' and 'coffee' appear to be *a posteriori*.

The Suma word for 'beverage' is *teki demo* (from *teki* 'drink' (verb) and *demo* 'thing, device'). It makes up part of the term for 'lemonade', along with *kusa belo* 'lemon'. The term for 'orangeade', *kisa belo semo*, is not constructed in a parallel fashion to the term for 'lemonade', as its last constituent is *semo* 'water' (*kisa belo* means 'orange') (cf. *kisa belo sapo* 'orange juice'). The Suma words for 'tea' and 'coffee' are in an *a priori* type pattern.

The following table contains terms for alcoholic beverages in Suma, most of which are compounds:

English	Suma	explanation
'beer'	biro (Eng.)	
'ale'	enga biro	*enga* 'England; English'
'wine'	vino (It.)	
'champagne'	sode vino	*sode* 'soda (pop)'
'whiskey'	vano	
'brandy'	vino vano	
'cognac'	franka vano	*franka* 'France'
'gin'	neda vano	*neda* 'Netherlands, Holland; Dutch'
'rye whiskey'	sero vano	*sero* 'cereal, grain'
'liquor'	alko semo	*alko* 'alcohol', *semo* 'water'

Table 5: *Suma Words for Alcoholic Beverages*

Below are words for alcoholic beverages in some other a priori languages:

	'beer'	'wine'	'liquor'	'brandy'	'rum'	'whisky'
Desa *Chat*		gocobo				
Kotava	ekot			lavajeb	xeyna	
Ro (1919)	pogac	pogal	pogab			pogam
Sona	Bir	vin				Uiski
Temenia	πιρα	λιαψιο	λικορε			

Table 6: *Terms for Alcoholic Beverages in Some* A Priori *Languages*

The Kotava word for 'brandy' contains *lava* 'water'.

Foster (1913) does not contain words for alcoholic beverages. All of the Ro (1919) words for alcoholic beverages begin with the sequence *pog* (and no other words begin with this sequence). Ro (1921) has the same words for 'beer', 'wine', 'liquor', and 'whiskey' as Ro (1919). Foster (1931) only has one word for an alcoholic beverage, *pogla* 'wine'.

The Temenia word for 'liquor' seems to be *a posteriori*.

A Posteriori and Mixed Languages

Now we turn to *a posteriori* and mixed languages. First we give just a small number of words meaning 'beverage':

	'beverage'
Glosa	bibe-ma, biberage
Int. IALA	biberage, bibitura
Interlingue	trincage

	'beverage'
Romániço	bibedo
Volapük	dlin
Voldu	drinko

Table 7: *'Beverage' in Some* A Posteriori *and Mixed Languages*

The Voldu word clearly comes from English, as may the Volapük word; Interlingue's root *trincage* also seems to come from a Gmc. source. Words from some other languages seem to be based on a form such as **bib*. The *-ma* in Glosa's *bibe-ma* means 'material, stuff, matter, substance'.

Below we present words for non-alcoholic beverages:

	'milk'
Algilez	mek
Ande	lez
Ardano	susu (Indon.)
Arlipo	lakto
Atlango	lakto
Auxil	lact
Ayola	milko
Esata	lec- (Sp.),[282] melk-
Esperanto	lakto
Eurolang	lact
Eurolengo	milk
Evroptal	pim (Estonian)
Farlingo	milko
Fremdu	laktu
Glosa	lakti
Id. Neut.	lakt
Ido	lakto

	'milk'
Mondlango	lakto
NOXILO	MyAAL
Olingo	laqto (Latin)
Omnial	lakte
Panamane	lat
Romániço	lacto
Romanova	lete
Sasxsek	milak
Sermo	lacte
Sintezo	lakto
Tal	lato
UNI	MIK
Uropa	lakta
Uropi	lik
Vela	miko
Virgoranto	milko
Voksigid	lakte[283]

---

282 In Appendix B of Bothi (2006) it is indicated that Italian is also a source for this word, but in Appendix C only Spanish is given as a source. This is not the only instance of discrepancy between the two appendixes on the source of a word, but in this case one might be dubious about the role of Italian, since the Italian word for 'milk' (*latte*) is not very similar to *lec-*.

283 Recall that Voksigid does not have underived nouns; this word is a verb meaning 'be milk'.

Int. IALA	lacte
Lingone	milko ("sort of PIE")
LFN	lete
LdP	milka

Volapük	milig
Voldu	milk
Welt. (V+F)	lact

	'tea'
Afrihili	isha
Algilez	cã
American	teu
Ande	tse
Ardano	txah (Korean)
Arlipo	teo
Atlango	teo
Ayola	teho
Dil	ti (Eng.)
Esata	tey-
Esperanto	teo
Eurolang	tee[284]
Eurolengo	té
Fremdu	teu
Glosa	tea
Id. Neut.	te
Ido	teo[286]
Ingli	te
Int. IALA	the
Ling	te
LFN	te[287]
LdP	chay (Hindi, Turkish)

	'tea'
Mondlango	teo
NOXILO	CEEI
Olingo	teo
Omnial	tee
Panamane	téeh
Panamerikan	te
Pandunia	ca
Pasifika	ca
Romániço	teo
Romanova	tei
Sasxsek	teh
Sermo	te
Sintezo	teo[285]
UNI	TEA
Unitario	tee
Uropa	teha
Uropi	tej
Vela	helabo
Virgoranto	teo
Volapük	tied
Voldu	teo

	'coffee'
Afrihili	εkawa
Algilez	kaf
American	cofeu

	'coffee'
Mondlango	kafo
Neo	kaf
NOXILO	CEEKA

---

284 Hunt (1998b) glosses this word as 'tea; plant/leaves of species Camellia sinensis, and drink made from them'.
285 This word is glossed in Dehée (2006) as 'tea (leaves; infusion)'.
286 Dyer (1924a: 367) glosses *teo* as '*(leaves and infusion)* tea'.
287 This word has a broader meaning than just the drink; it is glossed in anon. (2010d: 103) as 'tea *(plant, leaves, drink: species Camellia sinensis)*'.

Ande	keya		Olingo	qafo
Ardano	cofi		Omnial	café
Arlipo	kafo		Panamane	kaféh
Atlango	kafo		Panamerikan	kafe
Ayola	kafo		Pandunia	kafe
BL	kaf		Pasifika	kafe
Esata	kaf-		Romániço	cafeo
Esperanto	kafo		Romanova	cafe'
Eurolang	cafe[288]		Sasxsek	kafeh
Eurolengo	kafé		Sermo	café
Farlingo	kafo		Sintezo	kafo[289]
Fremdu	kafu		UNI	KOF
Glosa	kafa		Unitario	caffee
Id. Neut.	kaf		Uropa	kafa
Ido	kafeo		Uropi	kafa
Ingli	kafe		Vela	kafo
Int. IALA	caffe[290]		Virgoranto	kafo
LFN	cafe[291]		Volapük	kaf
LdP	kahwa (Arabic)		Voldu	kafe

	'juice'			'juice'
Algilez	jus		Olingo	suqo
Arlipo	suko		Omnial	suke
Atlango	juso		Panamane	juss
Ayola	suko (Rom.)		Panamerikan	sumo
Esata	jus-		Romániço	suco
Esperanto	suko[292]		Romanova	sugo
Evroptal	suk		Rug.	suks-
Id. Neut.	suk[293]		Sasxsek	sok[294]

---

288 Hunt (1998b) glosses this word as 'coffee; plant and seeds of Coffea arabica, and drink made from them'.
289 Dehée (2006) glosses this word as 'coffee (substance or drink)'.
290 This word also means 'café'.
291 This word also has a wider range of meaning than just the beverage; anon. (2010d: 18) glosses it as 'coffee (*plant, seeds, drink: species Coffea arabica*)'.
292 The Esperanto word *suko* is glossed as 'juice; sap' by Wells (1969: 148), the first meaning given for it in Waringhien (1970: 1045) is "Likvaĵo en la histoj de bestoj aŭ plantoj" ('Liquid in the bodies of animals or plants'). *Fruktosuko* means 'fruit juice'.

Ido	suko[295]
Ingli	jus
Int. IALA	succo[296]
Ling	jus
LFN	jus[297]
LdP	jus[298]
NOXILO	CEEU

Sintezo	suko
UNI	SOK
Uropi	suc
Vela	rahato
Volapük	vaet
Voldu	suk[299]

	'lemonade'
Esperanto	limonado
Eurolengo	lemonade
Id. Neut.	limonad
Ido	limonado
Int. IALA	limonada
LFN	limonada

	'lemonade'
Neo	limonad
Panamane	sitronáde
Sasxsek	limonad
Sintezo	limonado
Uropi	limonad
Vela	lemodo

Table 8: *Terms for Non-Alcoholic Beverages in* A Posteriori *and Mixed Languages*

The dominant model for terms for 'milk' is **lakt*, but **milk* is also a popular model. The latter is presumably the source for the *L* of NOXILO's *MyAAL*; the rest of the word is the radical *MyAA*, whose meaning we do not know (it is also found in e.g. MyAABA 'butter' and MyAAT 'meat'). Words with a form of (something like) **te* are in the majority among terms for 'tea'; another pattern is represented by e.g. LdPs *chay* and Pasifika's *ca* (in Pasifika, as in Algilez, <c> stands for [tʃ], in Pandunia it can be pronounced as [ʃ], [ṣ], or [ç]). The *CEE* in NOXILO's word for 'tea' seems to be the radical for beverages; it occurs in most words for beverages (though not in the word for milk, as we have seen). There is

---

293 This word also means 'sap', and thus has a broader meaning than just 'juice' in the sense of 'beverage' (one might assume it also covers this meaning). This may well be true of other words for 'juice' in this table.
294 This word means 'juice, nectar'.
295 The meaning of this word is also not limited to the sense of the beverage.
296 This word has a broader meaning than just the kind of beverage, as can be seen from the term *succo gastric* 'gastric juice'.
297 This word is glossed in anon. (2010d: 56) as 'juice *(fluid extracted)*'. It occurs in the terms *jus de orania* orange 'juice' and *jus de poma* 'apple juice, cider (non-alcoholic)'.
298 This word appears in the section of anon. (n.d. b) "Forms of Matter" rather than in the section "Foodstuffs, etc." and is given as the equivalent of English "juice (fluid extracted from something)". However, its meaning apparently covers 'juice' in the sense of a drink, since it is part of the terms *oranja jus* 'orange juice' and *vinjus* 'grape juice' (*vin* means 'vine, grape').
299 This word also means 'sap'.

also a dominating pattern among terms for 'juice', *suk*, but the **jus* pattern is not rare (perhaps it is where the *U* in NOXILO's *CEEU* comes from).

There is a high degree of uniformity among terms for 'coffee', though perhaps Ande's *keya* is *a priori*. The same is true of words for 'lemonade'.

Additional terms for non-alcoholic beverages in *a posteriori* and mixed languages include Algilez: *frutjus* 'fruit juice', *hitcok* 'hot chocolate'; Ande: *kaisa* 'cocoa'; Eurolengo: *oranjade* 'orangeade', *mineral aqua* and *aqua mineral* 'mineral water'; Fremdu: *oranjsuku* 'orange juice'; Neo: *mineralak* 'mineral water'.

Cider can be alcoholic or non-alcoholic; the following table gives some terms for it:

	'cider'
Arlipo	mosto
Ayola	tcidro
Esperanto	cidro
Hom-id.	cidro
Ido	cidro
Int. IALA	cidra

	'cider'
LFN	sidra
Romániço	cidro
Sintezo	cidro
Vela	cidoro
Volapük	podavin, pomavin

Table 9: *'Cider' in Some* A Posteriori *and Mixed Languages*

The LFN word *sidra* is glossed in anon. (2010d: 96) as 'cider (*alcoholic*)'; both of the Volapük words contain *vin* 'wine', so one might think that they refer to alcoholic cider. *Podavin* also contains *pod* 'apple' while *pomavin* contains *pom* 'fruit'. Volapük also has the word *podanuvin* 'sweet-cider' (built from *nuvin* 'must, unfermented grape-juice'). In the case of the other words in this table we do not know whether they mean alcoholic or non-alcoholic cider or both. There is not much variation among these words, as only the Arlipo and Volapük words do not follow a **cidr* type model.

Punch can also be alcoholic or non-alcoholic; below are a few words for it:

	'punch'
Esperanto	punĉo
Hom.-id.	punĉo
Ido	puncho

	'punch'
Int. IALA	punch
LFN	ponxe

Table 10: *'Punch' in Some* A Posteriori *and Mixed Languages*

There is no significant variation here.

We now examine some terms for alcoholic beverages:

	'wine'
Algilez	wãn
American	vin

	'wine'
NOXILO	CEEn
Olingo	vino

131

Ande	uain
Arlipo	vino
Ayola	vino
Dil	vin
Esata	vin- (Fr., It., Sp.), wayn-
Esperanto	vino
Eurolengo	vin
Evroptal	vin
Farlingo	vino
Fremdu	vinu
Id. Neut.	vin
Ido	vino
Ingli	wain
Int. IALA	vino
LFN	vino
LdP	vino
Mondlango	vino
Neo	vin

Omnial	vine
Panamane	vin
Panamerikan	vino
Romániço	vino
Romanova	vino
Rug.	vin-
Sasxsek	uin
Sermo	vino
Sintezo	vino
Tal	vino
UNI	VIN
Unitario	wino
Uropa	vina
Uropi	vin
Vela	vino
Volapük	vin
Voldu	vayn
Welt. (V+F)	vinon

	'beer'
Afrihili	owa[300]
Algilez	bir[301]
American	bier
Ande	bir
Arlipo	biero
Atlango	biro
Ayola	biro
Balta	bir
BL	bir
Esata	bir-
Esperanto	biero
Eurolengo	bier
Evroptal	bir
Farlingo	biro
Fremdu	biru
Glosa	bira[302]
Id. Neut.	bir

	'beer'
LdP	bira (Arabic, Turkish)
Mondlango	biero
NOXILO	CEEBI
Olingo	hopajo
Omnial	biere
Panamane	biére
Panamerikan	bira
Pandunia	bira
Romániço	biro
Romanova	bir
Sasxsek	bira
Sermo	bira
Sintezo	biro
Tal	biro
UNI	BIR
Unitario	bira
Uropa	bira

---

300 Afrihili also has the word *italawa* 'beer (stout)'.
301 This word is glossed as 'beer, ale' in Giles (2010b).
302 This word also means 'ale'.

Ido	biro[303]
Ingli	bir
Int. IALA	bira
Interlingue	bir
Ling	bir
LFN	bir

Uropi	bir
Vela	bero[304]
Virgoranto	biro
Volapük	bil[305]
Voldu	bir[306]
Welt. (E.)	birü

	'champagne'
Esperanto	ĉampano
Ido	champanio[307]
Int. IALA	champagne
Ling	shampan
Lingua	shampyn
LFN	xampanie

	'champagne'
Mondlango	campano
Panamane	shampánn
Sintezo	champanio
Uropi	campàn
Vela	fizo vino
Volapük	jamänavin

	'vermouth'
Esperanto	vermuto
Ido	vermuto
Int. IALA	vermut
Sermo	vermut
Sintezo	vermuto

	'grog'
Ayola	grogo (Eng.)
Esperanto	grogo[308]
Ido	grogo
Mondlango	grogo
Sintezo	grogo

	'liquor'
Esperanto	alkoholaĵo
Id. Neut.	liker
Int. IALA	liquor
NOXILO	CEELO
Romanova	licor

	'liquor'
Sasxsek	likora[309]
Sintezo	liquoro[310]
Vela	likero
Volapük	lig[311]

---

303 De Beaufront and Couturat (1908:25) have *biero*, but later sources such as de Beaufront (1925/2005: 78) have *biro*.
304 This word also means 'ale'.
305 This word is glossed as 'beer, lager beer' in Wood (1889: 24). Volapük also has the term *palbil* 'twice-brewed beer' (containing *pal* 'couple, pair').
306 This word also means 'ale'.
307 De Beaufront and Couturat (1908: 42) have *champano*, but later sources such as Dyer (1924a: 53) have c*hampanio*.
308 This word also means 'toddy'.
309 This word means 'liquor; liqueur'.
310 This word is glossed in Dehée (2006) as '(alcoholic) spirit, liquor'.
311 *Lig* can also mean 'strong liquor; liqueur'. Volapük also has the word *lufilavin* 'spirituous liquor, ardent spirits, intoxicating liquor, drinks'.

	'brandy'
Afrihili	apɛtɛkoni
Arlipo	brando
Esperanto	[312]
Fremdu	[313]
Id. Neut.	akuavit
Ido	brandio
Ingli	brandi
Int. IALA	brandy

	'brandy'
LdP	brendi
Mondlango	brando
Neo	akuavit
Uropi	brenivòd
Vela	vacabo
Volapük	filavin[314]
Voldu	brandi

	'cognac'
Esperanto	konjako[315]
Id. Neut.	koniak
Ido	konyako
Int. IALA	cognac
LFN	coniac[317]

	'cognac'
Panamane	koynáke
Romániço	coniaco
Sintezo	konyako
Uropi	koniàk[316]
Volapük	yägin[318]

	'gin'
Esperanto	ĝino
Eurolengo	jin
Fremdu	djinu
Ido	jino
Int. IALA	gin

	'gin'
LFN	jin
Mondlango	gino
Panamane	genébra
Sermo	gin
Vela	bacigo

	'rum'
Afrihili	apɛtɛmini
Arlipo	rumo
Esperanto	rumo
Eurolengo	rum
Id. Neut.	rum
Ido	rumo
Int. IALA	rum

	'rum'
LFN	rum
Mondlango	rumo
Sasxsek	rom
Sermo	rum
Sintezo	rumo
Vela	bacugo
Voldu	ron

312 Wells (1969: 57) glosses the Esperanto word *brando* as 'schnapps, brandy, spirits'.
313 Anon. (n.d. k) glosses the Fremdu word *konyaku* as 'brandy' in English, as 'cognac' in French, as 'coñac' in Spanish, as 'cognac' in Italian, and as 'conyac' in Catalan.
314 *Filavin* (which contains the words *fil* 'fire' and *vin* 'wine') is glossed as 'brandy, ardent spirits, distilled liquor, whiskey' in Wood (1889: 99).
315 Wells (1969: 101) glosses *konjako* as 'cognac, brandy'.
316 This word means 'cognac, brandy'.
317 This word is glossed as 'cognac, brandy' in anon. (2010d: 26).
318 This word is glossed as 'cognac, brandy' in Wood (1889: 379).

	'vodka'
Esperanto	vodko
Eurolengo	vodka
Int. IALA	vodka
LFN	vodka
LdP	vodka

	'vodka'
Mondlango	vodko
Olingo	vodqo (Russian)
Sermo	vodka
Sintezo	vodko
Uropi	vodka

	'whiskey'
Esperanto	viskio
Eurolengo	wisky
Id. Neut.	uiski
Ido	wiskio
Ingli	wiski
Int. IALA	whisky
Ling	viski
LFN	uisce
Mondlango	wiskio

	'whiskey'
NOXILO	CEEWI
Panamerikan	wiski
Sasxsek	[319]
Sermo	whisky
Sintezo	wiskio
Tutonish	brenvein
Uropi	wiski
Vela	felico
Volapük	filavin

	'cocktail'
Esperanto	koktelo
Hom.-id	kokteylo

	'cocktail'
Mondlango	koktelo
Neo	koktel

Table 11: *Terms for Alcoholic Beverages in Some* A Posteriori *and Mixed Languages*

In most cases here there is a high degree of uniformity: there is no significant variation among terms for 'vermouth', 'grog', 'vodka', or 'cocktail'.[320] The only non-uniform term among words for 'cognac' is Volapük's *yägin*. Only Vela and Volapük have significantly different words for 'champagne', both of which contain a root meaning 'wine'. The presence of this root is what makes Volapük's word different from most of the words for 'champagne', as its first component comes from the toponym *Jamän* 'Champagne'. There is little variation among words for 'gin', the two standouts being Panamane's *genébra* and Vela's *bacigo*. The latter word is in an *a priori* type pattern with Vela's word for 'rum', *bacugo*, which is one of the few non-uniform words with that meaning. Most words for 'whiskey' are also similar (leaving aside minor phonetic and orthographic differences), Vela and Volapük again not fitting in (with the former having another apparently *a priori* form). Recall that Volapük's *filavin* (from *fil* 'fire')

---

319 Sasxsek has a word *uiski*, but it is the name of the letter <w>.
320 We do not know whether the words for 'grog' are meant to have a specific sense or a general sense (i.e. 'liquor') or both.

also means 'brandy'. Volapük also has the term *filavin glönik* 'rye whiskey' (*glön* means 'rye').

We have collected many words for 'beer' and only two of them are not built along the lines of *bir. The fact that one of them is from Afrihili is not a surprise, since this language is based on African languages. As for Olingo's word, Jaque (1944) does not list *-*aj*- among the affixes of Olingo, but one might imagine that it exists in the language, perhaps inspired by the Esperanto suffix -*aĵ*-, although its meaning appears to be different from that of -*aĵ*- (which means 'a concrete manifestation of an abstraction; the external manifestation of an activity; a characteristic piece of behavior; the flesh of an animal' (Wells 1969: 31)). We say this because there are some words in Olingo that contain the sequence *aj*, e.g. *afranqajo* 'postage', *dupanajo* 'sandwich', and *suqerajo* 'candy'. *Hopajo* also seems to be formed with this putative suffix, attached to a root *hop- 'hop', although this root does not occur in Jaque (1944).

The -*ü* at the end of Weltsprache (Eichhorn)'s word for 'beer' (*birü*) is the suffix of nouns which denote "les fluides" ('fluids') (C&L 1903/1979: 296), in the sense of *fluid* which includes liquids and gases.

There also is not much variation among terms for 'wine', but this is probably due to the fact that the words for 'wine' in major western European languages are not very different. (The same explanation can be used for the uniformity of the terms meaning 'beer', and for some other sets of words as well.) However, we can distinguish between terms apparently based on French *vin* (or Italian *vino* or Latin *vinum*), which make of the great majority of the terms here, and terms apparently based on English wine, e.g. Ande's *uain*. There may also be the occasional case of a term built from (parts of) both models, perhaps Unitario's *wino* and Voldu's *vayn*. The origin of NOXILO's *CEEn* is not clear, but one might guess that its *n* is a borrowing of the last segment of the word for 'wine' of one (or more) of the major European languages.

Vela has a word for 'cherrywine', *bacupo*, which does not appear etymologically related to either its word for 'wine' or that for 'cherry', *cacano*.

Among words for 'liquor' only Esperanto's *alkoholaĵo* is obviously not based on the same model as the other terms; it contains the root *alkohol-* 'alcohol' and the previously mentioned suffix -*aĵ*-.

There is a fair degree of variation among words for 'brandy', but *brand is the most common general form.

Additional terms for alcoholic beverages in *a posteriori* and mixed languages include LFN: *sace* 'sake', *tecila* 'tequila', *xeres* 'sherry'; Neo: *kalvados* 'calvados'; NOXILO: *CEELOT* 'cheap distilled spirits', *CEERS* 'sake'; Romániço: *licuoro* 'liqueur', *absintio-licuoro* 'absinthe'.

Chapter 13: Describing the Weather in Artificial Languages

Weather affects all humans and, like natural languages, many ALs have words for describing various weather conditions. We shall be interested mainly in nouns from this semantic field.

A Priori Languages

Starting with *a priori* languages, we present some Ygyde nouns relating to weather; all of which are compounds:

English	Ygyde	roots contained
'weather'	ygoge	-*go* 'atmospheric', -*ge* 'environment'
'storm'	ygota	-*go* 'atmospheric', -*ta* 'war'
'rain'	ygogu, (SY) ygou	-*go* 'atmospheric', -*gu* 'liquid'
'downpour'	ykigogu, (SY) ykigou	-*ki* 'massive', -*go* 'atmospheric', -*gu* 'liquid'
'snow'	yfefe	-*fe* 'cold', -*fe* 'powder'[321]
'snowstorm'	yfegota	-*fe* 'cold', -*go* 'atmospheric', -*ta* 'war'
'hail'	ysofefe	-*so* 'big', -*fe* 'cold', -*fe* 'powder'
'hailstorm'	ysogofe	-*so* 'big', -*go* 'atmospheric', -*fe* 'powder'
'lightning'	ytogogy, (SY) ytogoy	-*to* 'ephemeral', -*go* 'atmospheric', -*gy* 'light'
'thunder'	yjygogy	-*jy* 'sonic', -*go* 'atmospheric', -*gy* 'light'
'cloud'	ygoko	-*go* 'atmospheric', -*ko* 'shape'
'fog'	ysagoko	-*sa* 'bottom' -*go* 'atmospheric', -*ko* 'shape'
'wind'	yjogo	-*jo* 'mobile', -*go* 'gas'
'tornado'	ygowi	-*do* 'pretty', -*go* 'atmospheric', -*wi* 'helix'
'rainbow'	ydogoko	-*go* 'atmospheric', -*ko* 'shape'

Table 1: *Some Ygyde Nouns for Metorological Phenomena*

---

[321] These two meanings of -*fe* seem to be an instance of homonymy, i.e. two different roots. While in the case of -*go*, which occurs in some other items in this table, the adjectival meaning ('atmospheric') and the nominal meaning ('gas') are close enough that one could claim one root is involved, this is often not the case, and the two meanings of -*fe* are sufficiently different that an analysis in terms of a single root is not plausible. (Another example of similar meanings is -*gu* 'wet' and 'liquid' and another example of quite different meanings is -*ga* 'lost' and 'money'). To our knowledge, the publicly available materials on Ygyde say nothing explicit on the question of the homonymy or polysemy of such roots; anon. (2009) presents adjectival roots and nominal roots in two separate lists.

The root -*go* 'atmospheric; gas' occurs in most of these words. The words for 'snowstorm' and 'hailstorm' were not constructed in a parallel way: while the former contains the same sequence of roots as 'storm' (meaning 'atmospheric war'), the latter does not and differs from the word for 'hail' only in having -*go* 'atmospheric' rather than -*fe* 'cold' as its second root (which one might find odd, since both could be said to be atmospheric and cold).

The following table contains Latejami nouns for meteorological phenomena, which again are compounds, and their "Etym[ology]" (from Morneau 2006):

English	Latejami	etymology
'weather, climate/ clime, elements'	tindafepi[322]	land/location/earth/natural/wild + bird/fly/ high/lift/ gas/sky/blue + non-living phenomenon
'rain/rainfall, shower, precipitation of water from the sky'	bofepi	fish/water/liquid/swim + non-living phenomenon
'snow'	cinjavi	chemical/clean/white + other natural substance
'snow/snowfall'	cinfepi	chemical/clean/white + non-living phenomenon
'flurries, snow flurries, light snowfall'	zucinfepi	minimal polarity + SNOW/SNOWFALL
'snowstorm'	kecinfepi	big/high polarity + SNOW/SNOWFALL
'blizzard, whiteout, severe snowstorm'	bicinfepi	maximal polarity + SNOW/SNOWFALL
'storm'	xondafepi	bad/undesirable + bird/fly/high/lift/gas/ sky/blue + non-living phenomenon
'lightning'	cekixogi	electric/shock/strike + see/light/evident/ show + non-living energy (mass noun)
'lightning bolt'	cekicugi	electric/shock/strike + see/light/evident/ show + non-living energy (count noun)
'thunder'	cefoyxogi	electric/shock/strike + loud/sound/hearing + non-living energy (mass noun)
'thunderclap'	cefoycugi	electric/shock/strike + loud/sound/hearing + non-living energy (count noun)
'cloud'	dabofepi	bird/fly/high/lift/gas/sky/blue + fish/water/ liquid/swim + non-living phenomenon
'fog'	cubofepi	low/under/on/support/foot/heavy + fish/ water/liquid/swim + non-living phenomenon

---

322 Morneau (2006) says, "*Tindafepi* literally means the weather at a particular time and place. Use the generic *lutindafepi* for the 'elements/climate/clime' sense".

'wind, air current'	dafepi	bird/fly/high/lift/gas/sky/blue + non-living phenomenon
'breeze'	fodafepi	small/low polarity + WIND
'cyclone'	jofepi	round/rotate/fat/full + non-living phenomenon
'hurricane, typhoon'	bijofepi	maximal polarity + CYCLONE
'tornado, twister, large destructive whirlwind'	kenjofepi	thin/narrow/finger/touch + round/rotate/fat/full + non-living phenomenon
'rainbow'	zinfepi	color + non-living phenomenon

Table 2: *Some Latejami Nouns for Meteorological Phenomena*

As in some words from other semantic fields, we see morphemes indicating "polarity" in several of the nouns here.

The next table shows some Suma nouns concerned with weather, most of which are compounds:

Suma	English	explanation
soto	'rain'	
desa soto	'drizzle'	*desa* 'thin'
luse soto	'hail'	*luse* 'ice'
seto soto	'sleet'	*seto* 'snow' (calque from Esperanto)
soto navo	'rainbow'	*navo* 'circle'
seto	'snow'	
favo	'cloud'	
lano favo	'fog'	*lano* 'land'
zino	'wind'	
vela zino	'breeze'	*vela* 'soft'
kosa zino	'hurricane'	*kosa* 'large'
vori zino	'cyclone, tornado'	*vori* 'turn, revolve, rotate'
lito semo	'dew'	*lito* 'night', *semo* 'water'
dobo	'lightning'	
debo	'thunder'	

Table 3: *Some Suma Nouns for Meteorological Phenomena*

The words for 'rain' and 'snow' are in *a priori* type pattern, as are the words for 'lightning' and 'thunder'. The Suma word for 'storm' is *zino seko*; although written as a separate word, *seko* is supposed to be a suffix meaning '-ness, -hood, -ism'.

In contrast to the languages mentioned above, Fitusa's weather-related vocabulary (and its vocabulary in general) is small; it has the roots *kom-* 'rain' and *kum-* and 'snow' (which would become nouns, verbs, or adjectives, depending on the suffix attached to them).

Now we shall present and discuss some weather-related words from several other a priori languages:

	'weather'	'rain'	'snow'	'hail'	'storm'
Desa *Chat*	desore	tigufi	jemaro		desuve
Kotava		muva	nolda	onotca	zivotc
Minyeva		figo	wali		
Ro (1913)	bicak	bigla[323]	bilak	bilad	bija
Ro (1919)	bicak	bigal	bilak		bijab
Ro (1921)	bicak	bigal	bilak		bijab
Ro (1931)			bilak		bija
Temenia	ηαχυαμυ		κελο πευπαυ	κιοκαψαψοα	τορεμεηετα

	'lightning'	'thunder'	'cloud'	'fog'	'wind'
Desa *Chat*		deqeqi	neyati		fifewu
Kotava		edi	rujod	sel	suka
Minyeva					klocu
Ro (1913)	bimak	bimam	bifka	bifaf	bidaf
Ro (1919)	bimak	bimam	bifab		bida
Ro (1921)	bimak	bimam	bif		bid
Ro (1931)			bifa		bida
Temenia			ηαε	ψαυμαοτε	ξοτοε

Table 4: *Nouns for Weather Phenomena in Some* A Priori *Languages*

Desa Chat also has the word *tipaje* 'frost'.

Kotava also has the words *apelk* 'cyclone', *canka* 'hurricane', *elada* 'hoarfrost', *korfi* 'rainbow', *xefto* 'thunderstorm', and *zarnda* 'dew'.

In addition to the nouns in the above table, Minyeva has the verb *cnagi* 'to rain (fall down in many little pieces), snow'.

The Ro (1913) words for meteorological phenomena begin with *bi*, the characterizing initial segments of words "[r]elating to the sky, weather, astronomy" (Foster 1913: 20). The Ro (1913) word for 'wind' begins with *bid*, which as a word by itself means 'air in motion' and is the characterizing initial sequence of words having to do with this idea. Other words containing this initial sequence are *bidab* 'zephyr', *bidac* 'breeze', *bidak* 'gale', and *bidal* 'cyclone'. The words for 'cloud' and 'fog' begin with *bif*, which as an independent word means 'cloudy weather'. Words for types of clouds begin with the word for 'cloud': *bifkac* 'cirrus', *bifkad* 'cumulus', *bifkaf* 'stratus', *bifkal* 'nimbus'. The

---

[323] We are not certain whether this word is a noun (or a verb); the same is true of the following two words in this line of the table, and of some other words of Ro (1913), as well as some words of Ro (1919), including those for 'rain' and 'snow', and of Ro (1921).

first three segments in the word for 'rain', i.e. *big*, make up the word for 'rainy weather'. Other words starting with these segments are *bigba* 'mist', *bigca* 'dripping', *bigda* 'drizzle', *bigma* 'pour', and *bignat* 'shower'. The word *bika* means 'changeable weather'. The words for 'snow' and 'hail', as well as that for 'frost', *bilaf*, begin with *bil*, which as a separate word means 'ice'.[324] The words for 'rainbow' and 'halo' are *bimas* and *bimat* respectively; note that they start with the same three segments as the words for 'lightning' and 'thunder'. The word for 'climate', *bical*, only differs from the word for 'weather' in its last segment.

Ro (1919) has the same words for 'weather' and 'climate' as Ro (1913), but some other words from this semantic field are different, as can be seen in the table above (although usually the differences are not great). The words for 'snow' and 'frost' are also the same as in Ro (1913), but they no longer completely contain the word for 'ice', since this is *bilab* in Ro (1919).[325]

As is true in other semantic domains, generally words relating to weather are the same in Ro (1921) as in Ro (1919), although the words for 'cloud' and 'wind' are somewhat different. In addition, Foster (1921) has two words which do not appear in Foster (1919); these involve the negative marker (-)*n*-: *bignal* 'drought' (cf. *bigal* 'rain') and *bijnab* 'calm' (cf. *bijab* 'storm').

Three of the four Ro (1931) nouns for weather phenomena are the same as the equivalent words in at least one earlier stage of the language; the one which is not, *bifa* 'cloud', does not differ much from the words for 'cloud' in earlier versions of Ro.

The Temenia term for 'snow' contains the words κελο 'ice' and πευπαυ 'white'. The verb meaning '(to) snow', πιεθι, is not etymologically related to it. Temenia also has the word ζυι 'mist' and the verb τεμαε '(to) rain'.

To our knowledge Hallner (1912) gives only three Scientific Dial System nouns for meteorological phenomena: *axtes* 'conditions of weather', *aetet* 'weather conditions affecting crops', and *axah* 'storm'. However, he does provide the verb *rora* '(to) rain' and a verb for '(to) snow', which is given as *loxa* on p. 146 but as *loca* on p. 155. However, there are words from this semantic field with more complex meanings, including the following:

Sci. Dial	English
Axtex	'The weather is hot and sultry'
Ayteb	'The weather is cool and refreshing and stimulating, and to work is a pleasure'
Aytec	'The weather is turning quite cold, requiring change of underwear'

---

324 The other word of this group is *bilac* 'glacier'.
325 The word for 'thaw' in Ro (1919) is *bilnab*, which is the word for 'ice' with the negative marker (-)*n*- in it. Ro (1921) also has this word.

Ayteg	'The thunder and lightning were terrible'
Aytej	'The rain is falling moderately'
Aytek	'It is raining, but just a sprinkle'
Aytev	'The wind kept up all night, holding off the frost'
Aetel	'The bright warm sun is melting the snow'
Aetev	'Weather conditions could not be better suited to fruit'
Aetew	'It is feared that the continuous rainy and foggy weather may prevent pollenizing and cause a fruit failure'
Aitek	'It is cloudy'
Aitem	'It is raining nearly every day'
Aiten	'It is raining almost every Sunday, enabling almost continuous undisturbed work during the entire week'
Aiter	'The September rain did some damage to raisins and dried fruit on trays'

Table 5: *Some Scientific Dial System Words Relating to Weather*

A Posteriori and Mixed Languages

We now examine *a posteriori* and mixed languages, beginning with their terms for 'weather':

	'weather'
Algilez	wev
Ande	hesta
Arlipo	vetro
Arulo	vetero
Atlango	vedro
Ayola	vetero
Esata	wed-, wedr-, temp- (Sp.)
Esperanto	vetero
Eurolang	wetter
Eurolengo	tempo
Farlingo	vetero
Id. Neut.	tempest
Ido	vetero

	'weather'
LdP	meteo
Mondlango	wetero
NOXILO	EnZA, EnZAA
Omnial	meteore
Panamane	véhda
Romániço	tempo
Romanova	tiempo
Rug.	tems-
Sasxsek	klimat[326]
Sermo	tempo, tempore[327]
Sintezo	vetero
UNI	TEM
Unitario	tempo

---

326 This word is glossed as 'climate, weather' in Nutter (n.d. b: 26).
327 Both of these words have other meanings, including 'time' in the senses of 'duration/extent of time' and 'point of time' and 'tense' in the grammatical sense.

Ingli	weda
Int. IALA	tempore[328]
Ling	temper
Lingone	wetro (Ger.)
LFN	clima[329]

Uropa	tempa
Uropi	verem
Vela	kizoto
Volapük	stom
Voldu	tempo

Table 6: *'Weather' in Some* A Posteriori *and Mixed Languages*

There are mainly general forms here, **temp* and **vet/der*, which are roughly equally common. The NOXILO word begins with *EnZ*, which seems to be a radical for words relating to weather, although none of the other NOXILO words presented in this chapter contain it. We would guess that it is found in terms relating to weather in general; other words with it include *EnZEL* 'temperature C' and *EnZIT* 'humidity'. The Algilez word for 'climate', *wevem*, consists of the word for 'weather' and the augmentative affix *-em*.

We shall now see terms for different types of precipitation:[330]

	'rain'
Algilez	rin
American	luv
Ande	lusta
Ardano	baraso (vb.), odano (vb.)
Arlipo	pluvo
Atlango	pluvo
Ayola	pluvetcare (vb.)
Esata	ren-
Esperanto	pluvo
Eurolang	pluv
Eurolengo	pluvor
Evroptal	dej

	'rain'
LdP	pluva[331]
Mondlango	pluvo
NOXILO	LOOn
Olingo	pluvo
Omnial	pluvar (vb.)
Panamane	plúvu
Perio	chibi (vb.)
Romániço	pluvo
Romanova	pluvia
Sasxsek	dus[332]
Sermo	pluvia
Sintezo	pluvo

---

328 This word also means 'time' in some senses and '(grammatical) tense'.
329 This word is glossed as 'climate, weather' in anon. (2010d: 22). The only other LFN word in anon. (2010d) which has 'weather' as a meaning is *aira*, which is glossed (p. 5) as "air; weather informal [sic]".
330 These terms are nouns (or can be used as nouns) unless otherwise indicated, except that the forms of Esata and Ruggles' Universal Language are roots.
331 *Pluva* is given as the noun meaning 'rain' in the *LdP-English Dictionary* (anon. 2010b), the *Classified Word List* of LdP (anon. n.d. b), and the *Русско-LdP Словарь* (anon n.d. c). However, Ivanov and Lysenko (2007) have *pluvia* rather than *pluva*.
332 This word is glossed as 'rain, showers' in Nutter (n.d. b: 12); it is also a verb meaning '(to) shower, rain'. Sasxsek also has the word *duso* 'rainfall, shower'; the suffix *-o* means a "[m]anifestation or instance of the action indicated by the root" (Nutter n.d. a.: 41).

Farlingo	pluvo
Fremdu	pluvu
Glosa	pluvi,[333] hieto (Gk.)
Id. Neut.	pluvi
Ido	pluvo
Int. IALA	pluvia
Ling	plov
Lingone	rayni (vb.) (Eng.)
LFN	pluve

UNI	PLU
Unitario	pluwio
Uropa	pluva
Uropi	liuv
Vela	gajo
Virgoranto	regno
Volapük	lömib, silavat[334]
Voldu	ren

	'snow'
Algilez	sno
American	nevu
Arlipo	nezho
Atlango	nivo
Ayola	nivo (Rom.)
Balta	nife (vb.)
Esata	nej- (Fr.), snow-
Esperanto	neĝo
Euransi	snegi (Serbian)
Eurolang	snow
Eurolengo	sno
Evroptal	sneg
Farlingo	nejo
Fremdu	snowu
Glosa	nivi, kiono (Gk.), nifa[337]
Id. Neut.	nev
Ido	nivo

	'snow'
LdP	snega (Russian)
Mondlango	nivo
NOXILO	LOOS
Olingo	nejo
Omnial	nive
Panamane	niéje
Perio	chubi (vb.)
Romániço	[335]
Romanova	neve
Rug.	niks-
Sasxsek	hidxfen
Sermo	nive[336]
Sintezo	nivo
UNI	SNO
Unitario	nikson
Uropa	niva
Uropi	snev

---

333 This word also means 'shower (rain)'.
334 Wood (1889) glosses *lömib* as 'rain, shower' (p. 187) and *silavat* (which contains *sil* 'sky, canopy of heaven') as 'rain, rain-water' (p. 305); the verb *silavatön* means 'to rain, shower'.
335 Morales (2010b) appears to give *nivo* as the Romániço equivalent of English *snow*, but Morales (2010a), which does not have a listing for *nivo*, glosses the Romániço word *nivajo* as 'snow'. Morales (p.c.) states, "*Nivo* is better translated as 'snowfall', from the verb *niver; nivajo* is the falling snow itself". The suffix *-aj-*, which is apparently contained in the latter word, means 'product, deed, result, part'.
336 This word is also an adjective meaning 'snowy, snow-white'.
337 With respect to *nifa* Springer et al. (2009: 49) say "prefer nivi".

Int. IALA	nive
Ling	sneg
Lingone	snewgo ("sort of PIE")
LFN	neva

Vela	vovo
Volapük	nif
Voldu	sneg
Welt. (V+F)	niv[338]

	'hail'
Arlipo	grelo[339]
Atlango	haylo
Esperanto	hajlo
Id. Neut.	grel
Ido	grelo
Int. IALA	grandine
LFN	graniza
LdP	aispluva
Mondlango	haylo
NOXILO	LOOH

	'hail'
Perio	chabi (vb.)
Romániço	grándino
Romanova	pluvia de jelo
Rug.	grqnd-[340]
Sermo	grandine
UNI	HAG
Uropi	gral
Vela	ragapo
Volapük	jod

	'sleet'
Glosa	pluvi-nivi, kalaza (Gk.)
Ido	greleto

	'sleet'
NOXILO	LOOTE
Romániço	nivgrándino

Table 7: *Terms for Types of Precipitation in Some* A Posteriori *and Mixed Languages*

Among words for 'rain' the general form **pluv* clearly is dominant. The most common pattern for terms for 'snow' is **nif/v*, but about a dozen words begin with *sne* or *sno*. Words for 'hail' vary to a large extent, as do the few words for 'sleet' that we have collected. The NOXILO words begin with *LOO*, which seems to be the radical for precipitation but also for some other meteorological phenomena, since the words for 'fog' and 'cloud; cloudy weather' also begin with it. At least some of these words appear to be partly *a posteriori*; for example, we would think that the S of *LOOS* comes from the English word *snow* and that the *H* of *LOOH* comes from *hail*. The three Perio verbs *chibi, chubi,* and *chabi* form an *a priori* type set of words.

The Sasxsek word *hidxfen* 'snow' contains *hid* 'water' and *fen* 'powder, dust; snow', i.e. *fen* alone can be used for 'snow'. The LdP word for 'hail' is a compound of the words for 'ice' (*ais*) and 'rain'. The Romanova term for 'hail' (as a noun) means 'rain of ice' (*jelo* being the word for 'ice').

---

338 Cf. the verb *ningan* 'to snow'.
339 *Greluno* means 'hailstone'; the suffix *-un-* means 'a part of some whole' according to Vitek (n.d.).
340 Ruggles (1829: 124) glosses this root as 'hail, frozen drops of rain'.

The Atlango word for 'raindrop' is *pluvikolo*; the suffix *-ikol-* means 'small particle of a whole' and also occurs in the word for 'snowflake', *nivikolo*. The LdP words for 'raindrop' and 'snowflake' are *pluvinka* and *sneginka*.[341]

Ling has the word *plovkad* 'shower' (*kad* means 'fall') and Panamane also has the noun *plúvindu* 'drizzle'. From the LFN word *pluve* 'rain' (both a noun and a verb) are derived the noun and verb *pluveta* '(to) drizzle, be misty; drizzle, mist' (with the diminutive suffix *-eta*) and the noun *pluvon* 'downpour' (containing the augmentative suffix *-on*).

The Konya word *pulun-wi* 'rain' apparently is a noun. However, it can be a whole sentence by itself with the meaning 'It's raining': Sulky (2005b), in which this sentence is contained, says, "It's common simply to utter a single noun or noun phrase in order to make an impersonal observation; in this case, the observation is '*rain*'".

Voksigid has the verbs *pluvi* 'be rain' and *esneve* 'be snow'. (Note that these apparently do not mean 'to rain' and 'to snow'.)

Terms for 'rainbow' in *a posteriori* and mixed languages usually do not contain the root meaning 'rain' in that language, that is, they generally follow a French type model than an English/German one. We see this in the following table, which shows components of some of these words:

	'rainbow'
Algilez	rinbow
Atlango	syelarko
Eurolang	pluv-arc
Fremdu	skayarku (*arku* 'bow, arc').
Id. Neut.	iris
Ido	pluv-arko, ciel-arko (*arko* 'arch, arc', *cielo* 'sky, heaven')
Int. IALA	iris, iride (both of these also mean 'iris (eye part)').
Ling	sjel-ark (*sjel* 'sky', *ark* 'bow; arch')
LdP	raduga (Rus.)
Mondlango	celarko (*celo* 'sky', *arko* 'arc')
Panamane	ráin-bówy
Romániço	celarco
Romanova	arco iris
Vela	gajozo
Volapük	Rellye (1888: 149) gives *lömibabob* as the word for 'rainbow' but Wood (1889: 277) has *lömöb*

Table 8: *'Rainbow' in Some* A Posteriori *and Mixed Languages*

---

341 The *Lingwa de Planeta Grammar* (anon. n.d. a: 28) says, "**The suffix -inka** denotes one small part of smth [= something]: ramla *sand* – ramlinka *grain of sand* ... pluva *rain* – pluvinka *drop of rain*".

The Panamane word appears to be a compound on the English/German model, but it does not contain its root for 'rain'; it was probably borrowed as a whole word from English. (Panamane's word for 'raincoat', *kapóut*, also does not contain its root for 'rain'.) The Vela word for 'rainbow' apparently is built from its word for 'rain', *gajo*.

A posteriori and mixed languages often have etymologically related terms for 'fog' and 'mist' or have the same term(s) for both meanings:

	'fog'	'mist'
Algilez	misem	mis
Ardano	cebet	
Arlipo	nebulo[342]	
Atlango	neblo	nyeblo
Ayola		
Esata	fog-, neb- (It.)	mist-
Esperanto	nebulo	nebuleto
Eurolang	nebel	
Eurolengo	fog	
Fremdu	fogu	
Id. Neut.	nebl	
Ido	nebulo	nebulo, nebuleto
Int. IALA	bruma, nebula[343]	
Lingone		misto (Eng.)
LFN	nebla	nebleta[344]
LdP	tuman (Turkish)	
Mondlango	fogo	
NOXILO	LOOG	
Olingo	nebelo	
Omnial	nebule, brume	
Panamane	nubelína	
Pandunia	jun[345]	
Romániço	nébulo	nebuleto[346]
Romanova	bruma	
Rug.	neb-	
Sasxsek	duman[347]	

---

342 What appears to be an etymologically related verb, *nebulon*, means 'to drizzle'.
343 *Nebula* also means 'haze'.
344 This word also means 'haze'.
345 This word also means 'cloud'.
346 *Nebuleto* also means 'haze'.
347 This word is glossed as 'fog, haze, cloud' in Nutter (n.d. b: 12).

147

Sermo	bruma,[348] nebula[349]
Sintezo	fogo
UNI	FOG
Unitario	nebula
Uropi	neb
Vela	fogo[350]
Volapük	fog, lutavat
Voldu	neblo[351]

Table 9: *'Fog' and 'Mist' in Some* A Posteriori *and Mixed Languages*

The Algilez word for 'fog' is made up of the word for 'mist' and the augmentative affix *-em*, while the word for 'haze', *miset*, contains *mis* and the diminutive affix *-et*. The Atlango words for 'fog and 'mist' are quite similar. The Esperanto word for 'mist', *nebuleto*, is derived from its root meaning 'fog' by the addition of the diminutive suffix *-et-*. Similarly, the LFN noun for 'mist, haze', *nebleta*, was built from *nebla* 'fog' and the diminutive suffix *-eta* and the Romániço word *nebuleto* 'mist, haze' apparently contains the root meaning 'fog' and the diminutive suffix *-et-*. The Volapük word *lutavat* 'fog, mist' is a compound of *lut* 'air' and *vat* 'water'.

The table below presents terms for 'cloud':

	'cloud'
Afrihili	oweli
Algilez	klād
Ardano	nube
Arlipo	nubo
Arulo	nubo
Atlango	klawdo
Ayola	nubo (Lat.)
Esata	nuv- (It., Sp.), nub-, klud-
Esperanto	nubo
Eurolang	nebulo
Evroptal	pilv (Finnish)
Farlingo	nubo

	'cloud'
Mondlango	nubo
NOXILO	LOOKLA[352]
Olingo	nubo
Omnial	nube
Panamane	volk
Pandunia	jun
Romániço	nubo
Romanova	nuve
Rug.	nub-[353]
Sasxsek	duman
Sermo	nube
Sintezo	nubo

---

348 This word also means 'brume'.
349 This word also means 'haze', and 'nebula' in the pathological sense. (Sermo has a different word equivalent to the English word *nebula* in its astronomical sense, namely *nebulosa* (which as an adjective means 'nebulous').)
350 This word also means 'cloud'.
351 This word also means 'nebula'.
352 This word also means 'cloudy weather'.
353 This root is glossed by Ruggles (1829: 142) as 'cloud, cloudiness'.

Fremdu	nubu
Id. Neut.	nub
Ido	nubo
Int. IALA	nube
Ling	nub
Lingone	neblo ("sort of PIE")
Lingua	nubi
LFN	nube
LdP	badal (Hindi)

UNI	NUB
Unitario	nubo
Uropa	nuba
Uropi	nolb
Vela	fogo
Volapük	lefog[354]
Voldu	klawd
Welt. (V+F)	nub

Table 10: *'Cloud' in Some* A Posteriori *and Mixed Languages*

In Ayola there are nouns for types of clouds: *ciruso* 'cirrus', *kumulo* 'cumulus', *nimbuso* 'nimbus', and *stratuso* 'stratus'. LFN has the words *cumulo* 'cumulus', *nimbo* 'nimbus', *siro* 'cirrus, and *strato* 'stratus',[355] and Sintezo has the words *kumuluso* 'cumulus', *nimbo* 'nimbus'. The Sermo word *nubilo* means 'storm cloud'. Ido has the word *nimbo* 'nimbus (rain cloud)'.

We shall now look at words for 'wind':

	'wind'
Algilez	wind
American	vent
Ande	hosa
Ardano	manglo
Arlipo	vento
Arulo	vento
Atlango	vyento
Ayola	vento
Esata	wind-, vent- (Fr., It., Sp.)
Esperanto	vento
Euransi	kaze (Japanese)
Eurolang	wind
Evroptal	tul (Estonian)
Farlingo	vento
Id. Neut.	vent
Ido	vento
Int. IALA	vento
Ling	vent

	'wind'
Mondlango	vento
NOXILO	GyEE
Olingo	vento
Omnial	vente, aneme
Panamane	vent
Romániço	vento
Romanova	vento
Rug.	vent-
Sasxsek	feq[356]
Sermo	vento
Sintezo	vento
UNI	VEN
Unitario	wento
Univ.-Spr.	vind
Uropi	vint
Vela	hoho
Virgoranto	vindo
Volapük	vien

---

354 *Lefog* is glossed as 'cloudiness, cloud' in Wood (1889: 170).
355 *Strato* has a range of other meanings; it is glossed in anon. (2010d: 100) as 'layer; coat (*as of paint*), coating; stratus (*cloud*); shell (*electron*)'.
356 This word also means 'breeze'.

Lingone	windo (Eng.)
LFN	venta
LdP	feng (Mandarin)

Voldu	wind
Welt. (V+F)	vent

Table 11: *'Wind' in Some* A Posteriori *and Mixed Languages*

Although various languages have been drawn on in creating terms for 'wind', a large majority of these terms have the form (something like) **vent* or **wind*.

In NOXILO *GyEE* appears to be both the word for 'wind' and the radical for words for winds and storms: the word for 'storm' begins with it, as do various other words, including those in the following table:

GyEEDI	'puffy wind'
GyEEHAR	'hurricane'
GyEEMA	'downward air current'
GyEEMAS	'downburst'
GyEEMOn	'monsoon'

GyEEn	'breeze'
GyEEP	'ascending current'
GyEET	'tornado'
GyEEU	'strong wind'

Table 12: *Some NOXILO Words Containing* GyEE *'Wind'*

The table below contains words for different types (or strengths) of wind:

	'breeze'
Algilez	windet
Ayola	brizo
Id. Neut.	bris
Ido	brizo
Int. IALA	brisa
Ling	bris
LFN	venteta
Panamane	brísa
Romániço	venteto
Rug.	hqr-
Vela	hohi

	'zephyr'
Esp.	zefiro
Ido	zefiro
LFN	venteta
Mondlango	zefiro
Olingo	zefiro
Sermo	zefiro[357]
Sintezo	zefiro[358]

	'gale'
Algilez	windem[359]
LdP	gro-feng[360]

	'sirocco'
Esperanto	siroko
Ido	siroko

---

357 This word means 'zephyr' in the senses 'west wind', 'soft, gentle breeze', and 'zephyr cloth'.
358 This word also means 'soft breeze'.
359 This word also means 'strong wind'.
360 This word also means 'strong wind'.

Rug.	hqr-		LFN	xiroco
Vela	hagako			

Table 13: *Terms for Types/Strengths of Wind in Some* A Posteriori *and Mixed Languages*

Some of these terms were derived by means of affixes. The Algilez word for 'breeze', *windet*, consists of *wind* 'wind' and *-et*; the word for 'gale, strong wind', *windem*, is built from the same root but ends with *-em*; recall that *-et* and *-em* are the Algilez diminutive and augmentative affixes respectively. The LFN word for 'breeze, zephyr', *venteta*, contains the diminutive suffix *-eta*. The Romániço word *venteto* 'breeze' was formed by attaching the diminutive suffix *-et* to the root meaning 'wind'.

One component of the LdP word *gro-feng* 'strong wind, gale', is the "augmentative particle" (anon n.d. a: 39) *gro-*, which is attached with a hyphen (recall that *feng* means 'wind').

Aside from such words the only terms which shows significant variation from others with the same meaning are *hqr-* of Ruggles' Universal Language (which means both 'breeze' and 'gale') and the Vela words. The Vela word for breeze, *hohi*, seems to be etymologically related to the word for 'wind', *hoho*, like the word for 'gust, squall', *hohogo*.

Sermo also has the word *austro* 'south wind, Auster'.

Let us turn to terms for 'storm':

	'storm'			'storm'
Arlipo	stormo		Olingo	ventevo
Atlango	[361]		Omnial	tempeste[362]
Ayola	stormo		Panamane	sturm
Esperanto	ŝtormo		Pandunia	tufan
Eurolang	tempest		Romániço	tempestato
Evroptal	groz (Ukrainian)		Romanova	tormenta
Id. Neut.	tempestad		Sermo	tempesta
Ido	sturmo, tempesto[363]		Sintezo	orajo[364]
Int. IALA	tempesta		UNI	BA-VEN[365]
LFN	tempesta[366]		Uropi	torm

---

361 The word *stormo* is given in Antonius (2009b) as the Atlango equivalent of "storm (with thunder and lightning)" and so presumably it would not include all storms in its meaning.
362 This word means 'tempest, storm'.
363 According to Dyer (1924a: 354), *sturmo* means 'storm, with thunder and lightning, thunderstorm; (fig.) tumult', while *tempesto* means 'tempest, gale, violent storm (with noise of elements)' (p. 368).
364 Dehée (2006) glosses this word as 'storm (with thunder & lightning)'.
365 This word consists of the augmentative prefix *BA-* and *VEN* 'wind'.

LdP	storma
Mondlango	stormo
NOXILO	GyEES

Vela	fahato
Volapük	tep[367]
Voldu	storm

Table 14: *'Storm'* in Some A Posteriori *and Mixed Languages*

There is a considerable amount of variation here, although the general forms **storm* and **tempest* are fairly common. The Olingo word for 'storm' apparently contains the root *vent-* 'wind' and the suffix for augmentation, *-ev-*.
The next table presents words for types of storms:[368]

	'cyclone'
Atlango	ciklongo
Esperanto	ciklono
Ido	ciklono[369]
Int. IALA	cyclon
LFN	siclon[371]
Mondlango	ciklono
Romániço	ciclono
Sermo	ciclon
Sintezo	ciklono
Vela	rapado

	'hurricane'
Atlango	hurakango, orkango
Ayola	hurikano
Esperanto	uragano
Id. Neut.	uragan[370]
Ido	uragano
Int. IALA	huracan
Ling	uragan
Romániço	huracano
Romanova	uracan
Sermo	huracan
UNI	ORK
Volapük	letep[372]

	'tornado'
Int. IALA	tornado
LFN	tornado
LdP	tornado

	'typhoon'
Esperanto	tajfuno
Mondlango	tayfuno
Sasxsek	taifun[373]

366 This word is glossed as 'storm, tempest' in anon. (2010d: 103).
367 *Tep* is glossed as 'tempest, storm, tumult' by Wood (1889: 342), but it is the only Volapük equivalent for the English word *storm* given in Wood (ibid.: 322). Both *letep* and *tep* are given as equivalents of English *tempest* (ibid.: 337). Volapük also has the noun *lustom* 'thunder-storm, storm, foul weather'. There is a related verb *lustomön* 'to thunder, to storm'.
368 The distinction between a type of storm and a type of wind is not clear-cut (at least for laymen); for example, a cyclone could be seen as a kind of wind rather than a kind of storm. No linguistic or other significance is to be placed upon our treatment of a meteorological phenomenon as one or the other of these.
369 This word is glossed as 'cyclone, tornado, typhoon: a violent rotary wind' in Dyer (1924a: 55).
370 This word is glossed as 'hurricane; tempest' in Holmes (1903: 130).
371 This word also means 'typhoon, hurricane'.
372 This word is glossed by Wood (1889: 178) as 'hurricane, great tempest'.
373 This word is glossed in Nutter (n.d. b: 48) as 'cyclone, typhoon, hurricane'.

NOXILO	GyEET
Romániço	tornado
Romanova	tornado
Sermo	tornado

Sermo	tifon
Sintezo	tifono
Vela	tifuno[374]

Table 15: *Terms for Types of Storms in Some* A Posteriori *and Mixed Languages*

There is very little significant variation among these terms. One word which is quite different from other words with the same meaning is Volapük's *letep* 'hurricane, great tempest', which consists of the augmentative prefix *le-* and *tep* "tempest, storm, tumult".

Other words of *a posteriori* languages for types of storms include:
  Esperanto: *fulmotondro*: 'thunderstorm'
  LdP: *snegastorma* 'snowstorm, blizzard'
  Mondlango: *blizardo* 'blizzard'
  Vela: *rabavo* 'blizzard'
We finish with words for some other meteorological phenomena:

	'lightning'[375]
Arlipo	fulmo[376]
Atlango	fulmo
Esperanto	fulmo
Eurolang	blitz
Evroptal	[378]
Fremdu	flaxu[379]
Id. Neut.	fulmin
Ido	fulmino
Int. IALA	fulgure[382]

	'lightning'
LdP	bliza
Mondlango	fulmo
Olingo	qilato (Malay)
Panamane	láihten, fúlmy[377]
Romániço	fúlmino
Sermo	fulgure[380]
Sintezo	fulmino[381]
Vela	jobo
Volapük	lelit[383]

---

374 This word also means 'tornado, hurricane'.
375 The meaning that we have in mind here is 'lightning', not 'flash of lightning'. However, some words which are glossed as 'lightning' in our sources, and which we have put in this table, might in fact have the latter meaning.
376 Arlipo also has the verb *fulmon* 'to lighten'.
377 Panamane also has the words *láiten-flash* and *fulmenáyu*, both of which mean 'lightning-flash'. Note that the <h> in *láihten* is not present in *láiten-flash*; each word occurs twice (in the form given here) in Amador (1936).
378 Evroptal has the word *blits*, from Low German, for which Le Masson (n.d. b) gives *éclair* ('flash of lightning') as the French equivalent.
379 This word is glossed in French in anon. (n.d. k) as 'éclair, foudre' (and just as 'lightning' in English), so it seems to mean both 'lightning' and 'flash of lightning'.
380 This word means '(flash of) lightning'. Sermo also has the word *fulmine*, which as a noun means 'thunderbolt; lightning' and as an adjective means 'fulmineous'.
381 This word means '(flash of) lightning, fulmination'.

Lingone	blisko (Slavic)
LFN	lampo

Voldu	fulmo

	'thunder'[384]
Arlipo	[385]
Atlango	tondro
Esata	tund-, twon- (It.)
Eurolang	donner
Evroptal	grim (Ukrainian)
Fremdu	grondu
Id. Neut.	toner
Int. IALA	tonitro
Ling	toner
LFN	tona
LdP	guruha (Indon.)
Mondlango	tondro

	'thunder'
Omnial	bronte
Panamane	tróinu[386]
Romániço	tónitro
Romanova	tronata
Sermo	tonitro
UNI	UPU
Unitario	tondro
Uropi	trom
Vela	jago
Volapük	töt[387]
Voldu	tondro

	'dew'
Arlipo	roso
Atlango	roso
Ayola	veso (Albanian)
Id. Neut.	rosi
Ido	roso
Int. IALA	rore
LFN	rosio
Mondlango	roso

	'dew'
Olingo	ambuno
Romániço	rosato
Sermo	rore, ros
Sintezo	roso
Vela	madazo
Volapük	töf[388]
Voldu	dyuv

	'frost'[389]
Arlipo	frosto

	'frost'
Mondlango	frosto

---

382 As far as we can tell, this word means both 'lightning' and 'flash of lightning'.
383 The word *lelitastal* means 'thunder-bolt, flash of lightning' (*stal* means 'ray (light)').
384 The meaning that we have in mind is 'thunder' and not 'clap of thunder'. However, some words which are glossed as 'thunder' in our sources, and which we have put in this table, might have the latter meaning.
385 The Arlipo-English dictionary in Vitek (n.d.) does not contain a noun meaning 'thunder' but it does have the verb *tondron* 'to thunder'.
386 Panamane also has the word tróin-kláppu 'thunderbolt'.
387 *Lelitaflap* means 'thunder-clap' (the noun *flap* means 'blow, hit, stroke').
388 This word also means 'dew-drop'.
389 Of course *frost* (in one sense) can occur in non-meteorological contexts, as in frost in a freezer. We cannot be certain that the words placed here mean 'frost' in its meteorological senses.

Atlango	frosto
Farlingo	frosto
Fremdu	frostu
Id. Neut.	frost

Panamane	jiasínda
UNI	HEL
Vela	zovo
Virgoranto	frosto

Table 16: *'Lightning', 'Thunder', 'Dew', and 'Frost' in Some* A Posteriori *and Mixed Languages*

There is a fair amount of variation among words for 'lightning', though words with the general form of **fulm(in)* account for about half of the total, with no other form occurring nearly as commonly. Roughly 50% of words for 'thunder' begin with *ton*. Among words for 'frost' the general form **frost* is clearly dominant; the pattern **ros/r* is the most common for meaning 'frost', and the words that do not follow it are quite different from one another. The table shows only words which our sources have glossed as 'frost', but we have also found the following terms:

    Arlipo: *brino* 'hoarfrost'
    Idiom Neutral: *glas-rosi* means 'hoar frost, white frost, rime'.
    Ido: *pruino* 'hoar frost, rime'
    LdP: *frima* 'hoarfrost, rime'.
    Volapük: *frod* means 'hoar-froast, white-frost, rime'

Chapter 14: Terms for Time Periods in Artificial Languages

All humans experience time and so it is not surprising that ALs, even those with small vocabularies, generally have words for at least some time periods. We will only deal with periods of fixed length, and thus not with words for e.g. 'moment' and 'era'.

A Priori Languages

We shall first look at *a priori* languages. The table below shows the Latejami words for periods of time, along with the "etym[ology]" for each one in Morneau (2006):

English	Latejami	etymology
'second'	zutovi	minimal polarity + DAY
'minute'	fotovi	small/low polarity + DAY
'hour'	cantovi	average polarity + DAY
'day'	tovi[390]	"'-tov' is the classifier for 'measure'"
'week'	taytovi	seven + DAY
'month'	ketovi	big/high polarity + DAY
'year'	bitovi	maximal polarity + DAY
'century'	jujufemi	zero/not/opposite/imaginary/magic + zero/not/opposite/ imaginary/magic + period of time

Table 1: *Latejami Words for Time Periods*

Most of these words contain a polarity modifier, with the word for 'day' being the most basic term. The etymology of the word for 'century' seems odd.

Next we see words from aUI and their components:

English	aUI	composition
'second'	ynAz	*ynA* 'minute', *z* 'part'
'minute'	ynA	*Yn*- 'little-, micro-',[391] *A* 'time'
'hour'	iAz	*iA* 'day', *z* 'part'
'day'	iA	*i* 'light', *A* 'time'[392]
'week'	EiA	*E* 'seven', *iA* 'day'

---

390 Cf. *kifemi* 'day(time), daylight hours' and *tofemi* 'date, day'.
391 There may be a difference (in phonetic value) between <y> and <Y>, but Weilgart (1979) sometimes uses one where the other would be expected, so no significance should be attached to the fact that <Y> rather than <y> appears here; this is the form as given in Weilgart (1979: 241).
392 Weilgart (1979: 97) says, "ia = day = light-time, or: the 24 hours from light to light".

| 'month' | ekiA | eki 'moon', A 'time' |
| 'year' | akiA | aki 'sun', A 'time' |

Table 2: *aUI Words for Time Periods*

Thus the aUI word for 'second' means 'part of a minute' and the word for 'hour' means 'part of a day'.

	'second'	'minute'	'hour'	'day'	'week'
Babm	decc	decf	dech	decn	dcak
Desa *Chat*	vonimi	cacoci	hagoha	hajera[393]	neroco
Fitusa	aipo	aifo	aiko	ailo[394]	aiso
Minyeva	tike	kope	pato	bani[395]	fectu
Ro (1913)	tab	tac	tad	taf	tak
Ro (1931)			tada	tafa	taka
Sona	riko	kori	hori	diri[396]	ridi
Suma	puko	piko	pako	temo[397]	7 temo
Temenia	ζεκυτο	μηυτο	τειρι	μηικε	λιυφυα

	'month'	'year'	'decade'	'century'	'millenium'
Babm	dcam	dcob		dodb	
Desa *Chat*	wutija	sanawi			
Fitusa	aito	aimo			
Minyeva	nesta	sejna			
Ro (1913)	tal	taq	taqzeb	taqzib	taqzob
Ro (1931)	tala	taqa		taqzaw	
Sona	mendi	tori			
Suma	moso[398]	tomo		seo tomo	
Temenia	ζυοξα	θυψαχυ			

Table 3: *Words for Time Periods in Some* A Priori *Languages*

---

393 We do not know whether this word means 'day (period of 24 hours)' or 'day (as opposed to 'night')', or both. Desa *Chat* also has the word *muvubi* 'date (day)'.

394 Fitusa also has the word *pato* 'day' (apparently as opposed to *pito* 'night').

395 *Bani* means 'day' in the sense of 'calendar day'. The word *veva* means 'day' in the sense of 'sunrise to sunset'.

396 *Diri* means 'day of 24 hours', while *irodi* means 'day' (apparently opposed to *vandi* 'night'; *iro* is the word for 'light; shine; lamp').

397 *Temo* means 'day (24 hours)'. Suma also has the words *meso* 'day of the week' and *lato* 'day (as opposed to 'night').

398 Since *moso* forms an a priori type pattern with *meso* 'day of the week' rather than with *temo* 'day (24 hours)', one might think that it can only mean 'one of the months of the year' (e.g. January) and not 'a period of roughly 30 days' (as in "He stayed in Paris for a month"). If this is the case, one might argue that it should not be in this table, as it is not a term like e.g. English *minute*, which means 'a period of 60 seconds'.

The Babm words for periods of time contain <d> and <c> or a second <d>; these combinations are characteristic features of words whose meaning involves "[t]ime and [c]alendar" (Okamoto 1962: 55).

Fitusa's words form a series: the length of the period of time denoted increases following its alphabetical order of consonantal letters, in which <p> is first, followed by <f>, and so on.

The Ro (1913) words for 'second' through 'year' consist of *ta* (which is the characteristic initial sequence of words whose meaning involves time[399]) followed by a consonant, in alphabetical order of the latter as the length of the period of time increases, but with some consonants not being used, e.g. there does not seem to be a word **tah*.[400] There is a word *tam* 'season', so it is part of this sequence, being longer than a month but shorter than a year. The words for 'decade', 'century', and 'millenium' consist of the word for year followed by the words for 'ten', '100', and '1000'.

The Ro (1919) words for 'second' through 'year' are the same as those of Ro (1913), but the year for 'century' has changed to *taqzaw*, presumably because the word for '100' has changed (to *zaw*). Also, Foster (1919) glosses *tab* as 'second, moment' (while in Foster (1913: 84) it is simply glossed as 'second'). Foster (ibid.) does not give words for 'decade' and 'millenium', but he does have the word *taqzayo* 'millenial', from which we can deduce that millennium would be **taqzay* (*zay* means '1000' and *-o* appears to be an adjectival suffix).[401] Ro (1921) has the same words for 'minute' through 'year'; words for longer periods of time are not given in Foster (1921). Also, *tab* is glossed as 'moment' in Foster (1921: 21); no word for 'second' appears there. As can be seen from the table above, the Ro (1931) words for 'hour' through 'year' are similar to those of Ro (1913) (and of Ro (1919) and Ro (1921)), the only difference being that *a* has been added to the end of each of them (Foster (1931) does not provide words for 'second' or 'minute'), while the word for 'century' is the same as that of Ro (1919).

The Suma words for 'second', 'minute' and 'hour' are in an *a priori* type pattern, as are the words for 'day' and 'year'. The Suma word for 'century' contains the word *seo* 'hundred'.

---

399 The sequence *te* is the characteristic initial sequence of words relating to "Relative Time" (Foster 1913: 85), e.g. *tebac* 'very brief', *ted* 'prospective time'.

400 We do not know of any words in Ro (1913) with *h* in syllable-final position (although <h> can occur there as part of a digraph); *j*, *n*, and *p* can occur in this position, so their absence in words of this series is mysterious, but they are also left out of the sequence of words for numerals: *zag*, *zal*, *zam*, *zaq* mean 'five', 'six', 'seven' and 'eight'; on the other hand *k* is left out of the sequence of words for numerals, but is present here in the word for 'week', while *g* occurs in the numeral sequence, as seen in the word for 'five', but is not found in this sequence.

401 Foster (1919) has the words *tag* 'daytime' and *taj* 'night', which could explain some of the gaps (in terms of use of final segments) in the Ro (1913) series of words for time periods; perhaps Foster was reserving space for these or similar words.

A Posteriori and Mixed Languages

We shall now examine terms for periods of time in *a posteriori* and mixed languages, going from the shortest to the longest periods. We therefore begin with terms for 'second':

	'second'
Algilez	sek
American	secondo
Amerikan	minlin
Ande	tin
Arlipo	sekundo
Atlango	sekundo
Ayola	sekundo
BL	skant
Esperanto	sekundo
Euransi	sâkone
Eurolang	second
Eurolengo	sekond
Farlingo	sekundo
Fremdu	sekundu
Glosa	sekunda[403]
Id. Neut.	sekond
Ido	sekundo
Int. IALA	secunda
Ling	sekond
LFN	secondo
LdP	sekunda

	'second'
Loglan	sekmi
Mondlango	sekondo
Neo	sekund
NOXILO	MyO (Chinese)
Olingo	sequndo
Omnial	sekunde
Panamane	sekúndy
Perio	cito
Romániço	secundo
Romanova	segundo
Rug.	tjlps- (Art.)[402]
Salveto	seconde
Sasxsek	sekon
Sermo	secundo
Sintezo	sekundo
Slovio	sekund
Uropi	sekùnd
Vela	seko
Virgoranto	sekundo
Volapük	sekun
Voldu	sekúnd

Table 4: *'Second' in Some* A Posteriori *and Mixed Languages*

There is a high degree of uniformity here, with the vast majority of terms being of the general form *sekund or something derived from it. The Perio word, *cito*, does not follow this pattern and may be *a priori*; in any case it makes up an *a priori* type set with the words for 'minute', and 'hour', *cuto*, and *cato* respectively. As indicated, the term from Ruggles' Universal Language, *tjlps-*, is an "artificial" root which is in an *a priori* type pattern with the root for 'minute', *tjlts-*, and with two roots for very short time periods, *tjlks-* 'third, or sixtieth of a second' and *tjlfs-* 'fourth, or sixtieth of a third'. The origin of Ande's *tin* is not

---
402 The letter <j> stands for the diphthong [aɪ].
403 This is also one of the Glosa words for the ordinal numeral 'second'.

clear; perhaps it is also *a priori*. Sasxsek has the word *sanausimxsekon* 'nanosecond', which contains the word *sanaus* 'billion' and the fractional numeral creating suffix *-im*.

Now let us look at terms for 'minute':

	'minute'
Algilez	min
American	minuto
Amerikan	minit
Ande	mi
Atlango	minuto
BL	mnit
Esperanto	minuto
Euransi	menati
Eurolengo	minute
Evroptal	minut
Farlingo	minuto
Fremdu	minutu
Glosa	minuta
Id. Neut.	minut
Ido	minuto
Ingli	minut
Int. IALA	minuta
Konya	manuti
Ling	minut
LFN	minuto
LdP	minuta
Loglan	minta
Mondlango	minuto

	'minute'
Neo	minut
NOXILO	NAATI (Thai)
Olingo	minuto (Eng.)
Omnial	minute
Panamane	minúty
Pandunia	minit
Perio	cuto
Romániço	minuto
Romanova	minuto
Rug.	tjlts- (Art.)
Salveto	minute
Sasxsek	minut
Sermo	minuto
Sintezo	minuto
Slovio	minut
UNI	MIN
Unitario	minuto
Uropi	minùt
Vela	mino
Virgoranto	minuto
Volapük	minut
Voldu	minút

Table 5: *'Minute' in Some* A Posteriori *and Mixed Languages*

Again there is little significant variation. This time Ande's word, *mi*, appears *a posteriori*, being the first two segments of the general pattern for most of the other words here, **minut*. Like its word for 'second', and most of its words for other time periods, NOXILO's word for 'minute', *NAATI*, comes from a non-European source, and is quite different.

The following table contains terms for 'hour'.

	'hour'
Algilez	uro
American	ûro

	'hour'
Loglan	horto
Mondlango	horo

161

Amerikan	ɤr	Neo	or
Ande	tor	NOXILO	XI (Korean)
Ardano	wato (Wolof)	Olingo	horo
Arlipo	horo	Omnial	hore
Atlango	horo	Panamane	stúndy
Auxil	hore	Perio	cato
Ayola	horo	Romániço	horo
BL	ler	Romanova	ora
Ceqli	hora (Sp.)	Rug.	tids- (Art.)
Esata	hor-, stun-(Dutch, Ger.)	Salveto	ore
Esperanto	horo	Sasxsek	hora
Euransi	hori, vaqta[404]	Sermo	hora
Eurolengo	ur	Sintezo	horo
Evroptal	hur	Slovio	cxas
Farlingo	horo	Tal	ctundo
Fremdu	[405]	UNI	ORA
Glosa	horo	Unitario	ora
Id. Neut.	hor	Uropa	hora
Ido	horo	Uropi	hor
Int. IALA	hora	Vela	horo
Interlingue	hor	Virgoranto	stundo
Konya	xesi	Volapük	düp
Ling	hor	Voldu	hor
LFN	ora	Welt. (V+F)	gor
LdP	ora		

Table 6: *'Hour' in Some* A Posteriori *and Mixed Languages*

This time there is slightly more variation, although the large majority of the terms follow a Latin/Romance type model, **(h)or*. Several languages' words are based on the German word for 'hour', *Stunde*. Not surprisingly, the Slovio word seems to have been taken from Russian. (The Slovio words for 'second' and 'minute' presumably also come from Russian (and/or other Slavic languages), but since the Russian words are quite similar to e.g. the English and French words, the Slovio words do not show significant variation from most of the other words for 'second'

---

404 Both of these words are glossed as 'hour' in Sztemon (2001b) and we do not know what difference (if any) there is between them. One might perhaps suspect that one of them is used in telling time (as in French *Quelle heure est-il?* 'What time is it?'), but we have no evidence for this.

405 Anon. (n.d. k) gives *oru* as the Fremdu word for 'hour', but everywhere else in the Fremdu website (of which the home page is http://www.lukleo.net/) the word occurs as *horu*.

and 'minute' in *a posteriori* and mixed languages.)The term for 'hour' in Ruggles' Universal Language, *tids-*, seems to be *a priori* and in an *a priori* type pattern with some other roots for time periods in the language, *peds-* 'day' and *kads-* 'week'.[406]

Next are terms for 'day'. In some cases our source for the language does not (explicitly) indicate whether the word for 'day' means 'day' in the sense of 'period of 24 hours' or in the sense of 'time when there is daylight' or both (we have already encountered this problem with the *a priori* language Desa *Chat*); in such cases we have put the word in the table below, although it is not clear that it should be used in the former sense; however, in the absence of any other word meaning 'day' in the language (or at least among the words given by the source), one might guess that words can be used in both senses.

	'day'
Afrihili	alu
Algilez	de[407]
American	dio
Amerikan	**da**[409]
Ande	den
Ardano	dagur (Icelandic)
Arlipo	dio[412]

	'day'
Lingone	deno ("sort of PIE")
Lingua	die
LFN	dia (completa)[408]
Ling. Int.	die
LdP	dey[410]
NOXILO	NE[411]
Olingo	tago

---

406 Not all terms in an *a priori* type pattern are necessarily *a priori*, since an *a posteriori* word could provide a general model for such a pattern, with other members of the pattern being the same except for changes in one or two positions.

407 According to Giles (2010b) *de* means 'day (24 hours)'; cf. the word *day* 'daytime (as opposed to night)'.

408 *Dia* is glossed in anon. (2010d: 33) as 'day (*not night*)', which might make one think that it cannot (by itself) mean 'day' in the senses of '24 hours' or 'calendar day', especially since LFN has the term *dia completa* 'day (24-hour period)' (ibid.). However, some terms, phrases, and sentences containing *dia(s)* may lead one to the opposite conclusion; these include *a 24 oras de la dia* '24 hours a day' (ibid.: 32), *a alga dia* 'one day, someday' (ibid.: 6), *a esta dias* 'nowadays, these days' (ibid.: 41), *plato de la dia* 'dish of the day' (ibid.: 80), and (from anon. 2010c: 41) *Me va reveni pos tre dias* 'I will come back in three days'.

409 Note that <**a**> (as in this word) is a different letter than <a>.

410 According to the *LdP-English Dictionary* (anon. 2010b) *dey* means 'day' "in all meanings". LdP also has the word *lumadey* 'daylight, daytime', i.e. 'day' as opposed to 'night', from *luma* 'light'.

411 NOXILO also has the word *DEI* (from English). Sentaro (2010b) gives *NE* as the equivalent of English *day* and of *date* and *DEI* as the equivalent of *day of the week*; Sentaro (2010c) glosses *NE* as 'date' and *DEI* as 'day'. Given the word *NE_RI* 'day's trip' and the phrase in Sentaro (2010c) *5 NE KAn* '(for) five days' (*KAn* means 'period') we believe that *NE* is the word which means 'day' in the sense of a period of time. There is also the word *PROIDE* 'daytime'.

Arulo	jorno	Omnial	die
Atlango	diyurno[413]	Panamane	jor
Auxil	die	Pandunia	din
Ayola	djurno (Rom.)[414]	Romániço	dio[415]
BL	tag	Romanova	di'a[416]
Ceqli	dey (Eng.)[417]	Rug.	peds- (Art.)
Esata	dey-, tag- (Dutch, Ger.), jurn- (Fr., It.)	Salveto	die
		Sasxsek	din
Esperanto	tago	Sermo	die, jorno[418]
Euransi	ruzi	Sintezo	tago[419]
Eurolang	day	Slovio	den
Eurolengo	dag	Tal	dago
Evroptal	den	Tutonish	dag
Farlingo	tago	UNI	TAG
Glosa	di, hemera (Gk.)	Uropi	dia
Id. Neut.	diurn	Vela	[420]
Ido	dio[421]	Virgoranto	dago
Int. IALA	die[422]	Volapük	del

412 Vitek (n.d.) specifies that *dio* means 'day' in the sense of '24 hours'. The word *zhorno* means 'day (as opposed to night)'.

413 Antonius (2009b) gives *diyurno* as the Atlango equivalent of *day* (24 hours) and *diyo* as the equivalent of *day* (*daytime*) but in Antonius (2009a) there is the phrase "Diyoy dil semango" 'Days of the week', which would make one think that *diyo* is not limited to meaning 'day' in the sense of 'time when there is sunshine', unless Antonius has made an error.

414 Cf. the word *dago* 'day (daytime)'.

415 *Dio* means 'day' in the sense of '24-hour period'; the word *jurno* means 'day (as opposed to night)'.

416 The word meaning 'day' in the sense of when the light of the sun is present is *jorno*.

417 This word means 'period of 24 hours'. Ceqli also has the word *dia* 'day (period of light)' (from Spanish).

418 Both of these words mean 'day (as opposed to night)' and 'period of 24 hours'; in addition, *die* means 'daylight'.

419 *Tago* is glossed by Dehée (2006) as 'day (of 24 hours)'; Sintezo also has the word *jorno* 'daytime, day (opposite of night)'.

420 Prist (1998b: 28) gives *dobo* as the Vela equivalent of 'Midnight to midnight' and adds "not 'dajo', that is daylight only"; on p. 57 he glosses *dobo* as '24 hours, midnight to midnight, a day'. However, on p. 28 there is also the following sentence, in which *dajo* seems to be used in the sense of 'span of 24 hours':
(i) Ji riv-i hi ca dajo-s ag.
    I arrive-PST here two day-PL ago
    'I arrived here two days ago.'

421 *Dio* means 'day (24 hours)'; the word *jorno* means 'day' in the sense of 'daytime'.

Konya	tiki
Ling	di

Voldu	dag
Welt. (V+F)	din

Table 7: *'Day' in Some* A Posteriori *and Mixed Languages*

There is a considerable degree of variation here: the pattern **di(a/o/e)* is fairly common, but so is the Gmc. pattern **t/dag*, several languages have borrowed the English word 'day' or seem to have used French *jour* and/or Italian *giorno* as a model, and other types of forms occur as well.

The table below shows terms for 'week':

	'week'
Afrihili	ajume
Algilez	wik
American	semano
Ande	qvn
Ardano	sament (Amharic)
Arlipo	semajno
Arulo	semano
Atlango	semango, viko
Ayola	semano
BL	sman
Dil	vik (Eng.)
Esata	wik-, sman- (Fr., It., Sp.)
Esperanto	semajno
Euransi	hadi
Eurolengo	seman
Farlingo	semano
Fremdu	wiku
Glosa	setimana, hebdoma (Gk.), septi-di
Id. Neut.	seman
Ido	semano
Int. IALA	septimana
Ling	seman
Lingone	wiko (Eng.)
Lingua	hebdomad
LFN	semana

	'week'
LdP	wik
Mondlango	weko
Neo	vek
NOXILO	WIIK (Eng.)
Olingo	semeno
Omnial	semane
Panamane	vok
Pasifika	semana (Sp.)
Romániço	septimano
Romanova	semana
Rug.	kads- (Art.)
Salveto	semane
Sasxsek	seman
Sermo	septimana
Sintezo	semano
Slovio	tiden
Tal	veko
Tutonish	vok (Ger.)
UNI	ET-TAGI
Unitario	semano
Uropa	deswa
Uropi	sedia
Vela	viko
Virgoranto	veko
Volapük	vig
Voldu	vik

Table 8: *'Week' in Some* A Posteriori *and Mixed Languages*

---

422 This word means 'day' both in the sense of 'day (as opposed to 'night')' and in the sense of '24-hour span of time' and in addition means 'daylight'.

Again there is not much uniformity, although a fair number of words have the form *seman or *v/wik or something similar. One of the Glosa terms for 'week' consists simply of one of its words for 'seven', *septi*, and one of its words for 'day'. Similarly, the UNI word for 'week' simply means 'seven days', as *ET* is 'seven', *TAG* is 'day', and *-I* is the plural suffix. The Uropa word for 'week', *deswa*, contains the root for 'day', *des-*, and *w*, which occurs in "Nouns-of-multitude" (Donisthorpe 1913: 41); it thus means roughly 'group of days'.

We shall mention just a few words for 'fortnight'. The Panamane word *foternáte* is not very different from the English word. Sasxsek also has the word *duvxseman* 'fortnight', which contains the word for 'two', *duv*, and the word for 'week.' The Volapük word, *telavig*, is constructed in the same way (*tel* means 'two').

We now turn to words for 'month':

	'month'
Afrihili	ɔsu
Algilez	mon
American	meso
Amerikan	munʃ
Ande	mun
Arlipo	monato
Atlango	menso
Ayola	monato
BL	mes
Ceqli	xar (Arabic)
Communia	mense
Esata	mont-
Esperanto	monato
Euransi	mone
Eurolang	month
Eurolengo	mond
Evroptal	mij
Farlingo	monato
Fremdu	mensu
Glosa	meno (Gk.), mense,[423] mestra (Gk.)
Guosa	uki[425]

	'month'
Lingone	monso ("sort of PIE")
LFN	mensa
LdP	mes
Mondlango	mono
Neo	mes
NOXILO	YE (Chinese)
Olingo	buluno
Omnial	mensue
Panamane	moáte
Romániço	menso
Romanova	mese
Rug.	stigs- (Art.)
Salveto	mense
Sasxsek	mas
Sermo	mense
Sintezo	monato
Slovio	mesiac
Tal	meco
Tutonish	mont
UNI	LUN[424]
Unitario	monato
Uropi	mon

---

423 This word also means 'menses, menstruation'.
424 This word also means 'moon'.
425 Igbinę̀wę́ka (1987: 9) gives the source of this word as "Ed/So". "Ed" stands for Edo, but Igbinę̀wę́ka does not give "So" in his list of abbreviations.

Id. Neut.	mens
Ido	monato
Int. IALA	mense
Konya	moni
Ling	mens

Vela	mono
Virgoranto	meno
Volapük	mul, yelamul
Voldu	mond
Welt. (V+F)	monat (Ger.)

Table 9: *'Month' in Some* A Posteriori *and Mixed Languages*

The most common general form is **me(n)s*, but the German model **monat* is not rare and is used by e.g. Weltsprache (Volk and Fuchs). Latin is the main source for the lexemes of this language, but C&L (1903/1979: 269) say, "Quelques mots allemands sont employés pour éviter l'équivoque des racines latines: … **buc** = *livre*; **monat** = *mois* (**mens** = t*able*)" ('Some German words are used to avoid the ambiguity of the Latin roots: … **buc** = *book*; **monat** = *month* (**mens** = *table*)'). Various other forms occur as well.

We now shall examine terms meaning 'year':

	'year'
Afrihili	afi
Algilez	yir
American	anıo
Amerikan	yır
Ande	uar
Ardano	tahun (Indon.)
Arlipo	jaro
Arulo	yaro
Atlango	anyo
Auxil	ane
Ayola	djaro (West Gmc.)
BL	lan
Ceqli	sal (Hindi)
Esata	yir-, hano (Fr., It., Sp.)
Esperanto	jaro
Euransi	sâle
Eurolang	an
Eurolengo	an
Europal	anue
Farlingo	yaro
Fremdu	yaru
Glosa	anua, eto (Gk.)
Guosa	á(r)dún (Igbo/Yoruba)
Id. Neut.	anu

	'year'
Ling	an
Lingone	yaro (Eng.)
LFN	anio
Mondlango	yero
NOXILO	SAAL (Hindi)
Olingo	yaro (Ger.)
Ominal	anue
Panamane	yáry
Pandunia	nen
Romániço	anuo
Romanova	anio
Rug.	skags- (Art.)
Salveto	ane
Sasxsek	nan
Sermo	ano
Sintezo	yaro
Slovio	rocx
Tal	lano
Tutonish	jaar (Ger.)
UNI	ANO
Unitario	anno
Uropa	anna
Uropi	jar
Vela	jiro

167

Ido	yaro		Virgoranto	jaro
Int. IALA	anno		Volapük	yel
LdP	yar		Voldu	yar

Table 10: *'Year' in Some* A Posteriori *and Mixed Languages*

Again there is much variation. The most popular general form is **an*, and a good number of words appear to be based on German *Jahr*; English *year* seems to be the source for several other words. Idiom Neutral also has the word *semestr* 'half-year' and Sermo has the word *trimestre* 'quarter of a year'.

Let us now look at terms for periods which consist of multiple years:

	'decade'	'century'	'millenium'
Algilez	axyir[426]	senyir[427]	
Amerikan	yɪrpɷ	yɪrlɷ	
Ande		ientiar	
Ardano		ciasa (Ganda)	
Arlipo		jarcento	
Atlango	dekado, dekemo, dekanyo	centuro, centemo, centanyo	
Ayola		tcendjaro	
BL		sekl	
Esata		seq- (Fr.)	
Esperanto	jardeko	jarcento[428]	jarmilo
Euransi	dahyari	sâtyari	hezyâri
Eurolengo	diésan	sentan	
Farlingo		sekulo	
Fremdu	yardisu	yarcentu	yarmilu
Glosa	dek-anua	hekto anua[429]	
Id. Neut.		sekul	
Ido	yar-deko	yar-cento	
Int. IALA	decennio	seculo	millennio
Ling		sekl	
Lingone	yardeko	yarcento	yarmillo[430]
LFN	desenio	sentenio	milenio

---

426 *Ax* means 'ten'.
427 *Sen* means '100'.
428 Piron (1981) says, "The current forms *jarcento* 'year-hundred' and *jarmilo* 'year-thousand' for 'century' and 'millennium', for example, follow the Gmc. model, not the Slavic and Latin models which underlay the older forms *centjaro* and *miljaro*".
429 *Hekto* means 'hundred'.
430 The Lingone word for 'thousand' is *mil*.

LdP		sekla	
Mondlango	dekado	yercento	
Neo		seklo	
NOXILO	TIOSAAL[431]	AHSEn, STOSAAL[432]	MILASAAL[433]
Ominal		secule	
Panamane	déhkada, zentúbya	siéke	
Romániço	anudeço	século	
Romanova		sieclo	
Salveto	decane	centane	milane
Sasxsek	desxnan	hekxnan	kilxnan
Sermo	decenio	seculo[434]	milenio
Sintezo	[435]	yarcento	
Slovio	desrocxie	storocxie	
Tutonish	jaarti (Ger.)	jaarhundr (Ger.)	
UNI		EON	
Uropa		ctwannwa	
Vela	dekado	batijo	
Volapük	yelbalsüp	yeltum	yelmil, milyelüp

Table 11: *'Decade', 'Century', and 'Millenium'* in A Posteriori *and Mixed ALs*

We see from the above table that there are two basic methods for creating words for periods consisting of ten, 100, or 1000 years, to borrow words for these periods which are (not obviously) related to the word for 'year', or to make compounds consisting of a word for 'ten', '100', or '1000' and the root/word for 'year'. About a dozen of the words for 'century' were created by the first method; thus for example the Blue Language *sekl* bears no etymological relation to its word for 'year' and was probably borrowed from French (in which language the words for 'year' and 'century' are also not etymologically related). The second method seems more popular. An example of a language using it is Salveto, in

---

431 *TIO* means 'ten'.
432 Sentaro (2010b) gives both of these as equivalents of English *century*, but under the "remarks" column says "century" for the former and "one hundred years" for the latter (*STO* means '100') and gives the Japanese gloss '世紀' for the former and '百年' for the latter. Given this, one might think that the former would be used in a context such as "the 20th century" (and indeed Sentaro (ibid.) gives *20DAI AHSEn* as the equivalent of *20th century*) and the latter used to mean a period of 100 years. However, Sentaro (ibid.) gives *1 AHSEn* as the equivalent of 'for a century', which indicates that *AHSEn* can also be used with this meaning.
433 *MILA* means '1000'.
434 This word also means 'world (= things mundane)'.
435 Sintezo has the word *dekado*, but it is glossed in Dehée (2006) as 'decade (1. period of ten days; 2. division of a book consisting of ten parts)'.

169

which the words for 'decade', 'century', and 'millenium' are made up of the word for 'ten', '100', and '1000' respectively (*dec*, *cent*, and (*une*) *mil*[436]) and *ane* 'year'. Similarly, the Sasxsek words for 'decade', 'century', and 'millenium' consist of the words for 'ten', '100', and '1000' respectively, the epenthetic vowel <x> [ə], and the word for 'year'.

The Amerikan words for 'decade' and 'century' have the reverse order; they consist of the word for 'year' followed by pʘ 'ten' or lʘ '100'. The Tutonish words are built in the same way, although all the elements are different, with the words for 'ten' and '100' being *ti* and *hundr*.

The Romániço word for 'decade' consists of the root meaning 'year', the word for 'ten', *deç*, and the suffix for common nouns in the language, -*o*. The word for 'century' was not built on this pattern, but apparently comes from Latin. Thus Romániço uses both methods mentioned above (for different words).

The Euransi words for 'decade', 'century', and 'millenium' begin with part of the words meaning 'ten', '100', and '1000' respectively, which are *dahma*, *satma*, and *hezra*. This is not a surprise, but it is interesting that, unlike words with the same meanings in some other ALs, the second part of these words is not the word/root for 'year', but the sequence *yari* (or *yâri* in the case of the word for 'millenium') (cf. the German word *Jahr* 'year').

The Volapük word for 'decade' was built in yet another way; it contains the word for 'ten', *bals*, and the suffix -*üp*, which Wood (1889: 396) glosses as "termination for names of periods of time".[437] Note that for some reason this suffix does not appear in the words for 'century' (which contains the word *tum* '100') or in one of the words for 'millenium'.

The Uropa word for 'century', *ctwannwa*, contains the *w* that we saw in the word for 'week' as well as *ctw* '100' and *ann-* 'year' and so means roughly 'group of 100 years'.

NOXILO also has the word *AHSENIS* 'half century' (*WAnNIS* means 'half').

In his book on Amerikan Molee (1888: 270) proposes a different system for the "division of the day", with a day consisting of 10 hours, an hour consisting of 100 minutes, and a minute being made up of 100 seconds. Under this system the Amerikan words for 'second', 'hour', and 'minute' would not be equivalent to those in other languages (their lengths being different) (although of course one could use Molee's system and e.g. English terms such as *hour*, in which case *hour*, *minute*, and *second* would not have exactly the same meaning as they currently do). Molee (ibid.: 269) also proposes a year of 13 months, with the months consisting of 28 days.

---

436 These are the words given in Lorenz (2010); Lorenz (2005) has different words for '100' and '1000', (*une*) *cente* and (*une*) *mile*.

437 Weltsprache (Eichhorn) also has a marker of nouns whose meaning involves time, namely the suffix -*i*, as in *nori* 'hour' and *nani* 'year' (C&L (1903/1979: 297) gloss *nani* as 'année').

References[438]

Anonymous (2007a) *Dictionary French - Kotava* [actually a Kotava-French dictionary]. At URL <http://www.international-language.org/dictionaries/dict_kotava_french.pdf>.

Anonymous (2007b) *Dictionary English - Kotava*. At URL <http://www.international-language.org/dictionaries/dict_english_kotava.pdf>.

Anonymous (2007c) *Dictionary Kotava - English*. At URL <http://www.international-language.org/dictionaries/dict_kotava_english.pdf>.

Anonymous (2009) *Use This Guide to Make Ygyde Compound Words*. At URL <http://www.ygyde.neostrada.pl/ygydec.htm>.

Anonymous (2010a) *Ygyde Language Introduction*. At URL <http://www.ygyde.neostrada.pl/index.htm>.

Anonymous (2010b) *LdP-English Dictionary*. At URL <http://lingwadeplaneta.info/files/ldpen.shtml>.

Anonymous (2010c) *Grammar of Lingua Franca Nova* (version of Sept. 27, 2010). At URL <http://ccgi.esperanto.plus.com/lfn/grammar.pdf>.

Anonymous (2010d) *Lingua Franca Nova English Dictionary* (version of Sept. 27, 2010). At URL <http://ccgi.esperanto.plus.com/lfn/disionario.pdf>.

Anonymous (no date a) *Lingwa de Planeta Grammar*. At URL <http://lingwadeplaneta.info/files/anglegram.pdf>.

Anonymous (no date b) *Classified Word List* [of Lingwa de Planeta]. At. URL <http://lingwadeplaneta.info/files/wordlist.shtml>.

Anonymous (no date c) *Русско-LdP Словарь*. At URL <http://lingwadeplaneta.info/files/rusldp.shtml>.

Anonymous (no date d) *Lingua de Planeta Lernikursa*. At URL <http://lingwadeplaneta.info/files/lernikursa.pdf>.

Anonymous (no date e) *Rikki-Tikki-Tavi* [Translation of Kipling's story into LdP, also with Spanish and Russian versions]. At URL <http://lingwadeplaneta.info/utf-8/rikki.html>.

Anonymous (no date f) *Short Dialogues and Texts in Lingwa de Planeta*. At URL <http://lingwadeplaneta.info/files/syaotextas.pdf >.

Anonymous (no date g) *Lessons for Romanova, the Auxiliary Language*. At URL <http://espadiamapas.t35.com/RNENGrammar.htm>.

---

438 We also include in this list some sources that we have used but have not referred to.

Anonymous (no date h) *Basic English-Romanova Dictionary*. At URL <http://espadiamapas.t35.com/RNENDictionary.htm>.

Anonymous (no date i) *Lexique Kotava → Francais*. At URL <http://www.kotava.org/fr/fr_ravlemeem_kt.php>.

Anonymous (no date j) *Basic Grammar of Mondlango*. At URL <http://www.mondlango.com/english/grammar.htm>.

Anonymous (no date k) *Wordaru* [Lukleo [i.e. Fremdu]-French-English-Spanish-Italian-Catalan dictionary]. At URL <http://www.lukleo.net/dico.php>.

Anonymous (no date l) *Dicionario Sermo-Anglese.* At URL <http://www.oocities.com/sermo_vulgaris/sed.html>.

Amador, M. E. (1936) *Fundaments of Panamane*. Imprenta Barcelona, Pueblo Nuevo, Panama.

Anderson, A. W. (no date) *A Planned Auxiliary Language*. Apparently self-published, no place of publication given.

Antonius, R. A. (2009a) *Atlango*. At URL <http://vido.net/atlango/>.

Antonius, R. A. (2009b) *Mikra Vortaryo Angla - Atlango*. At URL <http://vido.net/atlango/vortajo.htm>.

ApGawain, N., P. D. Hugon, J. L. Moore, and L. de Beaufront (2008) *Ido for All* (edition 1.6, revised and edited by Jerry Muelver). At URL <http://idomondo.org/ skolo.1.6.pdf>.

Attobrah, K. (1973) *El-Afrihili: Book 1* (2nd edition). Afrihili Centre, Akrokerri, Ghana.

Ayola Research Group (2007) *La Nuva Internaciona Lingo Ayola*. Available through URL <http://www.aiola.org/>.

Barral, J. (no date) *La langue fédérale de la societé des nations*. Librairie Visconti, Nice.

Berlin, B. and P. Kay (1969) *Basic Color Term: Their Universality and Evolution*. University of California Press, Berkeley, CA.

Bollack, L. (1900) *Abridged Grammar of the Blue Language* (English version by Professor Tischer). Editions of the Blue Language, Paris.

Bollack, L. (1904) *Premières notions de la langue bleue*. Éditions de la Langue Bleue, Paris.

Bollen, J. (no date a) *Grammar Lingone*. Available through URL <http://testground. net/ index.htm>.

Bollen, J. (no date b) *Vocabulary Lingone*. Available through URL <http://testground.net/index.htm>.

Bond, S. (1926) *Meso*. Apparently self-published, Wellington, Somerset.

Bothi, P.[439] (2004) *The New Personal International Language Esata* (Draft Edition 0.2). LiRiCo, Italy. Formerly available at URL <http://www.beginnersgame.com/ page_25.pdf >.

Bothi, P. (2006) *The New Personal International Language Esata* (Draft Edition 0.3). LiRiCo, Italy. At URL <http://www.beginnersgame.com/page_25.pdf>.

Brown, J.[440] (2007a) *Temenia: Introduction* (Version 4.1). At URL <http://www.temenia.org/docs/Introduction.pdf>.

Brown, J. (2007b). *Complete Grammar* [of Temenia] (Version 3.3). At URL <http:// www.temenia.org/docs/CompleteGrammar.pdf>.

Brown, J. (2007c) [Temenia] *Dialogues* (Version 2). At <http://www.temenia.org/docs/Dialogues.pdf>.

Butler, M. C. (1965) *Step by Step in Esperanto*. The Esperanto Publishing Co., Orelia, WA, Australia.

Cárdenas, C. (1923) *Hom-Idyomo* (English edition, 2nd edition). Apparently self-published, printed by Fischer & Wittig, Leipzig.

Couturat, L. and L. Leau (1903 and 1907/1979) *Histoire de la language universelle* bound with *Les nouvelles langues internationales*. Georg Olms Verlag, Hildesheim.

Davis, P. (1999/2000) *An Outline of the World Language Desa* Chat (version 3.0). At URL <http://www.users.globalnet.co.uk/~vidas/desa.htm>.

De Beaufront, L. (1925/2005) *Kompleta Gramatiko detaloza di la linguo internaciona Ido*. Krayono: Ponferrada, Spain. At URL <http://es.geocities.com/krayono/kgd.pdf>.

De Beaufront, L. and L. Couturat (1908) *English-International Dictionary*. Guilbert Pitman, London.

---

439 In this and the work listed next, the author's name is simply given as PAFU, but a search on the internet revealed that his name is apparently Pafu Bothi.

440 Brown's name is not given in this work, but he is the creator of Temenia and thus can be identified as its author, since he makes statements such as "But I chose to construct an IAL for several reasons..." in this document (p. 5). Brown's name is also not given in the following two references but again we assume that he is their author, as they are available through the same website.

Dehée, J. (2006) *Vokabulario di Sintezo.* At URL <http://f1.grp.yahoofs.com/v1/4O7UTFeNPs57jQV0T8YuYyVmzjyxyRkrk5qukyDJVupWLuZTMAPs61w19rAyc6i-vkyfQq1URX93qK7I_FSpEjMQLcM/Vokabulario%20%20di%20%20Sintezo%20%2010%2C000%20vorto>.

Dominicus, R. (1982) *SPL: An International Language Based on Simplified Latin.* Dominicus Publishing House, Wisconsin.

Donisthorpe, W. (1913) *Uropa.* Apparently self-published, printed by W. Stent and Sons, Guildford.

Dyer, L. H. (1924a) *Ido-English Dictionary.* Sir Isaac Pitman & Sons, London.

Dyer, L. H. (1924b) *English-Ido Dictionary.* The International Language (Ido) Society of Great Britain, London.

Elhassi, Z. (2008) *Ardano Course.* Available through URL <http://groups.yahoo.com/group/ardano/files/Ardano%20courses/>.

Fetcey, S. and the Comité Linguistique Kotava (2009) *Kotava: Grammaire officielle complète* (Version III.11). Available through URL <http://www.kotava.org/fr/fr_xekeem.php>.

Fisahn, S.[441] (no date) *Lingua Franca Nova: Grammar.* At URL <http://lingua-franca-nova.net/lfngrammar.html>.

Foster, E. P. (1913) *Ru Ro.* World-Speech Press, Marietta, OH.

Foster, E. P. (1919) *Dictionary of Ro the World Language.* World-Speech Press, Marietta, OH.

Foster, E. P. (1921) *Roap: English Key to Ro the World Language.* The Ro Language Society, Waverly, WV.

Foster, E. P. (1931) *Ro-Latin-English Vocabularium Dictionary.* Roia, Waverly, WV.

Gao, J. K. (2005) Singlish: Declaration of a Universal Language Based on Simplified English. At URL <http://www.scribd.com/doc/40523786/Singlish>.

Giles, A.[442] (2009) *Algilez Lessons.* At URL <http://homepage.ntlworld.com/a.giles7/Algilez%20Lessons.pdf>.

---

441 At the bottom of this webpage are the statements "Lingua Franca Nova par Dr. C. George Boeree e la grupo LFN. Paje rede par Stefan Fisahn" ('Lingua Franca Nova by Dr. C. George Boeree and the LFN group. Webpage by Stefan Fisahn'). We therefore suspect that Boeree was responsible for much of the content of the page.

442 Giles' name does not appear in this document, but since he is the designer of the language and since his name appears in other documents on Algilez available through the same website, one can assume that he is the author of it as well.

Giles, A. (2010a) *The Algilez Grammar*. At URL <http://homepage.ntlworld.com/a.giles7/Algilez%20Grammar.pdf>.

Giles, A. (2010b) *Algilez Vocabulary*. At URL <http://homepage.ntlworld.com/a.giles7/AlgilezVocab.htm>.

Gilson, B. R. (2009a) *The Orthography, Phonology, and Phonotactics of Voksigid*. Available at URL <http://viewsoflanguage.host56.com/voksigid/ortho.html>.

Gilson, B. R. (2009b) *Voksigid: Word List*. Available at URL <http://viewsoflanguage.host56.com/voksigid/words.html >.

Gode, A. and H. E. Blair (1951) *Interlingua*. Storm Publishers, New York.

Goeres, H. D. W. (2004) *Grammática Completa* [of Linguna] (*Teil 1*). At URL <http://www.linguna.de/old/html/teil_1_von_3.html>.

Hallner, A. (1912) *The Scientific Dial Primer*. Sunset Publishing House, San Fransisco, CA.

Holmes, M. A. F. (1903) *Diksionar de Idiom Neutral*. John P. Smith Printing Co., Rochester, NY.

Hunt, P. (1998a) *Eurolang Quick Reference*. Available at URL <http://web.archive.org/web/20011120073143/www.vision25.demon.co.uk/el/qref.htm>.

Hunt, P. (1998b) *Eurolang to English Dictionary*. Available at URL <http://web.archive.org/web/20011118135807/www.vision25.demon.co.uk/el/el-eng.htm>.

Igbinęwęka, A. (1987) *The Dictionary of Guosa Language Vocabularies*. Vol. 1. Guosa Publications, Ikeja, Lagos.

Ivanov, D. and A. Lysenko (2007) [Multilingual Dictionary of Lingwa de Planeta]. At URL <http://lingwadeplaneta.info/glossword/index.php> and following URLs.

Jaque, R. S. (1944) *One Language*. J. F. Rowny Press, Santa Barbara, CA.

Jones, G. (2006) *Minyeva: Reference Grammar*. At URL <http://minyeva.alkaline.org/grammar.htm>.

Jones, L. (1972) *Eurolengo*. Oriel Press, no place of publication given.

Kisa, S. E. (2009a) [Toki Pona] *Lesson 1: Letters and Sounds*. Formerly available at URL <http://en.tokipona.org/wiki/Lesson_1:_Letters_and_sounds>.

Knight, B. J. (2005) Toki Pona: The Language of Good – The Simple Way of Life. At URL <http://rowa.giso.de/languages/toki-pona/english/toki-pona-lessons.pdf>.

Kupsala, R. (no date a)[443] *Pandunia's Phonology*. At URL <http://www.kupsala. net/risto/pandunia/english/ phonology.html>.

Kupsala (no date b). *Guide to Pandunia*. At URL <http://www.kupsala.net/risto/ pandunia/english/guide.html>.

Landais, J. [444] (no date a) *Uropi Grammatik in destrì Table*. At URL <http://uropi.free. fr/pdf/gramfr.pdf> (downloaded May 19, 2010).

Landais, J. (no date b) *Vokem Uropi* [part 1]. At URL <http://uropi.free.fr/pdf/ vokem1.pdf> (downloaded May 19, 2010).

Le Masson, Y. [445] (no date a) *Grammaire de l'Evroptal*. At URL <http://www. evroptal.net/evroptal.pdf>

Le Masson, Y (no date b) *Lexique* [of Evroptal]. At URL <http://www. evroptal.net/php/skriva_mots.php?ACTION=READ>.

Lins, U. (2001/no date) "Oka Asajirô, ein japanischer Kosmopolit" in S. Fiedler and L. Haitao (eds.) *Studoj pri Interlingvistiko / Studien zur Interlinguistik*, KAVA-PECH, Dobřichovice, Czech Republic. (Internet version of book prepared by L. Haitao (no date), at URL <http://www.lingviko.net/db/>).

Lorenz, M. (2005) *Salveto Primer*. At URL <http://www.salveto.net/primer.htm>.

Lorenz, M. (2010) *Salveto Grammar*. At URL <http://www.salveto.net/grammar. htm>.

May, R. (2007) *The Alphabet and Sounds* [of Ceqli]. AT URL <http://ceqli. pbworks.com/The+Alphabet+and+Sounds>.

Molee, E. (1888) *Plea for an American Language*. J. Anderson & Co., Chicago.

Molee, E. (1902) *Tutonish*. Scroll Publishing Co., Chicago, IL.

Molee, E. (1915) *alteutonik, 1915*. Self-published, Tacoma, WA.

Monnerot-Dumaine, M. (1960) *Précis d'interlinguistique générale et spéciale*. Librarie Maloine, Paris.

Morales, M. [446] (2010a) *Dictionario di Romániço*. At URL <http://www. romaniczo.com/vocabularos/dictionario.html>.

---

443 This webpage and the following one do not have any date, but the "main page" in English for Pandunia, which links to these pages, is dated "2007-2009".

444 Landais is not stated to be the author of this reference, but we assume that it is by him, or someone associated with him.

445 Le Masson's name is not given in this or the following reference. However, since he is apparently the designer of Evroptal, and since no other names are given in these references, we assume that he is their author.

Morales, M. (2010b) *English-Romániço* [Dictionary]. At URL <http://www.romaniczo.com/vocabularos/en_dictionario.html>.

Morales, M. (no date a) *Alphabet and Pronunciation* [of Romániço]. At URL <http://www.romaniczo.com/gramatico/en_gramatico_02.html>.

Morales, M. (no date b) *Nouns* [in Romániço]. At URL <http://www.romaniczo.com/ gramatico/en_gramatico_04.html>.

Morneau, R.[447] (2006) *Latejami-to-English Dictionary*. At URL <http://www.eskimo.com/~ram/Latejami/Latejami_to_English.html>.

Nicolas, A. (1904) *Spokil*. A. Maloine, Paris.

Nutter, D. (2008a) *Pasifika-English Dictionary*. At URL <http://conlang.dana.nutter.net/index.php/Pasifika-English_Dictionary>.

Nutter, D. (2008b) *Ingli - English Dictionary*. At URL <http://conlang.dana.nutter.net/index.php/Ingli/Ingli_-_English_Dictionary>.

Nutter, D. (no date a) *Sasxsek: A Language for Earth*. At URL <http://sasxsek.org/files/sasxsek_eng.pdf >

Nutter, D.[448] (no date b) Sasxsek *Dictionary*. At URL <http://sasxsek.org/files/sasxsek_dictionary_eng.pdf>.

O'Connor, C. L. (1917) *American: The New Pan-American Language*. Apparently self-published, printed by the Hausauer-Jones Printing Co., Buffalo, NY.

Okamoto, F. (1962) *Universal Auxiliary Language Babm*. Tokyo.

Olson, A. (1950) *How to Speak Ling*. Self-published, printed by Caslon Press, Stockholm.

Piron, C. (1981) *Esperanto: European or Asiatic Language?* Available at URL <http://claudepiron.free.fr/articlesenanglais/europeanorasiatic.htm>.

Pleyer, M. (1990) *Unitario*. Unitario Press, Bensheim.

Prist, B. (1998a) *English-Vela Dictionary*. Apparently self-published, no place of publication given.

---

[446] Morales' name is not given on this webpage or associated webpages about this language. However, through correspondence with him we have established that he is the designer of the language, and the author of the webpages.

[447] Morneau's name does not appear in this webpage, but it is fairly clear that he is its author (for one thing, he is the designer of Latejami).

[448] We assume Nutter is the (major) author or compiler of this work, although his name does not appear anywhere in it.

Prist, B. (1998b) *Vela for Children.* Apparently self-published, no place of publication given.

Quiles, C. (with F. López-Menchero) (2009) *A Grammar of Modern Indo-European* (2nd edition, version 4.15). Indo-European Language Association, at URL <http://dnghu.org/indo-european-grammar.pdf>.

Rellye, J. (1888) *A Dictionary of the English and Volapük Languages.* L. Schick, Chiacgo.

Rodríguez Hernández, J. M. (2002) "Interlingvistiko: *Auxil*". *Gazeto Andaluzia* 68:15-19.

Rosenblum, B. (1935) *Fitusa.* Apparently self-published, no place of publication given.

Ruggles, J. (1829) *A Universal Language.* M'Calla and Davis, Cincinnati, OH.

Russell, B. (1966) *Suma* (3rd edition). Apparently self-published, Plainview NY.

Russell, B. (1967) *Hundred Suma Words in Fairy Tales.* Apparently self-published, no place of publication given.

Schleyer, J. M. (1887) *Grammar with Vocabularies of Volapük* (2nd edition, translated by W. A. Seret). Thomas Murray & Son, Glasgow.

Searight, K. (1935) *Sona.* Kegan Paul, Trench, Trubner & Co., London.

Sentaro, M. (2010a) *NOXILO Webpage 1.* At URL <http://www2s.biglobe.ne.jp/~noxilo/sub1a.htm>.

Sentaro, M. (2010b) *English/NOXILO/Japanese* [Dictionary]. At URL <http://www2s.biglobe.ne.jp/~noxilo/EN10k.htm>.

Sentaro, M (2010c) *NOXILO Webpage 6.* At URL <http://www2s.biglobe.ne.jp/~noxilo/sub1f.htm>.

Sotos Ochando, B. (1860) *Diccionario de lengua universal.* J. Martín Alegría, Madrid.

Sprague, C. E. (1888) *Hand-Book of Volapük.* The Office Company, New York.

Springer, M., et al. (2009) *Glosa Inter-reti Diktionaria.* At URL <http://www.glosa.org/gid/gid.pdf>.

Stadelmann, J. (1945) *Voldu Texbook.* Lit. y Tip. Vargas, Caracas.

Steiner, P. (1885) *Elementargrammatik nebst Übungsstücken zur Gemein- oder Weltsprache (Pasilingua).* Heuser's Verlag, Neuwied a/Rhein.

Stolz, T., C. Stroh, and A. Urdze (2006) *On Comitatives and Related Categories*. Mouton de Gruyer, Berlin.

Sulky, L. (2005a) *The Konya Language*: *Alphabet, Numbers, and Pronunciation*. At URL <http://www.oocities.com/HandyDad/konya/konya-alphanum.html>.

Sulky, L. (2005b) *The Konya Language*: *Sample Sentences and Explanation*. At URL <http://www.oocities.com/HandyDad/konya/konya-sentence.html>.

Sztemon, L. (2001a) *Euransi Grammar in Brief & Phrases*. At URL <http://ls78.sweb.cz/saynegi.htm>.

Sztemon, L. (2001b) *Short Comparative Euransi-English-Czech Word List*. At URL <http://ls78.sweb.cz/farhane.htm>.

Tacchi, G. (no date) *A Pure Language*. Publisher and place of publication unknown.

Talmey, M. (1925) *Arulo*. Ilo Press, New York.

van Steenbergen, J. (2010) *Slovianski – Phonology & Orthography*. At URL <http://steen.free.fr/slovianski/phono_ortho.html>.

Vitek, L.[449] (no date) *Bonveno al le pageni di ARLIPO!* At URL <http://arlipo.info/>.

Wainscott, E. (1975) UNI – *The New International Language: Supplement* (English Language Edition). Uniline, Cleveland, OH.

Wald, M. (1909) *pan-kel, leichteste Kurzsprache für den Weltverkehr* (4th edition). Apparently self-published, Gross-Beeren, Brandenburg.

Waringhien, G., ed.-in-chief (1970) *Plena Ilustrita Vortaro de Esperanto*. Sennacieca Asocio Tutmonda, Paris.

Weilgart, J. W. (1979) *aUI: The Language of Space* (4th edition). Cosmic Communication Co., Decorah, IA.

Weisbart, J. (no date) *Europal (Europäisch)*: *Kurze Grammatik und Begründung*. Printed by Michaelis u. Neumann, Berlin.

Wells, J. C. (1969) *Esperanto Dictionary*. Hodder and Stoughton, Dunton Green, Kent.

Wennergren, B. (2005) *Plena Manlibro de Esperanta Gramatiko*. At URL <http://bertilow.com/pmeg/elshutebla/pmeg_14.0.pdf>.

---

449 On this page Vitek is named as the designer of Arlipo, but no author of the page is given. However, it seems to be a reasonable assumption that he is its author.

Wilkinson, J. and T. A. Wilkinson (2010) *2010 Guide to Neo Patwa*. At URL <http://patwa.pbworks.com/Guide> (downloaded on May 20, 2010).

Wood, M. W. (1889) *Dictionary of Volapük*. Charles E. Sprague, The Office Publishing Co., New York.

Żygis, M. (2008) "On the Avoidance of Voiced Sibilant Affricates". *ZAS Papers in Linguistics* 49: 23-45.